Anthropology and Theology

Anthropology and Theology

Douglas J. Davies

Oxford • New York

First published in 2002 by
Berg
Editorial offices:
150 Cowley Road, Oxford, OX4 1JJ, UK
838 Broadway, Third Floor, New York, NY 10003-4812, USA

Berg is an imprint of Oxford International Publishers Ltd.

Library of Congress Cataloguing-in-Publication Data
A catalogue record for this book is available from the Library of Congress.

British Library Cataloguing-in-Publication Data
A catalogue record for this book is available from the British Library.

ISBN 1 85973 532 0 (Cloth)
1 85973 537 1 (Paper)

Typeset by JS Typesetting, Wellingborough, Northants.
Printed in the United Kingdom by Antony Rowe Ltd, Chippenham, Wilts.

Contents

Preface

The roots of this book lie in a class text first produced in 1986 to answer the needs of mature students working on the East Midlands Ministry Training Course, many of whom became clergy. I was then at the Department of Theology at the University of Nottingham, largely teaching the social anthropology of religion. During my twenty or so years there I also served as an honorary assistant priest in a variety of urban and rural Anglican parishes. When I first began university teaching in 1974 there was very little material available seeking to relate anthropology and theology, and it became part of my intellectual goal to address that overlapping territory. As the bibliography indicates, this resulted in a series of empirical studies on a variety of topics including Anglican church life, belief and priesthood, as well as on death and funerary rites in Britain and elsewhere. I also wrote a major study of Mormonism, employing many of the concepts expounded in this book, whose non-systematic and non-comprehensive intention is to stimulate thought and foster a way of thinking rather than inform on detail. This is more a 'notes and queries' than an 'introduction to anthropology and theology' type of book. Much has been omitted that some might think vital, such as myth, doctrine and truth, or gender and belief; but, in the space available, I have tried to deal with some basic questions left largely untouched by others.

My own initial training in anthropology at Durham University was followed by research at the Institute of Social Anthropology at Oxford, where I completed my first period of research on Mormonism under the supervision of Dr Bryan Wilson. I then trained for the Anglican Ministry at Durham, where, fortunately, a background in anthropology was appreciated and encouraged, most especially by John Rogerson, who taught me Old Testament, and was himself doing much to relate theology and anthropology in biblical studies. I thank him for his continued support and friendship over many years. As good fortune had it, this was followed by a long period at Nottingham University, where my research interests extended to Sikhism with Eleanor Nesbitt as a postgraduate researcher, to death rites in Britain with Alastair Shaw as my research assistant, and to aspects of church organization and popular belief and practice through the Rural Church Project. The other two directors of this research, largely on Anglicanism, were Charles Watkins and Michael Winter as geographer and sociologist respectively. Seldom could any major venture have been conducted with greater vigour, comradeship and delight, and I thank them for that, as I do our excellent research assistants Caroline Pack, Susanne Seymour and Christopher Short. The Leverhulme Foundation funded that work. Life and work at Nottingham were much enhanced by Professor John Heywood Thomas, with whom I taught Philosophy and Phenomenology of Religion, and whose continuing friendship, with that of Mair Heywood Thomas, I can but simply mention.

Within Durham's Department of Theology, I thank my present colleagues for their cordiality and commitment to scholarship, as well as several Durham Heads of Houses for their collegial hospitality. Most especially I thank my undergraduate and postgraduate students for their vivacity, enjoyment of life and critical attitude to what one says, especially Mr Ed Dutton, who provided detailed student criticism of this typescript. I must also thank Professor David Martin, both for his crucial comments on an earlier and very much longer version of this text, and for his friendship over the years. Finally I thank Kathryn Earle at Berg, whose initial query and subsequent support prompted this particular volume.

Douglas J. Davies
University of Durham

Introduction

This book fosters a conversation between the two intellectual worlds of theology and anthropology by exploring related, often paired, concepts that have usually been pursued separately within those disciplines, as in the cases of incarnation and embodiment, salvation and merit-making, and symbolism and sacrament. Three theoretical themes of anthropology, viz., gift-theory, ethical vitality and rebounding violence, are introduced and developed in a theological direction, and three further ideas, concerning rebounding-vitality, transcending-plausibility and the moral–somatic relationship, mark my own contribution to the debate. This book is neither a brief history of the anthropology of religion (cf. Bowie 2000) nor a dedicated theological search for models to illuminate sacred texts (like, for example Theissen 1982; Overholt 1996; and Chalcraft 1997). Nor yet does it seek to be what Morton Klass in his introduction to Salamone and Adams's *Explorations in Anthropology and Theology* calls the 'anthropology of theology', an idea that seems too forced at this stage of scholarship (1997:1). More simplistically, it is a development of topics from my own engagement in theology and social anthropology, with roots in an earlier class text (Davies 1986).

Life-studies

Theology is a formal reflection, description and account of religious experience, while anthropology presents theoretical interpretations of the life experience of particular societies in general. As 'life-studies', experience lies at the heart of each; but their fundamental distinction concerns the existence of God. Theology tends to assume that God exists, underlies religious experience, and is the basis for considered reflection, while anthropology tends to assume God does not exist and simply studies the reported experiences of people. I use the phrase 'tends to' because some theologians speak as though no deity exists, while a few anthropologists claim religious faith. Still, generally speaking, Christian theology could not function without belief in God, while anthropology operates perfectly naturally without it.

Introduction

As far as mutual interest is concerned, theology has utilized anthropology more frequently than anthropology has taken any interest in theology. Indeed anthropology has shown a high degree of inhospitality to theology, so that Klass could speak of the 'great divide' between them (Salamone and Adams 1997:39). Studies seeking to relate anthropology and theology are rare indeed (but cf. Salamone and Adams 1997). Mission-minded Christian groups have drawn upon anthropological approaches to cultural interpretation, not least to aid in bible translation; and increasing numbers of biblical scholars have utilized social scientific ideas in biblical interpretation and in seeking to comprehend the emergence of Christianity as a sect of Judaism (e.g. Atkins 1991; Overholt 1996; Chalcraft 1997). Lévi-Strauss's original anthropological interpretation of biblical myth did much to initiate this theological response (Rogerson 1974, 1978; Malbon 1984; Jobling 1984). Systematic theologians, by contrast, are reluctant to admit anthropological notions into their studies, and have tended to have philosophy as their dialogue-partner.

One long-standing critique of Christianity, rooted in the nineteenth-century philosophy of Feuerbach, sociology of Durkheim and psychology of Freud, argued that, while theology reckons to be about God, it is, actually, only about humanity. Many others have accepted that appearance and reality are quite distinct, suggesting that since it is too difficult for humans to think directly about themselves they use supernatural images for indirect self-reflection. This image–reality distinction is a recurrent motif in the history of thought. Plato could speak of ideal forms as distinct from their pale reflection in actual phenomena, much as Max Weber would, millennia later, speak of ideal types. Freud would distinguish between unconscious and conscious mental activities, while numerous Eastern traditions distinguish between appearance and reality. Modern science, too, speaks in its own way of microcosmic and macrocosmic realms lying beyond the perceptions of everyday life.

Most theologians define theology as a reflection on the divine as self-disclosed, as a revelation of himself – and, in the mass of theological writing until very recently, it was very much a revelation of 'himself'. The active and self-revealing God is a powerful creator making the world before, providentially, ruling a kingdom whose bounds are endless. This increasingly gendered perspective has become influential as a basis of interpreting theology as masculinely motivated; but I will not pursue it further, on the assumption that to impose any gender on God is a consequence of anthropomorphism in particular cultures and their linguistic forms. To define God as masculine is, initially, unfortunate; but then to insist on a feminine grammar of discourse only compounds the primal error.

Method

This unsystematic book, conceived as a conversation between theology and social anthropology, reflects Paul Ricoeur's apt description of situations where 'understanding and explanation tend to overlap and pass over into each other' (1976:72). There is no priority of speaker, and theology is not assumed to be queen of the sciences, using elements of anthropology in a servile fashion, any more than anthropology is taken to be the foundational source of truthfulness concerning humanity. Each is regarded as one way of considering life and experience, in the hope that the outcome will conduce to more than the sum of the parts.

This theological–anthropological conversation is far from easy, given our taken-for-granted assumptions, shared by family, friends and society, which confer a degree of certainty upon the way things are. Our very identity is rooted in this classification of the world and, if we hold to a religion, its commandments and ethical principles underpin our very sense of self. Theology develops from such religious and cultural roots, adopting a position of authority reinforced by historical culture, church-state, church-university, or social class contexts. Anthropology can disturb this state of affairs, especially through its comparative method and the theoretical analyses it brings to bear upon differing beliefs and practices.

Comparative Method

Because the comparative method assumes that the religious processes and practices of many cultures are comparable it tends to remove the sense of uniqueness of each, and fosters the notion of cultural relativity. For some this makes the venture what I will call 'difficult to think', a phrase needing some explanation. In everyday life we do not find it 'difficult to think'. We know how to approach issues, balance arguments and judge between ideas because our criteria of judgement have become second nature to us. If, however, we scrutinize those very criteria and ask after their validity we encounter the experience of something being 'difficult to think' – a kind of philosophical distress emerges when we try to examine the very classification of reality by means of which we normally think.

This reflexive thought is intrinsically difficult because it involves trying to think about thinking, and involves an encounter with inaccessibility. In practice we need some degree of distance from ourselves in order to think about ourselves, and it is just such a process that underlies ideas of projection as explored by sociologists of knowledge such as Alfred Schutz

(Schutz and Luckmann 1973) and Peter Berger (1969), as well as earlier philosophers such as Ludwig Feuerbach (1957 [1841]). In a similar vein the anthropologist Claude Lévi-Strauss discussed totemic objects as objects that were 'good to think', enabling groups to ponder their own human condition, albeit indirectly, through reflection upon mythical entities (1962). Through the emergence of historical, cultural and scientific forms of critical scholarship such forms of self-knowledge have become available, even if not always desired.

Belief and Methodology

One basic aspect of theological method concerns belief and the method of confessional theology, which starts from the assumption that God exists and, through a divine disclosure, has revealed truth to some privileged individual or group, making one formulation of belief and practice more authentic than others. How are such confessional approaches related to what is often, loosely, called 'academic theology' within university contexts? Each confessional theology possesses its own method: Catholic Theology is often grounded in the philosophy of Thomas Aquinas, with subsequent generations producing their own commentaries and developments, all under a degree of control from Rome. Similarly, Protestant Theology is grounded in the bible and in distinctive interpretations of it, with certain key theologians commanding authoritative status. In many countries, but not England, universities possess Catholic Faculties and Protestant Faculties fostering these distinctions. In 1879, for example, Pope Leo XIII made the study of Thomas Aquinas a necessary part of education for Catholic priests and, in Protestant Churches, the writings of Luther and Calvin have been similarly authoritative, as have later interpreters. One brief account of denominational theology in relation to academic theology is furnished by the Uppsala theologian Mattias Martinson, whose criticism of confessional theology in the Swedish Lutheran context affirms the possibility of theology as the practice of 'a broad form of human self-critique', but only when theology is the paradoxical means of hope and of knowing its 'own immense incompetence' in so doing (2000:361). His subtle argument on philosophy and theology's relationship is reflected, much less sophisticatedly, in this present book's attempted conversation between some anthropological and theological ideas.

While anthropological traditions lack formal confessionalism and possess no 'church' of anthropology, there exist various schools of interpretation and practice that can result in relative isolation as, for example, between cognitively focused and symbolically inclined scholars (Atran 1993:48; Keesing 1993:93). The key organizational distinction between theology and anthropology lies in the fact that anthropology does not possess a 'lay' following and has no responsibility towards a non-professional body – although, increasingly, anthropologists are seen as having links with and continuing responsibility towards the people they study. Throughout the following chapters some considerable emphasis will be given both to a number of classical texts and to a selection of recent studies that echo a kind of authoritative status within anthropology; and specific mention must be made of Rappaport's important and post-humously published volume, *Ritual and Religion in the Making of Humanity* (1999), to which we return in Chapter 5, and which I commend as the key anthropological complement to this volume.

Social Science as 'Theology'

Given the relative closeness between anthropology and sociology some comment is needed on the debate between some theologians and sociologists over John Milbank's thesis that sociology is really a form of theology in a disguise invented by secular scholars (cf. *New Blackfriars* 1992; Repstadt 1999:141–54). Milbank's argument, a form of philosophical theology, exhorts theologians not to borrow concepts from sociology, since 'all twentieth-century sociology of religion can be exposed as a secular policing of the sublime' (1990: 106). Milbank's crucial question is 'whether there can be *theology* . . . without mediation by the social sciences?' His answer is 'yes' (1990: 246). He is not the first intellectual believer to want to retain the purity of doctrinal discourse and church history; nor will he be the last. His profound conservatism speaks of 'upholding the fundamentally historical character of salvation: in other words, orthodoxy' (ibid.). While Milbank is wise to criticize any blind acceptance of sociological ideas as intrinsically more insightful or valuable than theological ideas, he is too eager to assume that the content of orthodox theology is revealed and divinely contained within a single tradition stemming from St Augustine, and that nothing particularly valuable comes to it 'from outside'. For him one specific Christian theology provides the meta-narrative, the great story of the way things are, and he stakes his claim – 'by faith' – to a place in this great history (1990:249). I do wonder, however, if the discussion of embodiment in this book and, in particular, the issue of perceived affinity between Christ and the believer described in Chapter 2 might not be somehow relevant to Milbank's personal conviction that the death of Christ allows a believer to 'really "see" sin' (1990: 399).

But what of perspective and distance? Many Christians are perfectly happy to live within the thought-forms, language and practice of their faith and to defend them against all comers; but other Christians appreciate how a degree of distance aids their own understanding of faith in much the same way as some anthropologists gain a new vision of their own society from having lived in another. Theologically speaking, for example, one of the properties of Reformation theology involves a form of 'distancing', in the belief that religion, itself, exists under divine judgement with the theologian existing at the boundary between theology and culture at large – a point creatively held and argued by Paul Tillich. Indeed, it is noteworthy that he, along with several other Protestant theologians who have engaged with the idea of culture, including Wolfhart Pannenberg, are absent from Milbank's encyclopaedic study.

Pannenberg's extensive *Anthropology in Theological Perspective* is, essentially, a philosophical theology of 'doctrines of man', and its engagement with social anthropology is limited and often relegated to footnotes even when considering the prime assumptions of theology and anthropology (e.g. 1985: 433, 482, 483). Pannenberg is weak when criticizing anthropologists like Geertz for their emphasis upon the symbolic nature of human life because he reckons such symbolic activity to be personal, whereas culture is communal (1985:318). This inadequately criticizes anthropology, which has long accepted that 'society' is prior to individual human life. It is also odd because Pannenberg generally appreciates the priority of society, as his appraisal of Durkheim shows (1985: 405). While the realm of reciprocity and Mauss's work – important work for this present volume – is largely ignored, Pannenberg accepts the place of religion in society as the domain within which human personhood develops. In particular, his approach to the fact that it is within 'religion' that 'the earthly life of individuals can become the embodiment of a personal identity and integrity that transcend life's limitations and weaknesses' (1985:480) relates closely to our analysis of embodiment and transcendence in Chapters 2, 6 and 8. Pannenberg exemplifies Protestant theology's attempt to address basic issues in social anthropology when developing a theological anthropology; but his underlying method inevitably subordinates the cultural perspective to theology. For him, theology cannot simply adopt data from social anthropology, but must 'appropriate them in a critical way' (1985:18). Indeed, what anthropology says about human life must be expanded to show that 'the anthropological datum itself contains a further and theologically relevant dimension' (1985:20).

Fieldwork and Methodology

While anthropologists seldom pursue any such expansion, that does not, usually, indicate any lack of existential concern shown in their commitment to the groups they study. From the early twentieth century anthropologists have favoured 'fieldwork', a method often described as 'participant observation', and one serving to validate the status of a social or cultural anthropologist. From the later twentieth century a growing awareness of the earlier influence of colonial power and the way in which 'native' peoples had been treated as 'subjects' of study led to an intellectual concern over the values and motives of scholars, and resulted in a 'reflexive' form of anthropology. Issues such as 'Orientalism', the way in which 'Western' scholars classified and approached 'Eastern' peoples, as well as a growing awareness of the male orientation of study, led to calls for a higher profile for the life experience of the anthropologist. Anthropology became increasingly alert to the narrative aspect of fieldwork at practically the same time that theology discovered narrative theology (cf. Chapters 2 and 6). This reduction of the divide between academic theology and the faith-reflections of ordinary believers echoed a change in the image of scholarly, aloof and professional anthropologists and in attitudes to the rights of 'ordinary' people and their access to the outcome of anthropological study (Bloch 1992b:127ff.).

Confessional Theology and Fieldwork Anthropology

Another similarity between theologian and anthropologist concerns the impact of life-experience upon them as practitioners of their craft, for in a sense, each is a 'convert'. The church-based life-persuasion of most theologians matches the influence of a people, group or community studied by anthropologists. Even if it is too extreme to compare worship for the theologian with fieldwork for the anthropologist, fieldwork remains important in the social science of religion for its effect upon individual scholars, and matches the religious experience that motivates the confessional theologian. Here, fieldwork anthropology and confessional theology bear a certain family resemblance rooted in experience and shared with others through accounts framed by their respective traditions. Sometimes, as in Liberation Theology in South America and elsewhere and, less obviously but just as powerfully, in local church life throughout the world, religious leaders are constantly influenced by the social experience of pastoral 'fieldwork'. At least, by acknowledging the relation between experience, opinion and thought, the anthropologist can appreciate the theologian's commitment, just as the theologian can see the experiential basis of the anthropologist's life.

Christianity and Culture

These life experiences bring the question of culture to the forefront as a crucial topic of interest to both theology and anthropology. Culture was one of the first concepts established by nineteenth-century anthropologists as the object of their study and echoes a long-standing theological concern with the organization of society. Theologians have, from the earliest days of Christianity as an emergent sect of Judaism, been self-conscious about belonging to a distinctive group with its own scheme of world-interpretation and ethics of action. Its growth as a Church in the Hellenistic world led, through Constantine's Empire, to the Christendom of medieval Europe. With the Protestant Reformation powerful states further accentuated the importance of a theological self-understanding of secular authority and power. Through the imperial colonialization of the Americas and elsewhere Christianity expanded into innumerable cultures and, with the extensive missionary activity of the eighteenth and nineteenth centuries, its politically powerful presence was marked through Christian denominations across the world and continues to be highly influential even in contexts deemed to be profoundly secular.

Christianity adheres to no single social theory applicable to all Churches at all times, despite individual apologists who would desire it; for Catholic, Orthodox and Protestants, in their Lutheran, Anglican, Reformed and Charismatic traditions, along with numerous independent groups, have all developed distinctive theories of faith and society. One of the ongoing tasks of denominational and ecumenical theology is to engage constantly with this issue, as witnessed by political, economic, ethnic and gender theologies. The late nineteenth and early twentieth centuries were typified by Christian social theory generated in relation to denominational divisions and the influence of Christian ideology upon public life. When J. H. W. Stuckenberg, for example, undertook to write what he saw as the very first *Christian Sociology*, he devoted time to explaining that 'Christian Sociology' could not be a version of Auguste Comte's 'positivist' sociology that denied the existence and influence of God. For Stuckenberg the Protestant Principle of biblical authority underlay what he described as 'the science of Christian society' (1881:34). While his was a worthy attempt at highlighting the importance of studying human beings and not simply studying God, as he saw theology largely intent upon doing, he achieved very little, especially when compared, for example, with the German historian of religion Ernst Troeltsch (1865–1923), who made an immense contribution to an understanding of how Protestantism had influenced Western culture. His posthumous *Social Teachings of the Christian Churches* (1931 [1912]) remains a significant account of religious group organization and of the process whereby established Churches accommodated to worldly values, only to attract sectarian protest against that compromise, one of the most influential examples of which came in Søren Kierkegaard's judgement of Danish Lutheranism in the mid-nineteenth century (Steere 1961:16). Under Troeltsch's influence the American theologian, Richard H. Niebuhr pursued the themes of denominational fragmentation and of Christian ethics (1929), while his brother, Reinhold Niebuhr (1943) exerted considerable influence through writing and personal involvement in political activity. Troeltsch also influenced Louis Dumont's anthropological study of the rise of individualism, beginning in early Christianity when the individual was emancipated 'through a personal transcendence' of people set in a community of equality but sensing a personal relationship with God (1986:31). Here Dumont's anthropology resembles Pannenberg's theological treatment of the 'autonomy of the individual' originating in the life of faith as expressed, not least, in the Reformation (1985:482ff.).

Many others have advanced Christian social theory, from theologians such as F. D. Maurice (1805–1872) and leaders like William Temple (cf. 1934) to literary figures such as T. S. Elliott, whose sense of growing secularization led him to the conviction that 'anything like Christian traditions transmitted from generation to generation within the family must disappear', with the remaining small body of Christians 'consisting entirely of adults' (1939:22). While so much could be said historically, philosophically and theologically, I identify four features of Christian social theory to enter our conversation between theology and anthropology, viz. (i.) the idea of Christendom, (ii) the two kingdoms, (iii) the sacramental world and (iv) the Christian individual.

Christendom

Emerging within the political reality of the Holy Roman Empire, Christendom extended from Charlemagne's coronation in AD 800 until its essential demise, as some would see it, at the hands of Napoleon in 1806. For a thousand years the Kingdom of God was intimately involved with human political regimes. The sixteenth century's Reformation yielded its own versions of this scheme, notably in German and British states, while, later, the founding fathers of the USA established a society free from state control of religion. Through American ideals of democracy and divine election this evolved a broad civic religion, giving the contemporary USA a sense of itself as a spokesman for Christianity, a new form of Christendom allied to military power. Even when Christians no longer think of power in terms of control, the very notion of the Ecumenical Movement, as a world-wide unity of Christians, conveys a sense of the extent of Christianity.

Two Kingdoms or One

A sub-theme of 'Christendom', the dichotomy between sacred and secular domains, has taken numerous forms with, for example, John's Gospel distinguishing between 'the world' and Christ's followers and Paul marking the 'flesh' from the 'spirit'. In the early fifth century Augustine explored the divide between Christian and world in *The City of God*, a response to the fall of Rome in 410 AD and influenced by Plato's earlier ideal city reflected in *The Republic*. Underlying many of these notions is the issue of humanity, either set to love God, neighbour and the righteousness motivating such commitment, or the self-love that detracts from ultimate social well-being (cf. Barker 1944:xiv ff.). In Protestant theology Luther developed the two-kingdoms theory of the kingdom of God and of the world. Kings and magistrates rule the worldly kingdom for the good of all, with the sword as their symbol of power. Strength, even wrath, are required to maintain in this domain an order that is ultimately validated through God's firm purpose expressed in the Bible. The other kingdom is ruled by God's word expressed in Bible, Christ and sermon, and is the sphere where grace and mercy reign. The power of the two-cities image is still evident today, as in Milbank's philosophical *tour de force* defending a traditional Christianity against sociological interpretation (1990:380ff.).

Psychologically and philosophically speaking this world-view of two domains is consonant with ideas of conversion as a transition from one realm to another, as explored in Chapter 6. Politically this reflects the sharp historical line separating state and Church in the USA, but joining them in English Anglicanism and in the Lutheranism of several other European countries. Only in 2000, for example, was the Lutheran Church of Sweden disestablished. This type of Protestant theory avoided a theological chasm between the sacred and the secular, while opposing the Catholic scheme of Church penetration of society through its sacramental system governing spirituality and ethics.

The Sacramental World

The theological method described as 'sacramental' relates the sacred and profane through a different kind of theological rationale, in which the sacred so relates to the profane that nothing lies beyond its reach. Traditional sacramental theology is rooted in Catholic spirituality and ethics and framed by the Mass, which ultimately validates the belief that God became human in the person of Jesus of Nazareth. This doctrine of the incarnation, asserting both a divine and a human nature in the one person of Jesus, views all earthly matter as a potential vehicle of and for the divine. The Mass, including the Eucharistic development of it in non-Roman Catholic Churches, maintains this sacramental view of the world; and at its heart lie the combined doctrines of transubstantiation and Eucharistic sacrifice. The Fourth Lateran Council of 1215 formally announced the belief that in the rite the bread became the body and the wine the blood of Christ. Following the medieval theological adaptation of the Aristotelian philosophical classification of the nature of things this distinguished between their 'substance' and 'accidents': the substance referring to the real and actual nature, and the accidents to the way something appeared to the ordinary senses. On this basis the Mass involves a divine miracle whereby the substance – the 'real' nature of the bread – becomes transformed into the substance – the 'real' nature of Christ; and so likewise with the wine and the blood of Christ. All the while their 'accidents' remain unchanged: bread looks like bread and wine like wine.

The doctrine of the sacrifice of the Mass, though much disputed, argues that to some degree or other the original death of Christ, interpreted as a sacrifice for the sin of the world, is represented afresh. This can mean that the original passion and death of Christ are depicted or that the very act of sacrifice occurs again in and through the rite of the priest at the altar. Whatever the doctrinal precision, there emerged an entire spirituality of devotion surrounding the Mass. Thomas Aquinas was partially responsible for this, having been given the responsibility for helping to frame the new ritual of the Feast of Corpus Christi in the 1260s. He laid a basis for subsequent debates over ritual in Western theology and, through it, for Western intellectualism's approach to the very idea of ritual. By explaining how the physical entities of bread and wine enabled the very body and blood of Christ to be available for the faithful he fostered a spirituality that easily frames an expectation of miracles. Just as the Mass involves a miracle of transformation, so God might visit any location, person, or event on occasions of divine disclosure, ensuring that Christian individuals inhabit a sacramental universe potent with possibility exemplified, for example, in the mystically scientific reflections of Teilhard de Chardin (1959, 1965). This Catholic priest, a palaeontologist prevented for much of his life from actively teaching his synthetic vision, wrote, persuasively, of looking 'at the world simultaneously from an evolutionary and a spiritual point of view', and enjoined others to 'establish ourselves in the divine *milieu*', where, 'we shall be within the inmost depths of souls and the greatest consistency of matter'. (1965:124, 127).

The Christian Individual

To Christendom, the two kingdoms and the sacramental world as models of religious life we can now add a fourth, that of the Christian individual. Though we could root this in Kierkegaard, often designated the father of existentialism, I will use Paul Tillich (1886–1965). There is a sense in which Tillich and Teilhard provide extreme examples of the logical tendencies of Catholic and Protestant theologies. If the miracle of grace for Catholics is rooted in the Mass, for Protestants it occupies the heart addressed by God's written and preached 'word'. If Teilhard extends that miracle to the realm of evolving matter at large, Tillich enhances it in the existential life of the individual believer. Yet, and this is the intriguing feature, both Teilhard and Tillich in their own ways seek to overcome any dichotomy between sacred and secular. Their resemblance lies in the ultimate disregard of any absolute distinction between the sacred and the secular, their difference in the process and focus of disregard: Tillich's existentialism operates in and through the individual and the perception of individuals, while Teilhard's sacramental perspective functions through its classification of the non-human realm of matter.

Tillich argues against any distinction of the 'two kingdoms' type. He sees his own form of existential theology as leading to 'the disappearance of the gap between the sacred and the secular' (1959:41). He defines religion as 'being ultimately concerned about that which is and should be our ultimate concern'. This means that 'faith is the state of being grasped by an ultimate concern', with God being 'the name for the content of the concern'. He is eager to stress that this is an existential definition and perspective and not some 'theoretical understanding of religion' (1959:40). This existential concern involves every moment and each aspect of life, with no option for the sacred–secular divide; 'every work day is a day of the Lord, every supper a Lord's supper . . . every joy a joy in God. In all preliminary concerns, ultimate concern is present, consecrating them. Essentially the religious and the secular are not separated realms. Rather they are within each other' (1959:41). But, in an essentially important distinction, he affirms that this reflects an ideal state, one in which we do not live. Unfortunately, the religious realm sets itself up as a distinct arena of activity, and the constraint of having to live caught between 'sacred' and 'secular' realms is the prime example of the 'estrangement of man from his true being' (1959:42). Even so, the sense of an ultimate concern is, actually and really, what each culture pursues. So it is that 'religion is the substance of culture and culture is the totality of forms in which the basic concern of religion expresses itself' (ibid.).

In a telling sentence Tillich expresses what could almost be taken to be a bridge statement serving well to relate theological and anthropological concerns when he affirms that 'he who can read the style of a culture can discover its ultimate concern, its religious substance': this charter impelled him to explore the style of his contemporary culture – that of industrial society – and brought him to the conclusion that human exploration of the technical aspects of life had conduced to a 'loss of the dimension of depth' of encounter with reality (1959:43). This was at the same time that, for example, the equally influential historian of religion, Mircea Eliade, was bemoaning the banalization of the world with its loss of mythical perception and presaged the 1960s as the decade of the twentieth century that dwelt most upon the idea and the experience of the 'secular' (1968).

Tillich's theological influence declined in the latter half of the twentieth century as conservative, evangelical and even fundamentalist religion expanded on the one hand and radical movements on the other. These varied from political activism in Liberation and Black Theology to a form of philosophical atheism combined with elements of traditional devotionalism on the other. Tillich's existential theology reflects human experience and the way individuals make philosophical and theological sense of life experience. It is not simply about philosophy or theology and it is not simply about political action. Perhaps there have been relatively few people who have been able to grasp the way in which his theology interfuses experience and be interfused by it. Misunderstanding always lies close to hand, as is the case with Tillich's key existentialist-based concepts of 'being' and of 'existence'. For Tillich God is being itself. God is the 'ground of being'. Humanity, by contrast, is rooted in existence. In this sense mankind experiences existence, while God is being itself. On that basis of thought God does 'not exist'. To say that God 'existed' would be to identify deity with humanity in a 'fallen' world or, in terms of existentialist theology, as being estranged. For many ordinary believers, however, the very statement that God does not exist is taken to indicate an atheistic utterance – something far from Tillich's intention. The point at issue here is that it is the method of theology to engage with life and experience and to do so in a way that sees that involvement as a participation in God. Each theological method does this through its own grammar of discourse, and tends to be associated with a particular type of religious practice. That framework of active participation provides an ethos for worship and for ethics and comprises that world of relationships with others within which a theologian thinks and acts.

The Dynamic World of Selves

From the political, sacramental and existential worlds of theological thought we move to that element of anthropology's consideration of human nature proposed by Bloch that brings the living individual into anthropological focus (1992a). No longer are we dealing simply with earlier sociological and anthropological preoccupations with roles, social status or social process, but with the added dynamic of life-changes that can best be classified as existential concerns.

Bloch depicts 'the vast majority of societies' as representing human life 'occurring within a permanent framework which transcends the natural transformative process of birth, growth, reproduction, ageing and death' (1992a:3). He typifies that transcending element in the idioms of violence and conquest effected through rites in which the natural vitality of everyday life is replaced by a higher-order vitality. 'In ritual representations, native vitality is replaced by a conquered, external, consumed vitality' (1992a:5). Encompassing several major theoretical concerns of the anthropology of religion, including sacrifice and the supernatural, he draws attention to 'power' as the crucial concept in the study of religion, arguing that new vitality is generated through contact with supernatural figures and leads to a transcending of the ordinary facts of life enshrined in birth, maturation and death. While he practically apologizes for bringing this more philosophical anthropology to bear upon social analysis at a time when wholesale interpretative possibilities are deemed impossible, his perspective seems to me a particularly fruitful approach to several aspects of contemporary religion in general and Christianity in particular.

Defining Religion

Trying to understand religion assumes, of course, that we have some notion of what it is. What often passes for anthropological definition of religion might, more properly, be viewed as no more than a 'summarized description' (Boyer 1994:34). Certainly, the variety of anthropological 'definitions' of religion moves from Tylor's intellectualist stress on belief in supernatural beings through Durkheim's sociological focus on unified system of beliefs and practices uniting people as a moral community around sacred things to Geertz's preoccupation with religion as a system of symbols providing particular moods and a sense of certainty about the world. More recently Boyer focused on human responses to counter-intuitive life situations as a basic, cognitive approach to religion. We will return to these approaches when appropriate; but, because it serves well to relate 'ritual' to this book's concern with embodiment, I will largely follow Geertz's definition of religion as a 'system of symbols which acts to establish powerful, pervasive and long-lasting moods and motivations in men by formulating conceptions of a general order of existence and clothing these conceptions with such an aura of factuality that these moods and motivations seem uniquely realistic' (1973:4).

This stresses the symbolic aspect of religion and tends to analyse cultures as a form of 'text' with various levels of interpretation (cf. Schneider 1993:55–82). While this makes some anthropologists describe him as a symbolist, this book highlights emotion, mood and the sense of the factuality of religion in Geertz's perspective and, in Chapter 2 for example, we move away from culture as a decodable text or language and set it alongside other forms of description of self-awareness within cultural frameworks in order to develop our interest in embodiment. One of the more poignant features of religion related to moods of embodiment is the sense of the reality of things that it conveys; yet here, too, caution is wise, when we recall Boyer's insight that religion often demarcates areas of life experience that contradict common sense and embrace counterintuitive information. This makes Geertz's 'conceptions of a general order of existence' and their enveloping 'aura of factuality' potentially but not ultimately problematic. For religious responses to life experience regularly address the problematic, troubling, bizarre and contradictory aspects of life, providing an enclosure for, and a mode of response to, them. It is this ability to respond to problematic areas through action that furnishes an extremely powerful adaptive feature of human life. When philosophy fails ritual may succeed. Here Christianity possesses a prized set of ideas bearing a family likeness to each other, and including notions of paradox, mystery and awe, each grounded in the practice of piety (Boyer 1994:36, 57).

For the devotee, order and a sense of reality are often greater for having engaged with the counterintuitive; and cultures with an established literary tradition, invoking philosophical ideas, often frame this domain in terms of truthfulness. One consequence of this awareness of truthfulness and reality is that devotees dislike having their religion described in terms that contextualize it through a higher-level critical interpretation, as though that account immediately relativizes and reduces its significance (cf. van Dijk and Pels 1996:245–70). Similarly, some theologians can be disconcerted when anthropological notions are used to interpret theological ideas. As has been already mentioned in relation to confessional theology and anthropological fieldwork, the emotional underpinning of intellectualism is very similar in both theology and anthropology, where experiences of life contexts relate to 'truth' in the sense of assured personal premises or thoughts about life. In contemporary life it is seldom politically correct to announce that one possesses the 'true' way of interpreting life, since 'truth' hints at a fundamentalism formally banned from much post-modern discussion. Yet, this life-view is more common than is admitted, and deserves more open reflection as part of an awareness of interest, conviction and engagement with colleagues at large.

It has been said, for example, that the main difference between Evangelical and Fundamentalist Christians in the USA lies not in the actual doctrines adhered to, but in the mode of adhering to them. I think this is largely correct, and is applicable to other forms of knowledge, including social scientific and scientific positions. Liberal, culturally relativist, post-modern and many other outlooks can be held in exclusivist or inclusivist ways, each relating differently to the counterintuitive aspect of life. Much depends, perhaps, upon the degree of fear inherent in a scholar's own grasp of the relationship between knowledge and personal identity. For theologians there always remains the question of status, and relationships within particular religious groups, and freedom of expression is not always guaranteed. For anthropologists too there are questions of peer acceptance within the profession of anthropology, as well as of their own status and identity as individuals related or not related to religious institutions.

The interrelationship between anthropological and theological interpretations of the world is not, then, an easy one. There is no 'question' to 'answer', but there is a real challenge. This challenge is not unlike that process of intellectual development when one's accepted world-view is exposed to other worlds and to the pestering question of human cultural relativity. Just how individuals respond to such periods of critical consideration depends upon many things. The desire to withdraw into the givenness of earlier certainties can be understood, as can the opposite trend of 'going native' and accepting the 'reality' of new experience. People will choose for themselves. This book, at least, offers itself as a kind of invitation to explore ideas in a conversation where themes of embodiment and salvation, human nature and the transcending of human nature, of the radical social nature of human relationships and yet of its basis in individuality all claim a voice. In certain respects this conversation between disciplines resembles Rowan Williams's grasp of theology as, itself, a venture drawing sometimes on 'celebratory, communicative and critical styles' depending upon purpose and context (2000:xiii). In the following chapters some of the topics drawn together from theological and anthropological worlds are treated sometimes in a reflective way, aware of the wonder of human beings and our cultures, sometimes rather didactically to make a point that may be unfamiliar to people, and some-times critically when indicating areas of inadequate treatment or of possible development.

Embodiment and Incarnation

Embodiment – the awareness of 'being' as a body – is the major theoretical perspective underlying this chapter and the entire book. Not only is embodiment concerned with how people talk about themselves, but also with how that awareness may be analysed. It combines basic information and the analysis of information. Anthropology is just beginning to study 'how people feel' and how 'somatic states' – states of the body, or *soma* as the body is called in Greek – might be classified and analysed (Blacking 1977:vii). Although gender is one vital aspect of embodiment, it will not be explored separately, for it possesses a literature of its own reflecting male and female forms of embodiment (cf. Bynum 1992), including the relationship of women and reciprocity within anthropological studies (cf. Irigaray 1997:174–89; Strathern 1998:22–42).

Embodiment is as interested in the posture of people's necks during prayer as in the content of their petitions, in the sensation of chanting as in the history of liturgical formulae. Embodiment also bears affinities to the idea of spirituality, itself an intriguing word of the early twenty-first century used as much in nursing and palliative care and in New Age circles as in its original ecclesiastical home. Theologically, 'spirituality' described 'spiritual formation' or Christian development through the practice of prayer within the ritual and daily life of devotees.

After establishing the important interfusing of doctrine and practice this chapter will argue that the idea of God becoming man in the individual, Jesus of Nazareth, makes sense to Christians because of an affinity between the spirituality of embodiment and the spirituality of the incarnation. These terms, embodiment and incarnation, spotlight the anthropological concern with the cultural medium of human life and the theological concern with divine–human relationships.

Systematic and Clustered Thinking

Another foundational aspect of our argument contrasts scholarly system-atization of belief with what ordinary people experience in clustered bits and pieces. Much academic theology and anthropology is logic-sentential, accounting for ideas, events and phenomena by describing and analysing them in a logical way expressed in formal sentences arranged to introduce, develop and conclude an argument. This 'logical approach' of formal education allows educated people to be described as 'disciplined' in thought, while academic disciplines are divided into particular 'subjects'. But ordinary life, religious or otherwise, is not so divided. Life lived is not as life documented, and, though some systematizing is justified, as scholars seek order and intelligibility amidst complexity, it is unwise to impose an artificial order on human experience. Proper attention must be paid to those human ways of thinking that produce ordinary forms of life and behaviour. Here psychological and neurological research, tentative though it is at present, enters the debate, not least in the theoretical idea of 'connectionism'. Derived from theories on brain function, connectionism argues that when problem-solving or dealing with many aspects of ordinary behaviour brain processes are not logic-like and two-dimensional, operating in 'straight lines' from one point to another, but are multi-dimensional, making connections between many sorts of experience and knowledge in working towards a response or some desired outcome. Associations between images, moods, words and information of all sorts are integrated until some desired response is reached. Memories, not just of names and places but also of smells and states of bodily feeling or moods, are all significant. We recall how we felt at a certain time and place, and these 'mood-memories' – as we shall call them – become influential over present responses and future decisions. A considerable amount of research is now available on the nature of mood and its relation to memory; but as technical debate it lies beyond the scope of this present book (cf. Frijda 1993:122.).

Systematic Theology and Non-systematic Faith

The ordered approach is represented in Systematic Theology, which integrates major doctrines on the basis of some guiding principle; and these rationales of tradition are, in turn, grounded in the practices and cultural history of particular groups. In terms of the sociology of know-ledge a systematic theology is the formal and ideological expression of the plausibility structure of a Church or community. In terms of Geertz's definition of religion Systematic Theology formulates 'conceptions of a general order of existence' while both scholarship and worship play their part in 'clothing these conceptions with such an aura of factuality that' their liturgically and ethically associated 'moods and motivations seem uniquely realistic' (1973:4).

Most people's practical belief is, probably, non-systematic; and this, in itself, demands some qualification of Geertz's definition of religion. While the formal training of priests involves systematic theology, it does not take long for them to learn, in pastoral ministry, that ordinary believers are seldom guided and informed by systematic doctrines, not simply because they have seldom studied theology but because ordinary life does not work in that way. Clergy, too, seldom operate upon the basis of Systematic Theology, for astute writers on priesthood acknowledge that 'the study of doctrine is a growth in sensitivity to the activity and presence of God rather than the learning of dogmatic assertions' (Martineau 1981:24). One classic Roman Catholic study of religious experience of more mystical kinds, Poulain's *The Graces of Interior Prayer,* began by distinguishing between studies that 'systematise all facts theologically' and his own account of 'very accurate descriptions' because the people he had in view 'do not desire these things' but want 'very exact pictures – I was about to say photographs – in which they can recognise themselves' (1921:xiii).

And if this applies to the regular worshipper, it applies even more to less regular participants. Wendy James raised the issue of the 'way in which partial and highly selective elements of that supposed entity "Christianity" may spread beyond the confines of formal teaching and the controlled transmission of belief and practice' (1988:132). Her example, on the spread of Christian ideas amongst the non-Christian Uduk in the Sudan–Ethiopian border area, concerned the medium of music and song, showing that a single song can avoid the complexities of Biblical texts, while different songs can produce contradictory messages. Because each song is self-contained this does not matter, since it is the singing that counts. She likens aspects of Christian hymns sung by people not necessarily given to Christianity to some Uduk ritual songs that are sung in a language from a neighbouring people that the Uduk do not actually understand. It is not only, for example, in the old Latin Mass or in some contemporary Western Sikh Gurdwaras that groups engage in sacred words they do not immediately understand, a fact that adds another dimension to the elements comprising a person's 'religious cluster'. While a systematic theology serves well as the formal idealization of a faith, practical religion involves behaviour related to clusters of belief – clusters that, in turn, are related to the wider systematic theology of a group, accentuating its style and mood.

Systematic Anthropology and Life as Lived

Anthropology entertains similar distinctions, as when Maurice Bloch asked why some anthropological discussions were questionable as far as the people studied were concerned (1992b:127–46). He reasoned that scholars over-systematized a society's way of life. When literate, those written about could not readily identify themselves and their way of life in what was written about them. Of course, there is a technical distinction that is relevant here, borrowed from linguists but widely used by anthropologists, in which they speak of the 'emic' and 'etic' approach to cultures. The emic view of life details the view held by people of themselves, while the etic perspective consists in the theoretical model of their life constructed by anthropologists, who seek the underlying pattern of values, the ideological template upon which a society operates. Although this distinction can, quite obviously, lead to a difference of accounting for a society, that was not Bloch's point, for he was still considering the 'emic' level of description, arguing that a systematized scheme of things was alien to the way in which most peoples actually live. Put simply, life does not feel as though it is lived according to some organizing blueprint, and to describe it as such is a mistake. His description of the distance between some anthropologists and the accounts they give and the people they study is highly reminiscent of the distance between many theologians and ordinary Christians, and may account for that degree of distrust often existing between them. While many traditional believers think that liberal theologians dilute the truth of faith, they also do not recognize their way of living their faith in what theologians write.

Cluster and Context

One cause of this distance lies in decontextualization, a distinctive feature of systematizing thought. Anthropology tends to be less guilty of that error than does systematic theology, owing to the context-specific nature of the groups studied, even though certain notions, such as kinship or even ritual, have occasioned debate on this issue (Needham 1974). Excessive theological decontextualization led to the later twentieth-century reaction explicitly called contextual theology, emphasizing the significance of local concerns and prompting groups to develop their own theological reflections. Chris Rowland, a contemporary Professor of New Testament Theology at Oxford, spoke of just such a 'growing gap between the use of the bible in adult theological education in Britain and its use in theology and religious studies departments and in most seminaries'

(Rowland 1997:44). His example of a biblical scholar committed to contextual theology in the form of Liberation Theology through personal experience in Brazil is unusual, at least within British biblical scholarship. Some other notable exceptions have been clergy committed to industrial mission and urban contexts (cf. Duffield 1997). Liberation Theology, engaged with the politics of justice in contexts of oppression, is a related concern, especially in the later twentieth century in South America. It overlaps with Narrative Theology or the Theology of Story (Navone 1977; Stroup 1981). Together these exemplify what I would call 'cluster-theology', developing groups of theological ideas relevant to particular situations. By sympathetic extension some have used forms of Liberation Theology within the Church of England to engage in practical action, typified in David Sheppard's book *Bias to the Poor*, a phrase that came to enshrine a theological idea on what God's preference might be (1983:145–58). One interesting example of contextual theology seems to invert this political concern, as when missionaries in the Sudan avoided translating hymns dealing with freedom – not least Spirituals such as 'Let my People Go' – at a time of some political sensitivity (Wendy James 1988:137).

While Liberation-like approaches accentuate the link between context and cluster, they can also slip into their own form of systematic theology related to power politics, gender oppression or the like; but the theoretically valuable issue remains the consideration of how beliefs are invoked, activated or ignored in different contexts. Certainly caution is demanded over what formal theology might decontextualize as syncretism, but what, in context, may be more a kind of *bricolage* of selected religious ideas and practices, as in Afro-Brazilian Condomble (Ryle 1988: 40ff.).

Such variability runs counter to the implicit assumption of the systematic theologian that 'the truth' is the same at all times and in all places. In practice, however, religious believers do not live and act as though that were the case. Here we must be careful, for a great deal hangs upon the emphasis given to the way we express our argument. I am suggesting that in practice people act as though one idea is important in one context and another idea in another context. The systematician will read this as a perfect example of the believer's drawing motivating doctrines from the total available scheme but leaving the entire system intact. My suggestion is that there is no 'system' as far as most religious believers are concerned; there are only clusters of belief, clusters constructed through life experience, through influential individuals among family, friends, teachers and priests. Boyer has expressed the same idea when arguing that 'anecdotes, memories, statements made by ritual specialists' help constitute the information held by people on topics like ghosts (1994:95).

This cluster-approach to belief, and also to theology, is particularly well suited to discussing embodiment, an important issue for priests and other practitioners who are trained in systematic theology, yet whose work is with formally untrained believers. As those mediating the 'great' tradition of systematic theology with the 'little' tradition of local practice, theirs is the task of mutual interpretation. Empirical data on contextualized beliefs in individuals are rare, and two examples will suffice: one concerns the Eucharist, the other death.

Faith Clusters

The eucharistic example, here as elsewhere in this book, is drawn from the Church of England, a rite reflecting the basic pattern of several major Christian traditions. In one study people were asked about some ideas that might be important to them when they attended the Eucharist. Presented with a variety of options, 86 per cent of the 168 interviewed said that they 'felt at one with God', 85 per cent said it made them realize what Jesus did for them on the cross, 73 per cent said they felt 'at one with themselves', 68 per cent that they felt 'at one with others' and 36 per cent that they 'sensed the presence of dead loved ones' (Davies *et al.* 1990:234ff.). There is nothing surprising about these responses, given the overall theological associations of the rite: what was informative was that age and geography made a difference. The older people were the more likely they were to say that they 'felt at one with other people': this was the response of 50 per cent of those aged 18–34, 56 per cent of those aged 35–44, 69 per cent of those aged 45–54, 70 per cent of those aged 55–64, and 80 per cent of those aged over 65. This suggests that the element of the Eucharist reflected in the ritual act of 'sharing of the peace', shaking hands or otherwise greeting each other, is likely to reflect different meanings for those taking part. Also the sense of what Jesus had accomplished on the cross, too, generally increased with age, with 70 per cent of the 18–34-year-olds choosing this element, and 90 per cent of the over 65 group. Geographical location of respondents also made a difference to the elements favoured. Those who felt 'at one with themselves' for example, varied from 91 per cent in the English Midlands to 61 per cent in the north-east of England. Even 'what Jesus did on the Cross' could vary from 75 per cent to 92 per cent in two different parts of central England (Davies *et al.* 1990:236–8). This was the variation in responses to a set of specific options specifically on the Eucharist: it is likely to be even greater on wider beliefs.

Death Clusters

My second example concerns life after death. In the same study of those on the active register of Anglican churches some 15 per cent expressed disagreement with the idea of life after death, and 13 per cent were unsure about it. As far as the idea of reincarnation, or coming back to this life as something or someone else, was concerned 4 per cent of the churchgoers thought that this was the case, and another 18 per cent were unsure about the possibility (Davies *et al.* 1990:226–7). In a quite different survey similar variation of belief occurred in relation to beliefs in life after death amongst members of major denominations (Davies and Shaw 1995). Many more variations of belief in relation to life circumstances and choice could be drawn from personal experience of most people, many of which could be shown to reflect that 'incorrigibility of the body', those pressures of our humanity that refer to biological needs or to a desire for particular places (Winquist 1995:34–44).

System versus Cluster

It is important to underline this wider world from which individuals draw their beliefs, attitudes and behaviours, since it is too easy to separate off the ordinary world of daily life and experience from 'religious' experience and 'religious' ritual, as Pascal Boyer, for example, has made clear (1993a:42). The historical development of doctrine has witnessed an ever-increasing definition of what the truth is believed to be, and that truth diverges as groups move apart; and the same can be said for much Christian ritual. While Boyer is correct, in one sense, in arguing that 'religious ideas are . . . a motley of representations drawn from numerous cognitive domains', his determined concern to establish a psychologically grounded basis for the cognitive processes underlying religious ritual – a venture with which I am sympathetic – should not ignore the historical constraints of theological debate that have brought a degree of cultural seriousness to the definition of what constitutes a ritual (ibid.).

Greek Orthodoxy, Roman Catholicism and Protestantism are not at one on many issues of doctrine, and especially on the church organization that implements what is believed to be the truth. Church history reveals an increasing systematization of belief and division between groups in relation to their own preferred system. In anthropology, too, there are different traditions of interpretation, and in a wave of self-analysis often described as 'reflexive anthropology', many contemporary practitioners show concern over anthropology's intimate alliance with major European societies, empires and values, not least male-oriented values, in its interpretation of cultural life. Anthropological and theological hermeneutics share some mutual sensitivities.

To draw attention to factors influencing methods and theories, whether in theology or anthropology, is only to express the obvious nature of our own historical and cultural formation. Such reflections could constitute the prelude for an extensive discussion of social and critical theory, that kind of cultural epistemology or theorizing about knowing what we know and how we know it that has over the last thirty years become an entire intellectual discipline penetrating many of the humanities and social sciences, and that can, all too easily, take the form of endless reflections on power, gender and language ending in a paralysis of mind. Indeed, there is a sense in which post-modern analysis is an example of the shift from both theological and philosophical 'systems' to the clustering of belief associated with the embodiment of particular thinkers. More illuminating as far as embodiment is concerned are analyses such as those of Zygmunt Bauman, which consider, for example, the drive for physically fit bodies or the tactile nature of relationships in contemporary urban life: the point is that social worlds produce bodies to their own liking (1995: 115ff.). Here it is sufficient to acknowledge such post-modern persuasions and to hint at the similarity between theologians who acknowledge the limits of language for describing God and anthropologists aware of the cultural and autobiographical limitations involved in seeking to understand another culture and to give an account of it to those of their own.

God Is Another Culture

Indeed, there is a sense in which God is another culture. Theology and anthropology share the fact of engagement with 'another', well aware of the inherent limitations of the self in appropriating it. This awareness involves an impulsion to engage with the other, believing it to be inevitably worthwhile. To know that one is human and seeking to understand God or that one is a person from one culture seeking to understand someone from another is to acknowledge something of one's limitations and of the relativity of personal understanding. But this is simply to know the constraining facts of life within which thinking and understanding occur. For all practical purposes the provisional attitude of searching, framed by a degree of humility, reflects Anselm's well-known theological idea that one believes in order that one might understand in a life in which faith seeks understanding – all grounded in embodiment.

Grasping the Body

Still, even this focus involves problems because, from the realm of anthropology it is obvious that each culture possesses its own idea of what persons are and how they come to be themselves. One of the first anthropologists to engage with the issue of the universality or locality of the nature of self-identity was Marcel Mauss, through his influential essay on 'the techniques of the body', a kind of phenomenology of bodily behaviour in relation to a sense of identity, presented as a series of propositions on how human beings acquire their own abilities to live and act in certain ways (1979 [1936]). Just how 'selves' are depicted the world over has been taken up by many other anthropologists (e.g. Carrithers *et al.* 1985; Strathern 1988; Wendy James 1998:14–15). The broad outcome of that research is that there is no single concept of the 'self'. Each culture depicts persons according to its own ideology, to its historical and cultural forms of life and to its environment, climate and ecology.

Against that background of cultural diversity it is risky to address the ideas of 'self' and of 'embodiment' in a rather general way; but I do so, not only for the benefit of those for whom these ideas are novel, but also because the world-wide nature of Christianity – despite innumerable local cultural influences and variants – often affirms similar clusters of beliefs and tends to decontextualize them in systematic ways. Christianity constituted one of the earliest forms of globalization, and its own standardizations have deeply influenced ideas of what constitutes humanity and humanity's destiny. Here we will, first, reflect on both official and popular reasons for a sense of the human partition of the self, then advocate the case of embodiment as a single entity, and, finally, consider the theological idea of the incarnation in relation to the idea of embodiment.

Partition of the Self

Human beings have long seen their ultimate destiny as lying beyond their bodies. The Christian tradition is no exception, with its belief in spiritual realities and the afterlife as a further development of the self in closer relation to God. It also announces that God actually became directly involved in human life through the person of Jesus of Nazareth. More than this, it depicts a scheme of salvation in which men and women may, themselves, become divine. This interlinked theme of human embodiment and Incarnation expresses the notion of salvation. In fact the Christian notion of the individual or of the self is, essentially, soteriological. Because practically all forms of Christian identity are salvation-related the notion of identity is immediately set within the framework of some Church or of some corporate scheme that is charged with the task of explaining why and how human identity is flawed, as well as how it may come to a state of salvation.

Traditional Partitions

Some kind of division within human individuality, identity or selfhood relates to this flaw and underlies a great deal of Western intellectual thinking about the human condition. In the wake of the classical Greek divide between soul and body Plato has many followers, accepting that the soul is the true location of ultimate values and of the real human self, a soul that separates from the body at death and leaves for non-material realms of truth. Combined with or at least related to it are notions of body and spirit drawn from traditional Hebrew sources and reflected in the New Testament. Sometimes the very existence of biblical texts referring, in an apparently tripartite way, to body, soul and spirit leads to an increased awareness of divisions within each human being, but without any certainty as to what they are.

In sociological thought Durkheim adopted the notion that each individual could be viewed in the abstract terms of *Homo duplex,* referring not to any soul–body distinction, but to the metaphorical sense in which society was represented inside each individual, along with a more personal and private sense of the person. Earlier, Simmel had arrived at a similar idea, arguing that human beings have 'the capacity to split' themselves 'into different parts and to feel that one such portion' constitutes the 'real self' (1997:182). The psychological view of Freud spoke of mankind's inner tripartism of id, ego and superego, and of an unconscious and a conscious mind. Other notions reinforce this general view, as with the idea of the real self as opposed to external social roles, or of the unconscious mind in relation to the conscious.

E. B. Tylor's seminal anthropological study, *Primitive Culture*, paid particular attention to what he called 'the doctrine of souls', borrowing the term 'animism' to define and expand the idea (1958 [1871]: 9ff.). Animism explored the distinction between 'Spiritualistic' and 'Materialistic' doctrines of mankind, as well as the human preoccupation with explanations of life and death, of dreams and consciousness. Tylor would have preferred to use the term 'Spiritualism' to cover the breadth of human interest in souls and their effect, but did not do so because of the prevailing influence of the word to describe 'a particular modern sect, who indeed hold extreme spiritualistic views' (1958:10). Still, for Tylor, beliefs in souls, 'from the philosophy of the savage thinker to that of the modern professor of theology', bear a very strong family resemblance (1958:85). If it was contemporary Spiritualism that stimulated Tylor's thought, as Ann Taves indicates in her excellent study of religious experience in the eighteenth and nineteenth centuries, other concerns with identity, mind, body and self sustained his work (Taves 1999:181, 198–200).

Inner-otherness

To continue this debate I take up the perceived interior division of the self through the term 'inner-otherness'. This topic involves debates on consciousness that lie beyond the scope of this book, ranging from whether computers may be conscious to popular ideas of 'out of the body' and 'near-death' experiences. Accounts of people floating from their bodies and being able to observe what is happening to it are extraordinarily reminiscent of Tylor's account of souls, sleep and the like. More socio-logically, Peter Berger also described how 'man produces 'otherness' both outside and inside of himself as a result of his life in society', suggesting that there are contexts in which an individual 'becomes strange to himself in certain aspects of his socialised self' (1969: 91–2). So, whether from Plato's philosophy, populist newspapers or sociological orthodoxy, there is much to encourage notions of inner-otherness, fostering the sense that there is more to individuals than their bodies.

Traditional Theologies

Christian theology also diverges on this topic. Traditional Catholic teaching posits a soul but, at its most abstract, it is not simply divided from the body. In his discussion of 'The Body in the Order of Salvation' Karl Rahner develops Aquinas to argue that the body is 'the self-expression of the spirit reaching out into time and space' (1972: 84). The import of this lies in the human awareness of an internal mystery reflected in Catholic liturgy, and not least in its funeral rites, which depicted the soul as leaving the body to be received into an afterlife prior to the final resurrection of the body. From the early to the middle twentieth century Protestant theologians have tended to avoid any soul–body distinction, talking more about a unity of the person and emphasizing the doctrine of the resurrection of the body as a divine miracle largely mirroring the divine power manifested in the original creation of the world, and avoiding issues of purgation of the soul after death.

But the 'soul' may also be purged before death through ascetic disciplining of the body. For, while emphasis has often been placed upon the soul, whose cultivation is vital to ensure its ultimate beatific vision of heaven, the body has presented itself as the arena within which that soul currently, though inevitably, has its being. This body, however, possesses needs and makes demands, especially for food and sex, the two areas that religion most forcefully addresses by rule and regulation. Historians of doctrine have shown how the soul–body duality became integral to much of the religious thought and practice of the early church fathers as the gnostic world-view 'permeated late antique thought, both Christian and pagan', yielding a 'doctrine of man as a sojourner in an alien universe whose true home is "above", whose life in this world should be one of mortification in preparation for death and the return of the soul from whence it came', making 'mortification the way of salvation' (Radford Ruether 1969:13,12). Something of this still haunts contemporary Christianity, even though some, albeit few, theologians prefer to see the body alone as the vital focus of their concern. So it is that within Christian traditions the soul and the body provide two rather different centres of gravity from which views of human life proceed. Secular concerns with the body also emerged in the later twentieth century as part of a consideration of well-being, to which we return below.

Inner-otherness and Power

One reason the idea of the soul appeals doctrinally is as the site of divine interaction with each individual; another is to validate human identity in ethical considerations of foetal development and abortion. Here, however, our prime concern is to do justice to that sense of self or inner-otherness that is characteristic of human thought and confers an awareness of depth and significance underlying the very meaning of life. Nowhere is it expressed more forcefully than, for example, in George Steiner's *Real Presences*, with its wager on that presence of God that sustains meaning within language, art and aesthetic awareness: 'there is language, there is art', he says, 'because there is "the other"' (1989:137). I consider this sense of 'the other' to be intimately related to the notion of 'inner-otherness' in significant ways, especially for religious groups. Methodologically speaking, one could interpret inner-otherness anthropologically through Durkheim's *Homo duplex*, as reflecting the internalized sense of society that an individual might perceive as the 'other' within. The very fact that language, the mother-tongue, is so deeply foundational to human views of the world and of self extends this emphasis upon the social element embedded within the individual life. More psychologically speaking, a similar process of internalization of images of authority figures could achieve a similar end. More philosophically speaking, the very human capacity to reflect upon life situations and to ponder options can give a sense of otherness, of a deciding centre that somehow lies above and beyond ordinary consciousness and approximates to the notion of the transcendental ego of philosophical phenomenology. Ritual activity also fosters the sense of inner-otherness, as people encounter levels of experience they cannot easily render in formal explanation. Though these issues are considered in detail in Chapters 5, 6, and 7, we can also emphasize here that much of the outcome of ritual activity affords a degree of satisfaction to participants that cannot be explained simply by the literal meaning of the words of the rites, a satisfaction captured in Ricoeur's astute observation that 'language only captures the foam on the surface of life', and in his call to a mindfulness of that certain something that is 'powerful, efficacious, forceful' in symbols, and that cannot simply be rendered in language (1976:63). Ricoeur the philosopher came to see, albeit later than most anthropologists, that 'within the symbol . . . there is something non-semantic as well as semantic' (1976:45). That non-semantic element relates to the human body, to its engagement with the world through ritual performance and to the sense of inner-otherness that is intensified through the very performance of ritual.

Inner-otherness and God

Basic Christian spirituality teaches people to pray by using language in relation to God much as they would in relation to other human beings. While philosophers of religion have analysed such religious language, my interest is in how language fosters a degree of inner-otherness. To speak to another assumes that 'I' have something to say. When moving from the act of speaking to one in which I consider the act of speaking I, myself, become aware that 'I' have something to say. Immediately we are engaged in a phenomenological analysis of the self considering itself, of an individual viewing itself as an object of itself. The notion of inner-otherness is one consequence of such a pondering self.

Inner-other Revelation

But, within the context of worship, Christians speak of moments of aware-ness of the presence of God almost as a tangible force. Although such experiences can be interpreted psychologically or even biochemically, to the believer they may finally validate the sense of inner-otherness – in particular, when devotees sense themselves as 'acted upon'. Their inner being seems to be passive before the active presence. The inner-otherness is transcended by the new presence. This experience matches the notion of revelation, when a message or an awareness appears to 'come' to believers, leaving them with the firm impression that there is something within them that has been visited by God. It is not at all surprising, then, that biblical authors should speak of the body as a temple of the Holy Spirit. Indeed, Paul's writings are replete with such a sense of inner-otherness, and it does not always take the same character. It can give him a sense of divine union or of alienation, as when he refers to himself as a wretched man who in a form of double-mindedness serves both the 'law of sin' and also the 'law of God' (Romans 7:24). By invoking the language of the Holy Spirit the inner-otherness need no longer be simply an awareness of self, but of self's awareness of the divine.

The Evil-other

The negative aspect of inner-otherness is also revealed in spirit possession, in the sense of being controlled by powers other than oneself. There is a long-standing stream within Christian thought, rooted in biblical stories of Jesus as an exorcist and of later accounts of possession by evil spirits, that personifies evil in the Devil. The Catholic Church has taken spirit possession and exorcism seriously, as have some other mainstream Churches, not to mention some contemporary Charismatic groups, for whom it is a major concern. Even the contemporary Church of England appoints specific clergy to act as exorcists in each diocese.

Anthropology has done a great deal to disclose the nature of this kind of spirit possession, showing how it usually relates to individuals who are relatively powerless and sense the weakness of their position over and against the strength of others. To be 'possessed' allows the marginalized individual a place at the centre of community or family focus, and confers a sense of worth. Such spirits are a further expression of embodiment, albeit a negative expression, as possession reveals a confusion in the dynamics of identity and of the way an individual's life is oppressed or contorted by circumstance. It is often possible to describe the categories of person in a society who are likely to be possessed, as Ioan Lewis has shown in his epidemiology of spirit possession, which notes the importance of the context of religious beliefs in a way that resembles my own point over the clustering of belief (Lewis 1986).

Credibility and Context

After Tylor's pinpointing of popular belief as opposed to official Christian theology (1958:492), the best-known modern anthropologist to explore the context-relatedness of ritual and rationales of belief was Evans-Pritchard. In *Witchcraft, Oracles and Magic Among the Azande* he drew attention to the 'plasticity of beliefs as functions of situations', arguing that for the Azande witchcraft beliefs, 'are not invisible ideational structures but are loose associations of notions' (1937:540). Evans-Pritchard, echoed by Bloch some fifty years later, noted that when ideas are brought together in a book and presented 'as a conceptual system their insufficiencies and contradictions' at once become apparent, while 'in real life they do not function as a whole but in bits'.

While it is right to question whether a 1930s account of a Sudanese tribe can be related to European Christian congregations of the early twenty-first century, I think it does provide more positive lessons than inappropriate analogies. Neither all congregations nor all forms of Christianity are the same, and it would certainly be the case that the more sect-like a group the greater the likelihood of its beliefs being integrated into a system and well known to most members, more than in larger denominations with professional hierarchies and extensive lay followings. Still, Evans-Pritchard's distinction between beliefs viewed as a 'conceptual system' and as 'functions of situations' remains instructive. Similarly, Sir Raymond Firth also identified the issue of the variability of belief, drawing attention to the way in which 'faith and scepticism in magical concepts and practices may appear side by side in different people, or even alternate in the same person in different periods' (1996: 134). This reinforces the idea that embodiment involves a complex set of variable responses to the environment and encourages a consideration of beliefs as clustered responses to immediate events and not solely as formal systems of abstracted ideas. Firth's teacher, Malinowski, was also keen to press the point that magic and religion are not 'merely a doctrine or philosophy, not merely an intellectual body of opinion, but a special mode of behaviour, a pragmatic attitude built up of reason, feeling and will alike' (1974:24). That particular description of what he saw as a 'sociological phenomenon as well as a personal experience' is one sound though partial description and definition of what I have been describing as embodiment. Another germane feature concerning the encounter of beliefs and practices involves the co-existence of 'gods and spirits' and the view that some kinds of sociological analysis have tended to marginalize spirits or the phenomena in which they are manifest (Mageo and Howard 1996:2ff.).

Certainly there is a degree of co-existence between Christianity, with its deity, and forms of Spiritualism, with their own access to spirits, in many contemporary European countries. One sophisticated approach to this area of spirit-worlds has been forged by Tim Jenkins in his timely *Religion in English Everyday Life*, through the idea of 'secrets' and the way secrets help establish and maintain relationships between people (1999:225ff.).

One example of evil in relation to embodiment, witchcraft and the maltreatment of individuals occurred in 1980s Britain rather than in 1930s Africa. At the request of the British Government's Department of Health, Jean La Fontaine subjected a widespread popular concern over Satanic abuse of children to critical anthropological analysis. She showed that many of the supposed devilish accomplices were 'vulnerable individuals, with deep needs for approval, relief from pain or explanation of their unhappiness' and, in about half the cases, she found the young people involved to have been 'maltreated, sometimes grossly' and concluded that Satanic abuse had not taken place (1998:188–9). Many accusations, often made by educated people, many involved in conservative Christian groups, and by numerous therapists, failed under critical anthropological analysis. Fontaine was able to show how this form of witchcraft accusation fitted a pattern when looked at comparatively, and shows just how important a topic of conversation this is between theology and anthropology.

Embodiment as Unity

From inner-otherness in relation to any notion of partition of the self, Holy Spirit or evil force, we now direct attention to inner-otherness as an aspect of embodiment, of the view of human being as subsisting in and as a body, and affirm that the sense of inner-otherness is part of the nature of embodiment. It is, however, hard to grasp the way people conceive of themselves as embodied individuals. It is not enough simply to speak of the images that people carry of their own personalities and bodies but, if we wish to extend the argument into theological territory, we also need to consider the wider picture of reality in which one embodied person encounters other similar persons and also reckons to encounter God.

There are many ways of approaching how profound social values come to be embedded in behaviour. Catherine Bell, for example, uses the phrase the 'social person' to refer to the 'complex and irreducible phenomenon' of the whole that results from the interplay of physical, intellectual and social dimensions of life (1992:96). This very term – social person – was one I used in my own prior study of salvation as a means of integrating rational and affective dimensions of life within each individual (1984a: 161). But even 'social person' does not give the immediate sense of the depth of feeling and acting demanded by the notion of embodiment.

Natural Symbols

Mary Douglas, an anthropologist well known amongst theologians, is helpful here through her work on the body as a kind of natural symbol (1970). Her essential ideas, enshrined in what she called 'the purity rule', remain of real use for interpreting embodied life, and embrace the realm of power, social control, bodily control, and the bodily expression of social values. Her rather oddly and rather misleadingly named 'purity rule' asserted that the greater the degree of control that a society exerts over its individual members, the greater will be the control each person will assume over his or her body. Physical appearance in dress, behaviour and speech expresses the degree of freedom possessed by that individual in the religious group. She spoke of 'grid' factors as those relating to the control of ideas and 'group' factors as concerning aspects of behaviour. The stronger the grid and group factors the greater the control of thought and behaviour in a religious movement. So, for example, in strict sectarian regimes both doctrine (grid factor) and ethics (group factor) will result in the wearing of similar clothes and hair-styles and in the use of similar patterns of speech amongst those who are likely to see themselves as brothers and sisters in a rather hierarchical scheme of things: personal freedom of thought and style of life are unacceptable.

Although some several biblical scholars have taken up Douglas's ideas, such as, for example, Robert Atkins, whose book *Egalitarian Community* (1991) was neatly subtitled 'ethnography and exegesis', indicating one form of relationship between anthropology and theology, Bruce Malina, with his reflections on ritual purity (1993:164ff.) and Howard Eilberg-Schwarz, who explored the body in the bible (1997:34–55), it is still worth describing her position in a relatively straightforward way. Society is depicted almost as a set of concentric circles, at the centre of which society and its values and beliefs are most 'concentrated' or explicit, becoming less forceful as we move through the outer circles. 'Society', as an abstract entity, comes to be symbolized in particular individuals or events invested with great significance and treated with deference. Accordingly we might think of the British Monarch, the Roman Pontiff or the President of the USA, along with their duly appointed representatives, as such embodiments of social value. When in their presence individuals are expected to behave in a controlled way, with speech and movement firmly mastered and highly stylized. It is as though the 'animal' nature comes to be entirely overlaid by 'cultural forms'. When outside those intense relationships individuals need not exert such control over themselves. Douglas explores the way in which various professions reflect their closeness to centres of social power in terms of their bodily control.

Many religious groups yield to Douglas's grid–group scheme. Some represent a high degree of control over both belief and behaviour, as in sectarian movements such as the Jehovah's Witnesses. Others are high on control of behaviour but not of belief, as in some orthodox Jewish and Quaker contexts; while yet others are low in control of both behaviour and belief, as in some of the larger denominations, such as the Church of England. It is less usual for a group to be high in control of belief but not of behaviour. Control of behaviour tends to be particularly strong when the group is explicitly aware of the need to maintain its boundaries against outsiders. Reflecting the Durkheimian tradition, Douglas sees the body as a microcosm reflecting each society, with the boundaries of the society reflected in the body itself, especially in food, excretory and sex rules. Conservative Jewish and Hindu groups, as well as, for example, Mormon groups, furnish good examples of bodily control reflecting social control over members. Numerous other examples might include the differential behaviour of social class groups in England and caste groups in India.

Bodies, Art and Theology

Embodiment views human bodies as being as complex symbolically as they are biologically. As symbolic bodies they afford access to political, economic, and other aspects of social life, including theology, and this is where Mauss's influence on embodiment is valuable. In Talal Asad's elaboration of Mauss he speaks, for example, of 'the ways in which embodied practices (including language in use) form a precondition for varieties of religious experience'. More than that, he affirms that 'the inability to enter into communion with God becomes a function of untaught bodies'. All this suggests that '"Consciousness" becomes a dependent concept' (1993:76–7).

The significance of this educative dimension of embodiment is hard to overemphasize. It embraces the importance of learning how to feel and how to foster particular emotions in the context of particular ideas. The alignment of idea, doctrine or belief with emotion is of paramount concern for religious traditions, and they largely achieve it without much explicit thought. The whole basis of worship and ethics functions in such a way that a particular spirituality – itself a particular mode of embodiment

– will be acquired through practice. Research on the ways in which embodied knowledge is acquired and developed remains a subject in its own infancy as far as anthropology is concerned. Christina Toren, for example, followed psychological ideas of cognitive development in children to argue that for 'young children ritual is *not* symbolic in the conventional anthropological sense', emphasizing that it takes time for children to appreciate that certain behaviour is not simply a practical act but one that 'expresses certain intangible meanings' (1993:147). This issue has been on a relatively long theological agenda ever since religious education specialists sought to relate Piaget's work on cognitive development to religious education (Goldman 1964; Hay 1990). Still, cognitive development is not the same thing as bodily knowledge, and research on this aspect of human awareness still awaits extensive development.

The very phrase 'practising Christian' touches this topic, for it is in action that a mode of being emerges. This makes the popular English expression, 'I can be a Christian without going to church' rather intriguing within British culture, implying that being a Christian is related to values that are open for anyone to practise in life at large. It also suggests that non-churchgoers have, on the one hand, not acquired a liturgically grounded Christian embodiment because, on the other, they have acquired their own form of embodied spirituality related to their own forms of practical morality in the family, at work, leisure and, perhaps, through their personal forms of prayer. It is certainly important not to assume that the notion of embodiment should be reserved only for ritualized endeavours.

Mainstream religious traditions involve basic patterns of practice acquired informally and elaborated through formal teaching. People learn how to pray by praying, they kneel, stand, enter into certain forms of speech and silence, they listen to music and singing and sing themselves. They learn how to make the sign of the cross, how to sit and a thousand and one other aspects of behaving, and all of this enters into their acquisition of symbolic knowledge as discussed in Chapter 7. The learning that is involved in 'our bodily felt sense' of the texts of liturgy lies at the heart of embodiment theory and, as D. M. Levin astutely observed in one of the best phenomenological-philosophical studies, there are ideas, such as 'charity', that 'we can really learn only by way of the bodily act itself' (1985:214). This is why the practice of a religion is key to 'understanding' the religion. But the kind of comprehension that comes from practice is not at all necessarily the same as the kind of knowledge that formal theological study conveys. This is one reason why a gap easily emerges between the devotees of Christianity and professional theologians. A survey of active churchgoers attending special Lent courses in Britain in 1986, for example, not only showed that many 'felt that theology is made too much of a mystery', but that only 37 per cent of these involved people felt that one of the essential features of the Church was to 'prepare people for eternal life', something that systematic theology might regard as basic to its scheme of salvation (BCC 1986:70, 12).

The same survey showed that 86 per cent felt that it was absolutely essential that the Church existed to worship God, something that is simply done rather than formally taught dogmatically. Still, in periods of rapid social and cultural change it is possible for breaks in transmission to occur or for new forms of activity to emerge. The liturgical reforms of both Catholicism and Anglicanism, for example, have not always shown explicit awareness of the power of embodied activity though, as in the 1980 *Alternative Service Book* of the Church of England, clear reference is made to the fact that 'Christians are formed by the way in which they pray' (*ASB* 1980:10). Indeed, until relatively recently the very subject of liturgy was very sparsely represented within British ecclesiastical and academic circles. When it was, it was more likely to be treated as a branch of doctrinal or historical theology and not to be well informed socio-logically or anthropologically. The *Alternative Service Book* instructed congregations to stand – inevitably with eyes open – whereas they had knelt with eyes closed for centuries. This shift in embodied activity in relation to the Eucharist occurred with minimum official comment (*ASB* 1980:32) and marked a change in the doctrinal emphasis upon mystery and the divine presence. Formerly the priest stood at the east end of the church at the high altar with his back to the people, who all faced forward towards him. It was as though God was located at some point beyond people and priest. With liturgical reform the priest came to stand in the body of the church either facing the people or surrounded by them. All shook hands or otherwise gave each other a 'sign of peace' at an appropriate point in the liturgy. The divine was now addressed as in the midst of the people rather than beholding them from his throne on high.

Concurrently, the emergent Charismatic movement believed the divine spirit to be self-evidently present as people prayed in glossolalia, received revelations and later, in the Toronto Blessing described in Chapter 6, might fall into a form of spiritual laughter. Charismatic embodiment was typified by the reception of these 'spiritual gifts' and in acts like raising the arms when engaged in singing or praying (Percy 1996: 89ff.). In both liturgical reform and Charismatic developments styles of embodiment affirmed the community of believers rather than a largely private and individual religiosity. In this, tradition 'spiritual gifts' are the physical manifestation of the power of God, and the Charismatic movement does through gloss-olalia or laughter what, for example, was done in the learned behaviour of 'religious weeping' in some earlier Catholic traditions (Christian 1982: 97–114).

New Age and Sunday School Divergence

In Asad's terms types of religious experience are intimately aligned with forms of bodily activity, and 'untaught bodies' are related to an inability to enter into communion with God. One consequence of this rather emphatic view for contemporary Britain concerns the radical change in the religious training of young children following the demise both of Sunday Schools and of religious assemblies at ordinary schools. The outcome yields generations of untaught bodies. Bodies that do not know hymns or how to sing them, and do not know prayers and how to kneel, sit or stand to say them. And this is occurring at the very time when, for example, major sporting events involve extensive singing ritual and the growth of New Age groups is given to the construction and practice of rites. While it is difficult to define New Age groups, it is easy to see their pragmatic and embodied qualities. They know more about the power of bodies performing ritual than they are concerned with systematized beliefs, as Paul Heelas has done much to show (1996:22ff.). In this they are a mirror inversion of the Churches, which know much about systematic theology but relatively little about embodied ritual.

Preaching Bodies

One historical example of a theologian who explicitly considered aspects of embodiment is the figure of C. H. Spurgeon, one of the greatest exponents of Protestant Evangelical preaching of the nineteenth century, widely travelled, though based in London, where he established The Pastors' College. There he instructed young preachers on 'Posture, Action, Gesture etc.' and, despite his protestations to the contrary, he regarded the mode of presentation of a sermon as of major import, validating it by invoking John Wesley's advice on 'Pronunciation and gesture' involving the posture of the head during preaching. Spurgeon devoted two extensive lectures to the topic, covering a great deal of ground. Not only does he observe differences in habit between 'races', and refer to Luther, Calvin and Dr Johnson, but he produces what might take a theologian by surprise in the form of extensive illustrations 'dictated' to his artist. One likens a preacher to a penguin, another contrasts the appearance of 'brimstone' and 'treacle'. So taken was he by these illustrations that the second lecture includes four pages of illustrations derived from advice to actors (1887: 137–43). Similar points can be made about popular preaching in early American frontier religion (Patterson 1982:225).

Art

While not all preachers are so carefully instructed, despite contemporary alertness to image and drama, there is a growing theological awareness of art, as exemplified in the exhibition 'Seeing Salvation', mounted in London's National Gallery in 1999 and attracting more visitors than any other exhibition in London. Some theologians now see that systematic theology and the philosophy of religion are not the only, or even the best, ways of handling theological issues. It might even be that a degree of arid tedium had entered these disciplines, making explorations into art and doctrine more fruitful fields of reflection.

Many academic disciplines come to a point when their stifling intro-version and minute re-analysis of already well-worked themes demand revitalization through interdisciplinary fertilization, as in the influence of social scientific ideas on biblical studies from the 1970s (Elliott 1995). That period of overlap took place when I was a student first of anthropology and then of theology, and prompted several of my early papers on, for example, glossolalia and charismatic religion (1976, 1984b), salvation (1978, 1984a), sacrifice (1977), social group organization and patterns of theology (1981), rites of passage in the training of priests and folk religion (1983a, 1983b, 1986). These led to my class text *Studies in Pastoral Theology and Social Anthropology* (1986), itself the germ of this present volume, which develops, expands and adds to the original ideas both of that 1986 product and of its 1990 revision. Against that background this book advocates an emphasis upon embodiment as another mode of engaging with theology, with theological ideas approached as much through bodies and behaviour as though texts, art or social organization.

Performing Ideas

Two ideas that are basic to this perspective of embodiment are *habitus* and *gestus,* which I have explored elsewhere in a detailed application to Mormon culture and need not rehearse here except to note Max Weber's early use of the idea of *habitus* and Pierre Bourdieu's development of the notion to describe situations in which the ideal values of a society come to expression in individuals (Davies 2000a:108ff.). Bourdieu's notion is similar to Tyson, Peacock and Patterson's notion of 'gesture', introduced to emphasize the importance of the way in which a religion is unfolded through the way people express their faith (1988). Practically the same point was made at the same time by Talal Asad, whose anthropological essay on embodiment itself derived from the theological work of Hugh of St Victor focused on the learning and control of structures of thought through action, all enshrined in the Latin *gestus* (1988:84).

With Douglas, these make it obvious that behaviour is a form of belief, that activity expresses a value system. This point is important in the light of traditional Christian theological approaches to theology as a venture in the systematizing, indeed in the over-systematizing of belief as formal and abstract expressions of religious ideas. Embodiment theory is one means of emphasizing the power of behaviour, especially in ritual contexts, to enshrine and express belief at one and the same time. It is a more powerful perspective than that of the 'performative utterance', a concept much employed by philosophers of religion to explain the significance of ritual. This, in fact, affords an illuminating contrast between the philosophy and the anthropology of religion in relation to ritual, for J. L. Austin introduced the notion of the performative utterance to account for the effect that specific sentences would achieve given particular contexts, and spoke of a certain 'force' inherent in the contexts framing such utterances (1961:220ff.). If the Queen of England utters the sentence 'I name this ship "The Centurion"' then it is named and ready for launching. If a shipyard worker did the same the day before it would have no effect. While this notion of performative utterance is useful, as we see in Chapter 5, it is also limited by the philosopher's own preoccupation with the power of language. Now, as deeply significant as language is, and there is no need to underemphasize its import, it still comprises only a part of human communication. In ritual contexts words accompany other actions, bodily movements and the architectural and other physical constraints of the ritual arena. Champagne, dynamic in its sparkle, pop and spurt, 'embodies' the performative utterance whether at ship launches or Grand Prix victories.

It is important, for example, to note the sense of excitement and nervousness, and the resolution of those heightened anxieties in ritual, to understand the fuller import of performative utterances. In many wedding ceremonies such excitement and its resolution is marked in posture, linguistic tone and action, with a shift occurring from the moments when tense bride and groom enter the ritual and make their vows to each other on to the moment when, in words that are never enscripted in the formal liturgical text, they may kiss each other and walk out to festive music. The beginning and the end moods differ. So too in many funerals, where the tension of the formal burial or cremation contrasts with the relaxed attitude of the subsequent reception. Such embodiment is often ignored in commentary, while it is observed in practice, as when prospective marriage partners are 'taken through' the service, as the English expression has it. This involves coming to the church along with appropriate family and supporting 'actors' and actually standing, sitting, walking, holding hands, kneeling and moving about the physical building. People are physically manipulated, moved and shown what to do and when to do it. This never happens at funerals.

In this way embodiment questions the primacy of profile of formal doctrine when considering Christian spirituality and practice. In reality, spirituality is a behavioural endeavour, and people 'become' Christian by behaving Christianly. The traditional formula, *lex orandi lex credendi*, is apposite in asserting that the traditions of prayer and of belief are mutually fostering. Here worship and ethics are obvious partners of embodiment in an ongoing process that is never complete. Just as musicians become musicians through performance, sports people such through playing and actors through acting, so Christians becomes Christian through worship, ethics and the life of faith in mundane events. Doubtless it is necessary for new converts to be given formal education in doctrine – indeed, new converts are often zealous for the formal truth of a faith. But, with time, beliefs become embodied, until the faith becomes not just 'second nature', as popular expression has it, but a new style of 'first nature'. Much more will be said about such notions of first and second nature in Chapters 5 and 6 when exploring rebounding vitality and conversion. We will not, however, consider the world of nature interpreted as 'first nature' and the social world as 'second nature' as in the literary philosophy of Georg Lukács (1971:62, cf. Martinson 2000:122ff.), nor the rather traditional Lévi-Straussian anthropological distinction between nature and culture; for our prime concern lies with the changes encountered by people in the course of their social life as they revalue their experience as embodied individuals.

Sex, Cloister and Family

One important area in which religious ideas are embodied is that of sexuality, with the element of the human–divine relation represented in Christianity's commitment to the ideal of love drawing from the same emotional sources as sexual attraction, commitments and desired self-fulfilment. It has been argued that 'falling in love is . . . akin to religious revelation', involving a sense of transcendence of the self through contact with a much desired other (Lindholm 1995:67). A key feature of this relation is manifested in the idiom of fulfilment through servitude. This loss of freedom in order to gain freedom is an essential paradox of Christianity. Peter Berger's insightful sociological consideration of theodicy emphasized the dynamics of masochism as an 'attempt to escape aloneness by absorption in another' (1969:64). In a telling contrast Berger set the 'astounding dispassion' with which some theologians seem to develop theories of suffering against their inner personal turmoil. 'Behind the calm mask of the theoretician' he sees 'the worshipper voluptuously grovelling in the dust before the god who punishes and destroys in sovereign majesty' (1969:65). While this vision serves as a timely reminder of the emotion-laden autobiographies lying unwritten behind every systematic theology and anthropological ethnography, it also highlights the power of emotion of those individuals for whom human relationships serve as a model for a relationship with God, albeit raised to a higher level of commitment, framed by asceticism and couched in terms of mystical union.

The balance between asceticism and family life has changed dramatic-ally over time. From the fourth century until the Protestant Reformation the ideal Christian life was ascetic, celibate and controlled, closely mirroring the life expected of monks, nuns and priests. The Protestant Reformation reversed this ideal type *Homo religiosus,* shifting the model of embodiment to the domestic arena of family and sexual practice, and, with married clergy, echoing the doctrine of the priesthood of all believers. Individuals become responsible to God without the need of mediating sacramental priests. Even in the Greek Orthodox sacramental tradition, for example, asking its married priests not to have sex before celebrating the divine Liturgy led to the impracticality of having daily celebrations of that rite (Muddiman 1996:118). The Protestant sense of immediacy of access to God did not take this sort of official path, but rendered sexual intercourse a normal part of life, running alongside prayer and worship. Some sectarian forms of Protestantism experimented widely with varied sexual practices.

This domestic ideal type of *Homo religiosus* is found in many religious traditions. The emergence of the religion of the Sikh Gurus in the sixteenth century led to a profound emphasis upon the householder as the basic form of piety. In marrying, producing children, and running households well – though always with an eye to the divine source of life – this contrasted with the traditional Hindu scheme of following a path of life from the initial celibacy of the student, through the stage of householder to a partial and, ultimately, to a final withdrawal from the social world prior to death. The Islamic preference, like that of Judaism and of Protestant Christianity, went for the householder model, albeit with firm laws of sexual and bodily control. The extreme development of the householder model of spirituality emerged in Mormonism, where marriage and procreation became not only the normal form of earthly life but were also posited as the scheme of existence in the eternal realms beyond death.

From the celibate fourth-century ascetic monk in Egypt's desert to the eternal king of an expanding celestial family of Mormonism, we have a spectrum of spirituality of the body that reflects the plasticity of thought of which a religious tradition is capable. This spectrum also exemplifies the complexity of the body when it comes to analysing its theological and anthropological significance. Two examples will demonstrate some of the issues involved in relating the body and social values: one takes my own notion of moral–somatic relationships, and the other Jonathan Parry's description of bio-moral phenomena.

Moral–somatic Relationships

I first introduced the idea of moral–somatic relationships in an account of the sociology of disasters, arguing that while psycho–somatic processes refer to associations between mind and body, 'moral–somatic' processes relate moral values and physical bodies (2000c:404–17). Here 'moral' does not refer directly to the noun 'morality', and is not synonymous with ethics, but follows the Durkheimian sociological account of society as a moral community. This remains valuable today, even though 'morality' often designates more specifically ethical concerns, and though many are so committed to notions of post-modernity, with its fragmented groups and isolates, that it is hard to speak of any society as a large-scale venture of shared values.

While it is undoubtedly true that many Western and Northern European states include numerous relatively isolated individuals leading single lives while tied to society at large through their jobs, leisure activities, consumerism or involvement with the media, there remain numerous subgroups, interest-groups, ethnically rooted communities and religiously divided traditions that do serve a focal function for their members. Still, post-modernity partly exists through the media and the power of stories, myths and the biographies of the famous and the afflicted, and it is in these stories that moral–somatic relationships surface. To come to the heart of the issue, moral–somatic relations are grounded in the social fact that human beings are social beings.

Social Context of Reciprocity

The greatest social fact, in Durkheimian terms, is the social nature of people. Durkheim is a sound source for considering the implications of just what this means, since the tradition that emerged around him, with Robert Hertz, Henri Hubert, Marcel Mauss and others, developed several key concepts in exploring the nature of society as a moral community. Prime amongst these was the concept of reciprocity, the mutuality grounded in the obligations inherent in the relationships underlying group life. Hubert and Mauss pursued reciprocity in relationship to sacrifice, as we see in Chapter 4, while Mauss's *The Gift* is the landmark study for numerous subsequent analyses of what has come to be called gift-theory, considered in detail in Chapter 3.

This social nature of humanity is not, of course, of limited provenance, for many have inevitably dwelt on the substantial significance of human mutual relationships, with Aristotle's roots of the Western tradition in the fourth century before Christ clearly addressing reciprocity in the mutual exchange of citizens, seeing it as that part of philosophical reflection deemed to be 'social science' (Aristotle 1963:101, 3). Indeed, Aristotle's argument that money needs to become a kind of independent standard by which different forms of exchange may be measured is echoed in Mauss's criticism of market economies more than two thousand years later. My purpose is not to furnish anything like a history of reciprocity, but simply to describe aspects of the anthropology of this basic feature of human nature in relation to theology.

Moral–somatic Dynamics

Within processes of reciprocity individuals generate not only aspects of their identity within community networks but also their sense of justice and issues related to salvation, as detailed in Chapter 6. Justice itself is an attribute of reciprocal relationships and, depending on the society, becomes more or less explicit as codes of law. Though open to philosophical, legal and sociological study, my focus lies on the relationship between the body and its contribution to the sense of well-being of an individual on the one hand, and the sense of justice experienced by an individual on the other.

Just as the notion of psycho–somatic factors assumes that states of mind are intimately associated with states of the body, so it can be argued that individuals experience a dynamic world of moral–somatic relationships. Lacking any accepted grammar of discourse for this topic, I will illustrate its scope to emphasize the feeling and emotionally responsive person, and not the abstract individual often at the heart of moral and legal philosophy. It is precisely the individual as an emotional being that lies at the heart of my concern with moral–somatic relationships, particularly individuals subject to injustice or the miscarriage of justice. Here moral–somatic relationships extend psycho–somatic interactions. It lies beyond my own competence to give any account of the processes by which these relations operate; my task is to indicate what I see as the crucial association between injustice and well-being.

Anthropologically speaking, social life presumes appropriate levels of reciprocity, with legal systems formalizing, controlling and correcting patterns of behaviour amongst individuals who are more than mere social actors within formal social systems. Individuals affect and transform both their own underlying biochemical systems and the social worlds of which they are a part. While this is as general a statement as possible about the interactions between abstract ideas and chemical responses, it expresses a growing body of research, not least that relating to grief, physical health and mental well-being (Stroebe and Stroebe 1987).

Individuals thrive or falter in terms of the treatment they receive at the hands of others, especially those institutions whose primary task is to foster the well-being of society. In contemporary Western societies, for example, institutions of law, involving both the judiciary and the police, along with the medical professions play a distinctively important part in human welfare. It is their anticipated task to do just that, and it is precisely if and when they fail that some individuals suffer distress. If in individual relationships people sometimes feel an injustice done against them such that it plays upon their mind, absorbs a great deal of their attention and affects their health, so too in public life. More public and negative are cases where a family loses a member by death in circumstances that they deem to be criminal, but where the legal system is reckoned to be at fault in failing to bring culprits to justice, as shown in Chapter 4 in my theory of offending death. It is problematic enough when people suffer the loss of another human being in ordinary circumstances; but when people say that they find it very difficult or impossible to continue with their lives because of the injustice they perceive to have befallen them a different situation emerges. It is precisely when the institutions that exist to foster well-being are deemed to be culpable that the greatest distress is experienced.

Nowhere is Durkheim's vision of the individual in relation to society depicted as *Homo duplex* more applicable than here. That double entity, of social identity and individual, biological, identity, witnesses social values penetrating the physical domains of people through the mediation of conscious self-reflection. If blushing is a simple example of such a bodily response to a social context, then we can begin to see the more complex cases of dismay when the anticipated reciprocity of social life fails. Just as people 'swell with pride' when their social world fosters them, so they may 'shrink', not with self-caused shame, but from the treatment they receive or fail to receive from institutions of authority. Vieda Skultans, for example, has shown the way injustice can take its toll on bodies in her subtle anthropological account of how 'resistance to authority in Soviet Latvia has come to be experienced as illness' (1999: 310).

Bio-Moral Life

Another powerful aspect of the moral–somatic relationship involving the integration of values and bodies concerns what Jonathan Parry in his magisterial study of Hindu life drew attention to when accounting for sin as a bio-moral phenomenon (1994). Although Hindu cosmology may differ significantly from Western Christianity it, too, regards evil as affecting the body. Parry's notion of the bio-moral dimension of life argues that the Western notion of the self as an 'autonomous, indivisible, bounded unit with an immutable bio-genetic make-up' differs from the South Asian 'individual' whose person is divisible and 'constitutionally volatile', made up of various substances, including food, that affect the moral state of that individual (1994:113). Accordingly, sin may emerge 'as excrement evacuated at death: it causes the body to rot with leprosy, seeps into the hair (which is why it is necessary to be tonsured on many ritual occasions) and makes the corpse particularly incombustible' (1994:127). This explains why there are rules over food just as there are rules over other aspects of behaviour: all affect morality, because the body and its moral state are essentially one. The same rationale underlies Western religious notions of the incorruptibility of saints and its inversion, when sin prevents the corruption of the body, as in popular Greek Orthodoxy's notion that great sin might prevent a body decaying or might leave the bones black rather than white (Danforth 1982:51). A related Protestant trend, sometimes given the name of Prosperity Gospel, is grounded in a related idea that believers can expect to be both healthy and generally successful if they obey God. The widespread growth of services related to healing, mentioned in Chapter 4, also echoes the moral–somatic dimension of embodiment, as do some eating disorders, involving connections between the body, an individual's self-appraisal, and relation to domestic power figures. Similarly, contemporary interests in diet, body and health increasingly propagate the idea that 'we are what we eat'.

Incarnation and Embodiment

Morality and embodiment also underlie the Incarnation, the doctrine that God became human in the man Jesus of Nazareth. This doctrine argues, first, that because Jesus was sinless he could be a sacrifice for sin and, second, that he genuinely entered into human experience. The paradox in this juxtaposition of intentions is that he was able to know the human condition without actually being a sinner like the rest of humanity, the unintended consequence of this being that while many Christians are keen to dwell on the mystery of the Incarnation, they are oddly ill at ease in comparing their life with that of Jesus. This raises the question of the relationship between the sense of personal embodiment and the incarnation conceived of as a form of embodiment.

While it is obvious that believers perceive a broad divide between the morality of their life and that of Jesus as Saviour, what of the similarities between them? Here I but sketch one response to this question, aware of the multiple theological and philosophical traditions lying behind this debate from the Church Fathers to contemporary existentialists, pinpointing the possibility of empathy between believer and the image of Christ grounded in the mystery inherent in the partial knowledge that individuals have of themselves. This 'personal' mystery echoes the divine mystery in Jesus as God-Man and is attracted to it. There is an elective affinity between the partial knowledge of self and the partial knowledge of God in Christ. Any Christological doctrine that so fully explained the nature of Jesus as both the Christ and the Incarnate Word of God that it removed such mystery might well cease to be effective in Christian piety. This rather large claim is not intended to argue for mystification and incredulity, but highlights the potent significance of the depth inherent in human embodiment, in inner-otherness, and its relation to the 'otherness' of God in the Incarnation.

Symbolic processes inherent in sacramental worship permit a wide variety of personal meanings and senses of awareness to be brought to doctrines such as the Incarnation. Those taking bread and wine, singing the hymns and sharing in silence possess varying opinions and differences in mood, yet ritual action accommodates their diversity within a single group. The power of symbols straddles beliefs, enabling the inherent mystery of each individual to be retained without abuse. More than that, the symbolic attractiveness and ritual efficacy of the doctrine of the Incarnation together validate the mystery of the self and demand this collective fellowship of believers. Identity comes to be broader than that of the isolated individual, and reflects the idea of a community of believers, variously understood as the Church, the Kingdom of God, the Body of Christ, the Christian community, etc. In this dual process of self-understanding and community involvement, just as in the interaction between human embodiment and belief in the Incarnation, both sides of the relational equation undergo some change. Preaching, sacraments and pastoral guidance allow individuals entry into contexts of mystery that become neither a puzzle of despond nor a cause for cynicism. For embodiment does involve a sensation of strangeness, one embracing the fundamental fact of the opacity of the self to the self, implying that individuals are never fully known to themselves, not least because, as far as believers are concerned, they conceive of themselves as set in relation with a God who is deemed not to be fully available to be known.

Language and Embodiment

One powerful aspect of embodiment is language itself. Positively, this involves the pleasure of self-expression in human relationships and the joy of self-expression in worship. Negatively it embraces the frustration of lack of words to turn feeling into a shared joy or sorrow. Until fairly recently the role of language as the medium for philosophical and theo-logical thought has dominated Western Christendom, not least through the medium of the sermon. Still, the sermon can also serve to activate other aspects of bodily engagement, not least at the Eucharist, when the message can help to integrate the various ritual symbols of altar, bread, wine, the waiting hands and tongue, all of which serve to create a leap of thought and an arc of faith. Preachers may touch the mind and alert the embodied self to foster those actions that trigger prime moods when the human embodiment of the believer meets the symbolic embodiment of God.

Sin and Guilt

One linguistic expression within the Eucharist involves the confession of sin; indeed, the conception of sin is a particularly powerful element of Christian embodiment, as has already been mentioned above in the context of possession and witchcraft, and as manifests itself again here in the less dramatic form of regular corporate confession, when individuals are encouraged to do something that ordinary social life often makes very difficult, viz., to admit to being in the wrong. This factor alone merits much more attention than we can give it here, not least for the several categories of person attending the eucharistic rite. Being in the wrong involves both an act of knowledge and a sense of confusion. It is known in different ways by children, teenagers, the newly wed, by the successful middle-aged and by the elderly. As far as the idea of embodiment is concerned, sin as an abstract idea of a transgressed code becomes manifest in a variety of ways, one of the most significant of which is guilt. This was approached in one early anthropological studies by Robert Hertz, who interpreted guilt as the 'manifestation of the action of society on the individual' (Parkin 1996:140). And it is in a most literal and physical sense that guilt can manifest itself on an individual, in feelings of shame manifested, for example, in blushing and other physical responses. Forms of social control often employ methods directly related to both shame and guilt, demonstrating the implicit power of embodiment. Some biblical scholars have applied such knowledge to their texts (cf. Bechtel 1991:47– 76). All the usual descriptions of the Christian tradition may also be used to describe this awareness of finitude, concupiscence, and oppressive guilt; but the power of the eucharistic context is that this total frame of embodiment is set in relation to the embodiment of God in Christ.

Word-body Power

Having emphasized embodiment in general, we can now consider language as one of its distinctive attributes that helps frame bodily activity. Language emerges from the diaphragm, lungs, throat and tongue as much as from the brain; it fosters awareness and conscious engagement with others, and is profoundly significant in the development of individual identity, including inner-otherness. The power of words in the construction of ideal worlds cannot be ignored. When combined with the ritual performance of established traditions, reinforced by priestly castes, the other world can become very real indeed, exemplifying Geertz's definition of religion as involving an aura of facticity.

Verbal religious formulae foster a degree of satisfaction. They afford comfort and answer the human need for meaning, especially in circum- stances where demonstrable meaning is not possible. They conclude varieties of religious reflection that, otherwise, deny conclusion. Perhaps one might even be justified in coining the awkward phrase, 'meaning-comfort words', to describe what I have in mind. 'Meaning-comfort' words are the linguistic opposite of the raised terminal tone of the rhetorical question. Music-like, they bring some group of ideas or issues to a satisfying resolution. They raise no further question and do not set off in some new conceptual direction. They typify contexts of worship rather than of the seminar or lecture, they comfort rather than challenge.

One classic example is the 'Gloria'. Regularly appended to Psalms and certain liturgical songs in Catholic traditions, the formula runs, 'Glory be to the Father, and to the Son and to the Holy Ghost, as it was in the beginning is now and ever shall be, world without end, Amen'. This verbal condensation unites domains of worship, doctrine and time. Worship is expressed in the ascribing of glory to God and doctrine in terms of the Trinity; and time, or sacred duration, is captured as past, present and future are verbally rehearsed.

–3–

Merit-making and Salvation

Why do so many Christmas sermons emphasize 'the real meaning of Christmas' against a background of innumerable presents that, presumably, express the false meaning of Christmas? Why expostulate against materialism when the festival's message concerns divine materialism in God's gracious assumption of humanity through the flesh of a woman called Mary? Anthropologically speaking, it is because the 'real meaning' is grounded in the 'inalienable gift' of Jesus as God's son, given but never given away, while other presents are 'alienable' gifts, purchased and passed on. To explain this distinction we introduce some anthropological theory on reciprocity and alienable gifts in this chapter, before developing it in Chapter 8, where the inalienable attribute is used to account for Christology.

Salvation in Christianity concerns the ultimate nature and destiny of humanity in relation to God as flawed human nature is transformed by God as spelled out in Creeds, theologies and liturgies. Human negativity and its correction can also be accounted for more anthropologically, as in my earlier study of salvation and the sociology of knowledge (1984a). But now the focus falls on 'merit' in the development of embodied human identity approached through the underlying social matrix of reciprocity.

Intrinsic to human development within networks of relationships are patterns of reciprocity, a theoretical term accounting for the exchanges, services and gifts helping to constitute society and fostering individual embodiment. Around reciprocity, as the pivotal centre of this chapter, we also analyse the allied notions of merit-making, grace and salvation and, to a lesser extent, the related issues of love and mysticism. These will, however, only be preliminary explorations, leading into the successive chapters and preparing for the final summation of the argument in Chapter 8.

Merit

Merit lies at the heart of much religion. Grounded in the very nature of the social world of relationships through which individuals develop their own embodied sense of identity, merit becomes the medium for expressing and transcending the imperfections of existence.

Marcel Mauss's theory of reciprocity provides a foundation for approaching merit in both its secular and religious forms (1954 [1925]). He took the social world to be an extensive network of relationships developed and maintained as people feel obliged to give, to receive, and to give back, all in a threefold process of reciprocation. The content of reciprocal acts may vary from the explicit gift to the care parents give to children and, later, adult children give to parents. Such 'gift'-exchange marks the existence of a particular relationship and reflects an aspect of identity within a network of relationships. This threefold process of giving, receiving and giving in return not only provides the conceptual foundation for our discussion of gifts, but also poses the prime problem for our even more crucial analysis of the idea of grace.

Grace is a central concept of Christianity: it is as central to theology as, for example, the notion of culture is to anthropology. Grace describes God's nature and the mode of divine activity in relation to humanity. Grace becomes problematic through the apparently conflicting demands and logic of reciprocity. The issues involved in these complexities lie at the heart both of more abstract Christian ideas of salvation and of practical pastoral concerns, as John Elford has shown (1999:92ff.). Here, however, we begin simply with Mauss's scheme of the threefold social obligation, and only when this proves inadequate will we pass on to Mauss's 'fourth obligation', fully analysed in Chapter 8.

The Demand

For Mauss, reciprocity is driven by an imperative demand inherent in individuals as social beings. Existing in groups and relating through various interactions, they mark their place within social networks through symbolic exchanges. What is given must be repaid, for there is something in a gift that demands a return gift in sets of spiralling interactions throughout life, and even after death in some cases. His conviction that gifts are not inert stems from the fact that they symbolize and express the dynamic nature of human identity and social status.

Gifts Galore

The diversity of symbolic exchanges is as wide as human nature is broad. Birthday and Christmas presents mark relationships between parents, children and relatives, as well as between employers, employees, customers and suppliers. Even the explicit absence of Christmas gifts, as amongst Jehovah's Witnesses, expresses religious ideas. Wedding gifts and rings constitute special exchanges; but, interestingly, funerals seldom involve presents. The formal expression of sympathy in cards or the neighbourly provision of food – themselves forms of reciprocity – are not matched by overt funeral presents, largely because relationships with the dead individual are being broken and not fostered, withdrawn from and not entered into. The wedding, by contrast, is the prime arena for generating relationships between strangers, and it was no accident that the French anthropologist Claude Lévi-Strauss interpreted the provision of a bride as a prime form of symbolic exchange (1969 [1949]). Certainly he made more sense of that than Derrida's literary-philosophical reflections on Mauss, which contribute practically nothing on the place of reciprocity in human life (Derrida 1997:121–47).

It is, then, quite obvious that the many sorts of communication taking place through symbolic exchange typify human beings as reciprocity-rooted members of society as a moral community. And it is to merit as a key product of this moral domain that we now turn, by giving the concept some definitional substance, considering some Buddhist and Hindu examples, and, then, exploring it in relation to grace in Christianity.

Rational-moral Imperative

The anthropological assumption that humanity is radically social mirrors the theological commitment of much of the Hebrew Bible's account of the inherent duties and responsibilities of human beings. Humanity's social nature adds a dynamic moral charge to the rational aspect of life, resulting in a complementarity between a moral and a cognitive imperative. This means that people seek both moral and rational sense in their life and world, with their interpretation of life becoming a moral interpretation. This is precisely the contribution religion has, traditionally, made to life, and is one major reason why the debate between science and religion is potentially problematic, since many scientific explanations of events come without any implicit moral values and, as such, reflect but half of the total human scheme of 'knowing'. This is no fault of science, given that science came to be pursued in its 'pure' form, decontextualized in its laboratory from ordinary social life. The consequences of scientific knowledge, however, spill over into everyday life at innumerable points and, once there, demand moral interpretation. This has never been more apparent than in contemporary issues of genetics, human reproduction and disease.

In societies exhibiting increasing secular tendencies an opposite phenomenon can occur, when religions offer moral interpretations that are no longer generally acceptable. Indeed, amidst issues of post-modernity that assume fragmentation of groups and the demise of shared commitments, one needs to be distinctly aware of the subtleties of the word 'society' in the contemporary world, appreciating the need to think in terms of sub-groups, sub-cultures, distinctive communities, religious communities or even work contexts as locales within which reciprocity and obligation operate and within which merit, as we will now analyse it, functions. One could also pursue merit-like phenomena in wider social and political life where status is accorded to people, as in the British honours system. Here, however, our exploration of merit deals narrowly only with traditional theology and its relation to some contemporary Christian groups.

Merit as Commodity

In terms of definition I will regard merit as a type of commodity, the product of social rules obeyed and available for the benefit of designated individuals; as a positive moral value it enhances the status of those who fulfil their social obligations. Although lying beyond the scope of this book, merit probably influences people's well-being in terms of what I described in the previous chapter as a moral–somatic process. John Davis, too, in his illuminating study of exchange has also briefly alluded to 'the immaterial reward', to 'that inner sense of well-being and the external reputation that comes from acting rightly' (1992:16).

Since society's survival depends upon collaboration, it is not surprising that some benefit is accorded to those enhancing social goals. Accordingly, devoted commitment to group expectations does yield a status that is merit-infused. Whether in the family or at work, individuals are praised and prized when they further shared ideals by embodying them in their practice, and are blamed and deemed unworthy of benefit or reward when they contradict those ideals. These are the basic social facts of life.

Status-merit and Destiny-merit

To show how these facts affect religious life I create two sets of concepts related to merit. First, I adapt the familiar sociological terms of 'achieved' and 'ascribed' as usually applied to status to create the categories of achieved merit and ascribed merit; then I coin the terms 'status-merit' and 'destiny-merit' to account, respectively, for aspects of ordinary social life and of religious notions of salvation. Accordingly, status-merit may advantage an individual in the more secular networks of social power, just as destiny-merit influences an individual's present and future well-being. Rewards accorded to individuals by society at large and by the religious world in particular show a close family resemblance. Just as social approbation is deemed beneficial in ordinary social life, so divine approbation is reckoned to carry positive consequences in terms of the future progress of life and destiny, as the following brief examples demonstrate.

Moral-commodity: Merit in Buddhist and Hindu Contexts

Robert Hertz's early anthropological study of sin, including the sacrificial issues of expiation, fear and guilt (1994 [1922]), has been related to some other anthropological studies by David Parkin (1996: 123–52). Here, however, I wish to draw attention to two other significant essays in which Obeyesekere (1968) and Tambiah (1968) raised fundamental questions about the making and use of merit in Buddhist societies. Tambiah's notion of ethical vitality is particularly important, for it describes a form of moral energy generated through ritual activity in the Theravada tradition of Thai Buddhism, where young men and boys may become monks for short periods of time. In doing so they are said to make merit that can be used to benefit their parents and ancestors through a process of merit-transfer. It is this phenomenon of merit-transfer that makes sense of viewing merit as a kind of moral commodity that can be generated and made available for future use. This is also a kind of vicarious action. Adults know they have broken basic Buddhist precepts many times and have accrued much sin, and, in this system as in many others, sin is deleterious to one's current welfare and future destiny. Here sin appears as a negative moral com-modity accumulated through breaking the moral code, and the offsetting of such sin against its moral opposite – merit – remains a long-standing religious equation in the ethical-judgemental religions of the world.

So, although Buddhist adults accumulate sin by breaking precepts, they may also reap some benefit when their children make merit by observing them. Having kept the rules and reaped the reward, children may share merit with others. In particular, these youngsters have controlled their sexual energy and, as Tambiah suggests, 'in a sense it is the sacrifice of this human energy which produces ethical vitality which can counter karma and suffering' (1968:105). This powerful idea demonstrates the deeply rooted nature of moral rules, the value placed on them, and the credit they bring to those who keep them.

Tambiah sets this entire scheme of merit-making, including the giving of gifts to monks by the laity, within the reciprocity of Thai life, ordinarily governed by strict ideas of reciprocity. In normal life like begets like, one gift results in a similar response; but in religious exchange physical behaviour generates metaphysical goods. The total process of reciprocity, in which merit is made and used in daily life, becomes extended into the religious domain, where not all meet their obligations. In cultures possessing a division between monks and laity it is demonstrably obvious that the possibility of achieving the highest realms of obligation is impossible for the laity. In relation to that, Obeyesekere suggested that the uncertainty Buddhists feel about their destiny has been countered in two major ways, by belief in saviour figures who assist believers, especially in northern Mahayana traditions, and by belief in merit-transfer, dominant in South Asian Theravada traditions. Obeyesekere's aside on the theme of astrology and its importance in Buddhist and Hindu cultures, where this *karmic* scheme makes the future uncertain, is also perhaps worthy of further investigation for Western cultures. I would suggest that it is the intrinsic sense of a merit system in relation to uncertain outcomes that makes astrology, fortune-telling and spiritualism a significant aspect of popular religion. This search for a degree of certainty amidst an otherwise uncertain world is not unrelated to the notion of the Protestant Ethic. The Hindu counterpart brings the concept of obligation into the domain of *karma*, that impersonal process of moral reciprocity grounded in the social system of caste and of caste duty. Indeed, *karma* represents a highly developed notion of reciprocity, in which moral causes result in moral effects through the system of transmigration of 'souls' in the round of existences of *samsara*. In Simmel's sociological terms, this power of moral values describes the 'yearning . . . to find the meaning of life', and 'yearning' helpfully highlights the combined intellectual and emotional thrust of individual destiny (1997:184).

Another aspect of merit in Indian life involves pilgrimages to local or national shrines as part of a 'merit pattern' of activity described by Bhardwaj, where richer people travelled furthest and sought more intangible benefits, while the poorest travelled least and sought more immediate benefits (Turner and Turner 1978:239, citing Bhardwaj 1973). Some from Christian cultural backgrounds find this moral system of *karma*, where destiny works by a process of moral cause and effect devoid of a divine and personal judge, difficult to grasp. Even within Buddhism's ideological scheme local variants may personify this operation of merit, as in Fürer-Haimendorf's description of the Sherpas' conceiving of merit as being kept in a record by 'two anthropomorphic beings, acting respectively as a person's good and evil genius' (1969:183).

But, whether in the impersonal scheme of *karma* or the personalized system of judgement of the Judaeo-Christian-Islamic scheme, notions of reciprocity and merit are equally influential. And this is without covering the historical cases of Zoroastrian or ancient Egyptian ethics and salvation. Still, it is worth bearing in mind Fürer-Haimendorf's contrast between cultures emphasizing a 'mechanical balancing of merit and demerit' and those grounding sin in 'dramatic outrages against a divine moral order': the latter he sees as conducing to a sense of pollution that prevents some religious activity or other (1969:189).

Obligation

But, for Buddhism, it is obvious that while obligation underlies the dynamics of reciprocity it remains paradoxical, as Sherry Ortner's study of Sherpa culture shows when arguing that the indigenous ideal of the good life was 'being free of debt to anyone' (1978:67). The image is of a culture where each individual and narrowly conceived family group seeks success in and through personal endeavour by avoiding demands and obligations to others, in a form of cultural protection of the self. For Ortner 'the basis of merit may be stated more starkly – absolute impersonality . . . The point cannot be stressed too strongly: The basis of merit, and of other modes of seeking salvation as well, is antirelational' (1978: 37, 38). The paradox is that merit needs to be made socially, yet its goal is individual. Ortner explains its resolution, in this Mahayana tradition, in the fact that the ultimate goal of salvation brings the 'saved' individual to a stage where compassionate love of others is of paramount importance. One aspect of what might be explored as the existential grief of Buddhism lies in its transformation into compassion, with the image of the compassionate Buddha providing a ready help for those who otherwise cannot achieve any serious degree of spiritual advancement. The supernatural power of the Buddha comes as a relief, a possibility amidst impossibility and, in terms of the dynamics of spirituality, it functions as grace does within Christian experience. The import of Ortner's work is that people believe merit can be made by them in and through ethical acts, and that this merit will be of personal benefit in the total process of salvation. As other scholars have shown for Buddhist societies, this goal is more likely to be a better reincarnation after death than ultimate nirvana, but that does not change the basic desire for betterment (Southwold 1982:146).

In the different cultural context of millenarian movements Kennelm Burridge similarly argued for a sociological definition of salvation grounded in the idea of unobligedness, when the one great desire is to be free of the demands and commitments that normally entangle individuals (1969:7). Indeed, the desire for isolation is one possible expression of self-centredness and of the hope for self-fulfilment as voiced by D. H. Lawrence: 'Lord, as the only boon, the only blessedness, leave me intact, leave me utterly isolate and out of reach of all men' (Lawrence and Skinner 1963:379). In terms of Christian theology, however, this longing for existence beyond reciprocity contradicts doctrines of creation and salvation and yet echoes the call of love. This paradox, too, deserves some explanation and, if possible, resolution.

Christian doctrines of creation and salvation are fundamentally relational. Hebrew creation myths and patriarchal narratives of the Old Testament show God deciding to create the cosmos and to establish relationships with each part of it through a series of commandments and covenants. Israel is called to obedience and covenants within an ethical basis of life directly related to the promise of salvation. God will bless this obedient people, as the law and the prophets attest, while poetic and wisdom literature add themes of love and devotion to human–divine relations. The religion of Israel appears as a complex interplay between these themes of law and love, of commandment and devotion, albeit with a degree of tension that not only continues in the New Testament, with its discussions of faith, but also in numerous theological debates over the succeeding centuries and millennia as the duty of obedience encounters affirmations of the free love of devotion. Traditionally this is expressed as the distinction between 'works and faith'.

The key point lies in the relational element between God and humanity, whether in the covenant and law motifs or, even more germane for Christianity, in the doctrine of the Incarnation. In Jesus the notions of covenant and law, of love and devotion come to complementary conclusion. Indeed, this area has spawned more orthodoxies and anathematized heresies than any other site of theology, a sure sign of its significance.

These Christological debates are not without parallel when expressing the intimacy of relation between deity and humanity in the life of individual Christians, especially in terms of the Holy Spirit as a divine presence effective within personal life. Whether in the baptismal sacramental language of Catholic traditions or in the Protestant discourse of personal conversion the individual's body is deemed to be renewed by or a temple of the Holy Spirit. While that spiritual presence may well involve inner transformation of particular sentiments, it also emerges in a degree of commitment to the group comprising the Church.

One aspect of the obligation born from group commitment within Catholicism involves the sacramental control of religious benefits. John

Fulton has outlined both the 'sin cycle' of ordinary members and the 'spiritual sickness', popularly called 'scruples', amongst more dedicated Catholics in pre-Second Vatican Council times (2000a:14–20). He sketches a world of relative uncertainty over one's love for God, where sin is aligned with aspects of sexuality that would make people sinners much of the time and demand repeated use of the Confessional to remove accrued sin prior to receiving the Holy Communion at the Mass – all with the hope of going to heaven after death. Fulton incisively describes ordinary Catholic life as grounded in a Church whose liturgical language the people did not understand, whose sacred objects they could not touch and whose priests were relatively distant individuals controlling the gate of grace. After the close of the Second Vatican Council there was a desire for greater openness to lay involvement and a shift in describing the nature of Confession; but, still, the picture Fulton paints reflects a long-standing pattern of piety that was not changed in a day.

There is an interesting tension inherent in the longing for existence beyond reciprocity and the desire for a love-union with the divine that renders obligation redundant. Even the apocalyptic visions of heaven depict a social world of collective adoration and worship with no 'privacy'. One resolution of the conflict between the desire for freedom and the desire for love comes in the Christian belief that God's 'service is perfect freedom'. This initially strange view is explicable once experiences of love are deemed to be transformative of the self and of one's view of others, with grace as the power transforming the desire for freedom from obligation into the voluntary commitment to obligation.

Grace

In terms of the Pauline tradition of the New Testament, its Patristic and classic extension in Augustine and its Lutheran affirmation in the Reformation, grace appears as a divine attribute and action. Grace reflects both the nature and action of God in a generous outpouring of creativity underlying not only the multiplicity of created phenomena but also the profundity of salvation. Couched in terms of love, grace is seen as an inexhaustible flow of acceptance and validation of those God created and redeemed. This ideal of creation and salvation is continued in Jesus of Nazareth, the personification and embodiment of grace. In the theological description of God as a Holy Trinity the grace reckoned to mark the interaction of these divine persons is but an expression of the being of God. When God then acts towards humanity it is by a natural extension of that intrinsic Trinitarian gracefulness.

Medium and Message

Theologically, one might expect the human response to God also to be treated in terms of 'being', so that the medium and its message might cohere; yet this is seldom the case. Karl Barth, for example, illustrates this paradox of grace and gift, for though he stresses the grace of God as intrinsic to God's Trinitarian being and action towards mankind, yet even he finds his argument coming to be embedded in the discourse of gift, reception and obligation. Barth proclaims, and much of his theology appears as declaration of the fact, that God created man (*sic*) for the 'prior purpose, that there may be a being distinct from Himself ordained for salvation, for perfect being, for participation in His own being, because as the One who loves in freedom He has determined to exercise redemptive grace – and that there may be an object of this His redemptive grace, a partner to receive it' (1956: 9). He goes on to discuss the 'character of man's obligation and commitment to Him' as one in which God 'binds man to Himself' through grace (1956:488). Perhaps it is through the use of contrast to emphasize a point or the inevitability of relational language that terms like 'object', 'partner to receive', 'obligation' and 'commitment' all bespeak a grammar of discourse of reciprocity that, however slightly, transforms the message of grace. Had Barth stopped with the phrase 'participation in His own being' then any potential misunderstanding over reciprocity would have been avoided, for there is a sense of mutuality inherent in the word 'participation' that is absent in 'obligation and commitment'.

Although I am intentionally pressing this issue, perhaps even to breaking-point, the problem with Barth's discussion of grace in relation to human fulfilment in salvation is that it locks into ideas of gift-giving and receiving. This accentuates the dissonance between the medium and the message, for the medium of reciprocity does not well serve the message of grace. The idiom of gift-giving is not appropriate for expressing grace, at least not in terms of Mauss's threefold obligation. But Christian tradition, including much of the New Testament, has long adopted gift-giving and reciprocity when discussing grace in salvation. While there is an inevitability over this, given the embeddedness of the language of reciprocity in ordinary social relationships, the potential inappropriateness of the medium for this message must be raised. Confessional theologians can assess the weight of this argument for themselves once they see, clearly, the theoretical issues involved in consonance or dissonance between medium and message.

The Eucharist

The Holy Communion Service in the 1662 Anglican *Book of Common Prayer* exemplifies the reciprocal model in relation to grace. It does so because, as the outcome of the 1549 and 1552 services with all their weight of Reformation and Catholic theological debates, it reflects the increasing effects of Reformation theology upon the newly established English Church, forged as it was from traditional Catholicism, but without entirely adopting the wholesale theological and ritual reform of European Protestantism.

The opening prayer, one of the most perfectly formed of all Anglican devotions, asks God to 'cleanse the thoughts of our hearts by the inspiration of Thy Holy Spirit, that we may perfectly love Thee, and worthily magnify Thy Holy Name'. Here divine inspiration and human love are mutually related without obvious reciprocity. I emphasize this because it could be argued that inspiration is a prior gift to which love is the reciprocal act; but that would be an excessive interpretation, seeing reciprocity in any event or phenomenon involving two partners. A similar perception of spiritual realities underlies the prayer for the majesty of the monarch in which 'we humbly beseech Thee so to dispose and govern the heart [of the monarch] that she may ever seek Thy Honour and Glory, and study to preserve Thy people committed to her charge'.

It is in the next prayer, for the 'Church militant here in earth', that reciprocal language begins to appear, as God is besought, 'mercifully to accept our alms and oblations, and to receive these our prayers which we offer unto Thy Divine Majesty'. God is asked to bless the universal Church, Christian rulers, parliamentary officers, local Church leaders and 'especially this congregation here present', that all may 'hear and receive Thy holy word: truly serving Thee in holiness and righteousness all the days of their life'. In the following confession people repent of their sins, and ask for forgiveness for their past life so that they may, hereafter, serve and please God in 'newness of life'. The absolution announces God's forgiveness, mercy, pardon and deliverance from sin, along with divine strength for living.

As the liturgy moves into what is popularly called The Prayer of Humble Access the theme of worthiness and merit is introduced, to remain in high profile until the close of the rite. The people admit that they 'do not presume to come to this Thy Table . . . trusting in our own righteousness, but in Thy manifold and great mercies'. The point is put with great power in admitting that they are not even 'worthy so much as to gather up the crumbs under Thy Table'. Yet they come because God's very character – indeed His 'property' – is 'always to have mercy'. On that basis they ask that they may 'so eat the Flesh of Thy Dear Son, Jesus Christ, and drink His Blood' that their sinful bodies and souls may be made clean and washed through it, to the end that they 'may evermore dwell in Him, and He in us'. Although the idea of unworthiness is emphasized, it quickly passes into the idiom of forgiveness through mercy that leads to a mutual indwelling. This is a distinctive feature of spirituality, and constitutes an alternative model of mutuality from that of reciprocity. What is more, the idiom is arrived at through the images of eating and drinking, to which we return in greater detail in Chapter 4. Indeed, this liturgy may be said to consist of two models of relationship, one of indwelling derived from the act of eating and drinking and another of reciprocity expressed in the gifts that are offered and received. This distinction prepares us for our discussion of inalienable and alienable gifts in Chapter 8.

The main prayer of consecration now makes this increasingly obvious. God is addressed as the one who 'of Thy tender mercy didst give Thine only Son, Jesus Christ, to suffer death upon the Cross for our redemption'. The priest asks that 'we may receive these Thy creatures of bread and wine . . . and be partakers of His most Blessed Body and Blood'. Coming to the absolutely central act of the rite the priest rehearses the words concerning Christ, 'Who in the same night that he was betrayed, took bread; and when he had given thanks He brake it, and gave it to his disciples, saying, Take, eat, this is my body which is given for you'. Similar words follow for the wine, as the 'blood of the New Testament which is shed for you and for many for the remission of sins'. Here the images of gift, of the givenness of the body become bread, and of the wine become blood, are paramount, for these 'gifts' become the basis for remembrance. And remembrance is central to the rite, and is of particular interest to the anthropology of religion because its significance has been taken in two quite different directions by Catholic and Protestant traditions. This is worth emphasizing, because it is easy to stress the more Catholic and sacramental theological interpretations of the Eucharist because of their easily accessible notions of sacrifice, while the more Protestant forms, especially those that are often described as purely memorialist, are viewed as somehow less symbolically and ritually rich, which is far from correct. For whether interpreted in the more Catholic sense, of actual mystical participation in the body and blood re-offered by the priest in what is deemed to be the sacrifice of the Mass, or in the more Protestant form of a mental act of faith that raises the historical death of Christ in the contemporary mind of the believer, the symbolic mind of devotees is actively engaged in relating the doctrinal realm with the personal context of the believer. Within the Anglican tradition this particular prayer offers scope for each of these schools of thought to interpret the words in line with their respective traditions. More particularly, as far as our analysis is concerned, the gift language is presented in such a way that it directs attention more towards an onto-logical sense of a participation in God (through inalienable gifts) rather than towards future sets of reciprocal acts (in alienable exchanges).

Then follows the eating of bread and drinking of wine, as each receives the elements from the priest, who states that the body and blood of Jesus Christ was 'given for you' and that they will 'preserve your body and soul unto everlasting life'. The elements are consumed. The two prayers that follow this administration and participation in the elements stress the more reciprocal theme, with its notion of merit, on the one hand and the incorporation or indwelling ontological sense of union with God on the other.

The first asks God to accept 'This our sacrifice of praise and thanks-giving' and, emphasizing the 'Merits and death of Thy Dear Son Jesus Christ', asks that all may be freed from their sins. The people 'offer and present' to God their 'souls and bodies, to be a reasonable, holy and lively sacrifice', and ask that they may be filled with 'grace and heavenly benediction'. Then, as though the point had not already been made forcefully enough, they admit once more that it is despite the fact that they are 'unworthy', through their 'manifold sins, to offer unto Thee any sacrifice', that they still ask God to accept the praises that it is their 'bounden duty and service' to render him. The theological stress on grace is rehearsed yet once more, in the request that God should not weigh their merits, but pardon their offences. Here the burden of the sense of unworthiness is great, and is balanced only by the merits of Christ and the sacrifice of his life. In a strongly reciprocal sense human error is balanced by divine blessing, creaturely unworthiness by divine merit.

The second prayer takes a different course and, although it makes explicit reference to the hope of God's everlasting kingdom, 'by the merits of the most precious Death and Passion' of God's 'dear Son', the stress falls not only on being fed with spiritual food and assured of God's favour and goodness, but also on being 'very members incorporate in the mystical body of Thy Son, which is the blessed company of all faithful people'. The prayer requests that believers may be so assisted with grace that they 'may continue in that holy fellowship, and do all such good works' as God may have prepared for them 'to walk in'. The theological and devotional weight of meaning lies on the incorporation motif, an element that would have evolved a great deal by the time the next set of liturgies emerged in 1980 and 2000, as is explored in Chapter 4.

The penultimate liturgical moment of the 1662 rite, the *Gloria in Excelsis,* praises the divine glory and acknowledges Christ as redeemer, with a final assertion that it is He that takes away the sin of the world. Then, in the closing blessing, the priest requests that God's peace should keep the hearts and minds of believers in the knowledge and love of God, and blesses the people in the name of the Father, Son and Holy Spirit.

Inhering Conflicts

Even this brief consideration of one eucharistic rite reveals a degree of ambivalence present in the use of reciprocal language when relating grace and reciprocity. The differences between religious traditions often depend upon the place of human endeavour in the scheme of salvation, and this is profoundly true for Christianity, whose theological history moves around the weighting given to merit in the ongoing life of faith.

In the liturgy just considered a very high profile is given to the 'merits' of Jesus Christ, because its underlying theology of sacrifice deems Christ to be the morally perfect and sinless victim slain for the sins of the world. His capacity as saviour depends not just upon what might be deemed the neutral status of sinlessness, but upon the extremely positive status of being merit-full. In this Christian tradition merit remains the prime moral commodity; but, whereas in Hinduism and Buddhism it has to be generated by many individuals, in this Christian tradition it is generated by the one person, Jesus. His is the ethical vitality achieved through obedience, and it is of the highest order because his fulfilment of law led to death, itself interpreted as sacrifice.

This is not to say that other merit-concepts do not exist; they do, in many sub-sets of belief and undercurrents of piety and theology, affirming a divine aid that transcends human merit-making. The paradoxical presence of forms of grace alongside religiosities of merit hints both at conflict and hope. Indian notions of *karma* and *samsara*, the trans-migration of the unperfected life, are not far removed from the notion of the day of judgement as originating in Zoroastrianism and extended in Judaism, Christianity and Islam. But even *karma* can be offset by the divine love-union with Krishna.

In Christianity the priority of grace underpins Paul's influential theology of salvation, exemplified in the biblical Epistle to the Romans, where human achievement is worthless before the totally elective love of God. The fifth century witnessed Augustine set against the Pelagian advocacy of human responsibility and effort in attaining a life morally acceptable to God. That Pauline idea, echoed in Augustine, comes to fullest Christian cultural significance in Luther's clarion call in the early sixteenth century, when he hammered the pattern more clearly than ever in the doctrine of Justification by Faith. This explained the relation between God and humanity while arguing against the notion of Indulgences, a concept explored in the final part of this chapter in relation to the treasury of merit of the Catholic Church. Luther argued that Paul had 'by one cast of his thunderbolt' established grace and shattered any idea of merit, so that 'there is no such thing as merit at all' (Luther 1957:296).

In his epoch-making treatise on the 'Bondage of the Will' Luther specified the two broad types of merit as classified by Catholic theology: congruent merit and condign merit. Congruent merit (*meritum de congruo*) referred to individuals acting 'congruously' or to the best of their ability, and meriting reward because of that; while condign merit (*meritum de condigno*), or the merit of worthiness, referred to people who were already justified by God and who could be said to be in a state of grace, and who then could set about their own achievements, for which they should be accorded an eternal reward. There is a real element of uncertainty involved in the Catholic view that, while it takes grace to begin the overall process of inclining towards God, it remains useful to speak of human endeavour in terms of merit. Central to condign merit is the belief that people might create or earn more merit that was required for their own personal destiny. By what were called acts of supererogation such surplus merit could be made and 'deposited' in the Treasury of Merit of the Church, to which we return below. Here we simply note that, for example, the Church of England in its own version of the Protestant Reformation dedicated its fourteenth Article of Religion to 'Works of Supererogation', declaring that, 'Voluntary works, besides over and above, God's Commandments, which they call Works of Supererogation, cannot be taught without arrogance and impiety . . . whereas Christ said plainly, When ye have done all that are commanded to you, say, We are unprofitable servants.' Such reflections not only gave birth to Protestantism, but fostered many subsequent sects that would develop grace and merit in ways of their own.

Intense personal motivations and social constraints surround this theological pivot of merit in the religious life of both Catholic and Protestant theologians. Barth astutely observed that it is those, like Paul and Luther, who have known a distinctive and totalitarian regime of life that are best able to break into another quite different set of commitments. Paul's Judaism, in which the merits or sins of the fathers could be visited upon their descendants, and Luther's Catholic monasticism were transcended and, at the same time, were contradicted in the new vision of faith and life that appealed to many of their contemporaries (Barth 1956:4). Rahner's work, itself always mindful of the social context of faith, is also sensitive when dealing with the theology of Indulgences, and sets the question of grace and merit within the total framework of the Church as the active agent in the sacramental system that transacts salvation (1972:8).

Death and Merit

Death and the afterlife have provided the most crucial context for merit in Christianity, especially when aligned with the notion of the immortal soul. Reinhold Niebuhr, amongst the more influential of American Protestant theologians of the twentieth century, saw with great clarity that 'all the plausible and implausible proofs for the immortality of the soul are efforts on the part of the human mind to master and control the consummation of life'. He emphasized how people 'try to prove in one way or another that an eternal element in the nature of man is worthy and capable of survival beyond death' (1943:306). While alluding to John Baillie's theological view that Plato's notion of the immortal soul is but 'a more philosophical version of the more primitive and animistic sense of a shadowy survival after death' (ibid.), Niebuhr highlights how little can be said about any future state. Still, he affirms belief in the consummation of life, his sense of certainty amidst logical constraints grounded in the view that earthly, embodied, life must be related to any future identity planned by God and not an inevitable outcome of human worthiness. He cannot entertain an eternal identity grounded in the popular combination of worth and an immortal soul.

For heavenly or earthly life, the notion of merit attracts human interest, appealing to both sense and reason. Attempted descriptions of events influencing life or afterlife are insufficient, for people want to know what causes those situations – they seek reasons touching on identity and the worth of individuals. Merit helps interpret worthiness, it links identity and causation of events within any number of distinct cultures – for moral codes vary considerably, as Fürer-Haimendorf showed for societies of different levels of cultural development (1969). Our concern lies with merit and problems of suffering and evil, a key theological topic, both in the philosophy of religion and in applied pastoral contexts.

Merit, Identity and Justice

Some tragedy befalls an individual, who immediately responds with the question 'Why me?' The distressed person seeks an answer that satisfies the demands of emotion as much as the inquisition of reason. Misfortune is perceived as an attack upon identity, and the victim finds no justifiable cause to explain it. But, sometimes, the same logic operates to remind the sufferer of some particular event or fault that caused this trouble. Now the response is, 'I know why this has happened to me.' So it is that positive and negative aspects of merit influence popular belief, as an inherent justice of life is assumed to render to each as each deserves, and protest is registered when that scheme is contravened, with life seeming chaotically senseless. The supposedly natural balance of moral acts and their reward is disrupted. Van der Ven, in his empirical approach to Pastoral Theology, has even cited research supporting the popular 'assumption of a just world' by which people lead their lives (1998:168). This reciprocity is similar whether in popular Hinduism, Buddhism, or Christianity. It supposes that there is a scheme somewhere that ensures justice in the realm of moral act and consequence; and if this is contradicted a crisis of confidence is triggered over the balanced nature of reality or over the justice of God. At such times evil may be perceived as malevolence, individuals being understandably unhappy with mere mechanistic explanations of their trouble.

Justice and a sense of responsibility together express the moral–somatic dimension of life in connection with illness, for people perceive their bodies and material reality as arenas within which moral balances are executed. Just as some question the suffering of the 'innocent', so others readily acknowledge suffering when they think it proper as a punishment for evil committed in the past. This response is often found in connection with bodily ills, including those of children and babies. Personal history may be recalled, and long-past events identified as the source of the required malefaction; there may even be a desire to be punished for a moral lapse. Whether in the positive or negative form, these expressions of merit relate to reciprocity, morality and embodiment.

Such situations can become quite acute for committed Christians if life is suddenly thwarted, and their sense of balance is quite thrown, with things no longer seeming to work together for their good as they rather expected they would or should, given their devotion to God. The cherished identity as a child of God, as an intimate with the Heavenly Father, is challenged. Many devotees seem to anticipate preferential treatment from God because they are Christian, reinforced perhaps by many biblical references to the rewards that God gives to faithful servants. This widespread confusion is fostered by the ambiguity of the word 'gift' in popular Christian teaching.

In terms of our discussion so far there would seem to be no such thing as a 'free-gift'. In daily life all gifts presume a response, while a free-gift implies a lack of necessity of response; 'free-gifts' would destroy the nature of reciprocal schemes of giving. In general terms, gifts are contrasted with necessary payments, as in the case of wages, and such is the form of argument that Paul follows in Romans. His is an unfortunate usage that can slightly mislead a casual reader. At first glance it seems as though the gift of the Spirit, which conduces to new life in a state of salvation, is a pure act of God's generosity that is quite undeserved by the recipient and that does not involve any return gift. Indeed, the whole argument about good works seems to assert the impossibility of making any gift to God. But Paul is quite emphatic in Chapter 12 that the life of faith is a process of response in and through a sacrifice of self. The divine grace has to be matched by faith, for grace and faith belong to the same total scheme of reciprocity, and that scheme is grounded in a mutuality of appropriate realities.

In other words, grace and faith belong to the same logical type of attitude and act. At the individual level of life this means that love must be active in order to be love, faith active to be faith; and that is only possible in response to grace, which is a divinely creative act. The idea of good works is rendered inappropriate, because works belong to a different logical type than grace and faith. Grace and faith operate upon the logic of generosity and mutuality. Accordingly, the notion of reward will assume a different significance in each scheme. In the 'works–wages' system a reward is an unearned benefit. In the 'grace–faith' system a reward is an extension of generosity intrinsic to love relations. The difference is precisely that which informs the parable of the workers in the vineyard, when the latecomers are paid the same as those who have laboured all day long (Matt. 20:1).

Trust and self-disregard are crucial for interpreting this parable, for grace and faith are set against endeavour and the logic of equal returns. The returns of love are not proportionate, and do not constitute normal reciprocity. In essence, faith and trust oppose works and mechanical consequence. Even the expectation that good will accrue to the believer is a misguided remnant of the old logic of reciprocity. Rahner usefully deals with this theme when posed in the guise of why God allows us to suffer. He directs the believer to the unconditional trust in a God whose intrinsic mystery does not admit of any certain answer. Indeed, the lack of an answer is precisely what embraces trust and betokens love (1972:15).

Power of Obligation

We have established that identity subsists within obligations of social force binding person to person in everyday life, and have seen that gift-theory is but one means of reflecting this. It is only when cultures elevate the notion of the private self or question the status of an enduring self that the desire for non-obligation is possible. It is doubtful whether the notion of self is constant at all times and places, it may even vary within the same individual at different periods of life. Buddhist societies initially focus on ideals of self, albeit while ultimately working towards the realization that no permanent self exists; and it may well be that schemes for eliminating obligation will be fostered where notions of self are believed to be false. Hence the significance of Ortner's stark assertion that impersonality and an anti-relational stance lie at the heart of the Sherpa merit schema. So it is that ordinary social reciprocity may predispose people to think that religious values operate on the same basis.

But religion often asserts that reality is at variance with the way ordinary life is lived. Both Buddhism and Hinduism argue that ordinariness is to some degree an illusion, while Christianity asserts the radical discontinuity between the way people live and the way God wills existence. This discontinuity is focused in Jesus as the Christ of God, whose Incarnation marks the bounds between fallen and redeemed Humanity. But here we must be careful: for once Christianity espouses the Incarnation as the critical means of understanding both God and human life, it is easy to assert that all things mortal and material have been taken up into Godhead and have thus been transformed. The doctrine of the Incarnation becomes the basis for validating all things mundane, as is often the case in sacramental theology. Only one aspect of this problem needs consideration at this point: viz., how the Incarnation affects the notion and practice of reciprocity. In strictly exegetical terms this is an interesting issue, not least because the Gospel of John uses ideas of giving and gift to interpret the Word becoming flesh.

When C. K. Barrett, for example, comments on John's belief that God loved the world to the extent that He gave His Son for its salvation, he adds that 'Love seems to be, for John, a reciprocal relation' (1955: 180). He also suggests that sometimes John uses ideas of love to refer to God's spontaneous and gracious relation to humanity and sometimes of humanity's sense of response to God's favours; but Barrett detected a slight discrepancy here, and it is an important point for our argument, when he says that man is not moved by 'free unmerited favour to God (which would be impossible), but by a sense of God's favour to him' (idem., original brackets). Here gift and love seem to cause a problem in the normal process of reciprocity, where duty and obligation are paramount. As an exegete Barrett has sensed the issue of discrepancy of categories and of the problem that we pose in Chapter 8 as inalienable and alienable gifts. Bultmann's comments on these Johannine verses omit the element of reciprocity, but what he does say is equally as important: 'For only the man who overcomes the offence of Jesus' humility and who perceives his exaltation in his death, can see in Jesus the Son sent by the Father' (1971:153). This marks a reversal of meaning, an inversion of values, in a revelation of God, an interpretation we could easily analyse through the rebounding conquest motif. The expression of doctrines of salvation through everyday notions of reciprocity can easily blur the idea of divine grace, which is seen as yet another version of human exchange, with the inversion of values not being achieved. In terms of Bloch's model, the conquest of reciprocity will not have been accomplished.

Grace Transcending

Such a conquest of reciprocity affords a powerful model for approaching the idea of grace and shows the usefulness of the practical dialogue between anthropological and theological ideas. Ordinary life is grounded in formal reciprocity but, in the life and teaching of Jesus, it is brought to a point of destruction and is replaced by the life of grace. Accordingly, one way of considering Pauline theology is in terms of the conquest of reciprocity and its accumulated merit and its replacement through the rebounding conquest of grace. Merit is transformed into grace in Christ. In the *Acts of the Apostles* the means by which grace takes effect and the conquest achieved is through the Holy Spirit, the power that follows from Christ's resurrection. The old nature of converts, grounded in reciprocity and described in terms of 'law', is replaced by a new nature symbolized by 'spirit'. In the new-found power of 'spirit' the convert sets out to conquer the old nature wherever it may be found.

Rebounding Vitality

The concept of 'rebounding vitality' is one way of depicting this process. I first introduced this hybrid term, derived from Bloch's 'rebounding conquest' and Tambiah's 'ethical vitality', in a brief study of the 'conversion' of Peter in *Acts*, arguing that 'the life of Christ generated that ethical vitality which, symbolised in the resurrection and conceptualised as merit, provided the energy for rebounding violence, symbolised in the coming of the Holy Spirit, which both empowered the new Christian community to evangelise and validated its emergent soteriology' (1995:212). Here the moral power (vitality or merit) generated by a designated person comes to be the force driving the existential change (conversion or enlightenment) associated with contact with supernatural powers that bring individuals to revalue their lives and to seek to transform those forms of old identity when found in others.

This idea brings an additional element to Bloch's basic thesis. For him it was contact with some supernatural power that provided the impetus for existential change and the motive for the consequent 'violent' action of conquest directed towards others; but, as Bloch indicates, there is no basic reason why his scheme should only be interpreted in religious contexts. It would also be feasible to interpret 'supernatural' in terms of charismatic leadership, and to see political movements as effecting changes of identity through association with a powerful leader, this leading to a movement of conquest over others. Military conquests and evangelistic campaigns bear more than a verbal resemblance to each other. Still, we remain with religious groups and with reciprocal processes of salvation. Here the nature of merit as a form of 'saving capital' in the soteriological sense cannot be ignored, nor can the significance of sacrificed lives. For the nature of merit is intrinsically personal, having to do with the expenditure, and even loss, of the self. This is the case in minor acts of self-abnegation during Lent, in the temporary Buddhist boy-monk, and in the sacrificed Messiah of early Judaeo-Christianity. Indeed, it is intriguing to see just how similar are the grammars of discourse of money, market, merit, self and sacrifice, as we see for sacrifice in Chapter 4 and for the Christian treasury of merit below.

Love-salvation

Another approach to merit and salvation, avoiding the conquest idiom, is that described by Paul as the 'more excellent way of love' that shifts the focus from the self as a victim to be vanquished and transformed to the self as lover and beloved. Freedom replaces obligation, and the sense of union displaces the crude opposition of reciprocal selves. The 'other' is not used as a means of good for the self, but is intrinsically desirable. The closeness of lover and beloved engenders a language of unity, just as, in the Christian confession that Christ lives in and through the life of the believer, a sense of 'indwelling' renders reciprocal models redundant. This was, for example, just how the mid-twentieth-century theologian Reinhold Niebuhr handled the idea of love, arguing that while 'love may elicit a reciprocal response and change the character of human relations' it 'cannot require a mutual response without losing its character of disinterestedness' (1943:256). So, too, when Emil Brunner speaks of the believer's 'most important duty' of 'pouring the vitality of love into the necessarily rigid forms' of social order (1937:233). Yet these theological discussions of love work on the assumption that a form of conquest has already occurred, and that the description of relation is, therefore, a description of a state of grace.

Love and Reciprocity

Romantic love is a topic open to a great variety of interpretation, with anthropological, biological, psychological, literary, theological and historical views playing their complementary parts or else vying for primacy (cf. Jankowiak 1995). It is of interest here only in relation to duty and obligation amongst lovers, whose sentiments transcend the apparently petty world of others, lovers who think their love unique, as innumerable songs attest. It does not matter that experience shows how such love may change, fail or shatter: for the moment it is incomparable. Indeed, for a few, romantic love remains dynamic for a lifetime; but for most it changes, as life takes its pragmatic path of duty and obligation. The prime attribute of romantic love, whether in simple human relationship or else in human perceptions of the divine, lies in the transcendence of obligation. The power of the other to attract one's life-attention or to exact any number of acts of privation is paramount, and ordinary expectations of obligation and commitment are deemed not only unnecessary but ignoble.

From Love to Marriage Presents

Even when romantic love is given positive cultural significance it tends to be framed by formal commitments expressed in ritual, reinforced in forms of legal obligation and communally marked through many gifts. Dowry, bride-price, paying for weddings and for presents all bear witness to this economic dimension of romance. Changes affecting marriage obligations are reflected in Christian marriage vows, as in the subtle shift from the covenantal 'with all my worldly goods I thee endow' to the more existentialist English 'all that I have I share with you'. A much advertised contemporary shift in commitments is marked in marriage contracts between the rich and famous, ensuring the economic benefit of one of the partners should the other act unfaithfully. That sort of explicit arrangement emphasizes the obligation that has long been deemed to be part of the marriage bond, albeit more implicitly expressed, not least in prime marriage symbols, as with the wedding ring that, in Western cultures, came to symbolize the relationship between the two partners of a marriage. Until the later decades of the twentieth century the ring was given by the man to the woman, who wore it permanently. In the 1662 *Book of Common Prayer* this was very much the case, as he said to her: 'with this ring I thee wed, with my body I thee worship and with all my worldly goods I thee endow'. By 1980 the *Alternative Service Book* makes provision for the bride also to place a ring on her husband's finger, using the same words he had used for her ring: 'I give you this ring as a sign of our marriage. With my body I honour you, all that I am I give to you, and all that I have I share with you, within the love of God, Father, Son and Holy Spirit.'

The rise to prominence of two rings expresses the change in status of women between the two societies, but maintains the prominence of 'gift' markers of social relationships. The wedding ring is, then, one form of gift, an object used symbolically to mark a particular kind of relationship. But, in terms to be fully explained in the final chapter, is it an alienable or an inalienable gift? Has its nature changed with time? Certainly, it reflects something of the paradoxical element in human life, when obligation and romantic love are juxtaposed and partially framed by separation and divorce.

Mysticism and Dual Sovereignty

Romantic love also mirrors those forms of mystical faith in which devotees sense a close mutual unity expressed in love-language, echoing sexual intimacy and intimating a vision of grand totality. This expression of love-mysticism for ever haunts legalistic and reciprocally focused Christianity, hovering in the wings to redeem rule-bound situations. Its distinctive yet often ignored characteristic lies in the absence of idioms of reciprocity, as exemplified in George Herbert's seventeenth-century 'Love bade me welcome'. Welcomed to a feast, the guest draws back, sensing unworthiness, ingratitude, sinful unpreparedness and shame. But the host, 'quick-eyed Love', observes the subtle recoil and, rather than let the guest's shame 'go where it doth deserve', asks if the guest is not aware of 'who bore the blame'? Acknowledging that the host has, indeed, done so, the guest responds in gratitude, yet still in the blame-language of reciprocity, and begs to serve at table. This the host will not endure:

'"You must sit down", says Love, "and taste my meat."
So I did sit and eat.'

Within several lines of this, the reciprocal language of obligation is
denatured to yield the language of love. Quite starkly, when fearing even
to look upon the host, the guest is rhetorically reminded 'who made the
eyes but I?' So too with food, it is no question of one eating and one
waiting at table: they both must sit and eat (Gardner 1972:132). The host
is the creator of vision and the very partner at table. Here mysticism,
rooted in love, denies the necessity, the possibility and even the propriety
of reciprocity and obligation. Because of this, mysticism becomes a
problem for religious institutions depending upon systems of authority
and rule-governed reciprocity to produce desired identities. One means
of analysing the relationship between authority and mysticism within
religious groups lies in Needham's process of dual sovereignty or
complementary governance within society at large (1980:63ff.). This
principle of dyarchy or dual-rule sets legal or jural and 'mystical' control
as complements. The larger the religious group, the more likely it is to
be able to draw upon both forms of influence to yield an integrated
community of believers, as I have detailed for Mormonism (2000a:199–
208). While Needham uses 'mystical' to designate religion in general, I
use it, more traditionally, to refer to that sense of a 'direct way to God'
(R. M. Jones 1909:v). For both mystical and jural forms of authority
operate within religious institutions as well as in society at large, where
the power politics element often draws from its mystical complement for
its own validation of power.

Godelier's study of social relationships and gift-exchange, to which
we return below, also suggests that groups depending upon types of gift-
exchange for their existence possess certain phenomena that legitimate
their wider operations. His analogy is of the gold kept by banks to
guarantee, or at least legitimate, their paper money supply, despite the
ultimate deficit involved. He speaks of 'keeping-for-giving', of the fact
that there must be a creditable base to validate what else is done (1999:33).
Slightly analogous is the 'intellectual capital' laid down by scholars in
their early work, which validates and legitimizes very many subsequent
activities not directly linked to their foundational studies.

Merit-capital

Ecclesiastically, these mystical aspects furnish the 'valuables' and
'treasures' that constitute a Church's spiritual capital and legitimize its

political and authoritarian control. The Roman Catholic Church has been particularly successful in providing niches for mystics and saints whose lives express a close relation to the holy, while its capital of embodied holiness allowed it to engage successfully in political and authoritarian control of its membership. Viewed as economic 'goods', such religious phenomena become significant for the historic Catholic notion of the 'treasury of merits' that gained currency in the eleventh century in connection with the Crusades.

The treasury of merit is grounded in a sense of reciprocity, and anticipates some benefit from obedience to God. The lives of Christ, Mary and the saints at large all yield merit. The contemporary Catholic Church clearly sets merit firmly within the superseding context of grace, understood as the '*favour*, the free *and undeserved help* that God gives us to respond to his call to become children of God' (original italics). Similarly, merit is the 'recompense owed by a community or society for the action of one of its members', to which humanity has no 'strict right', because ultimately everything comes from God: 'even the merits of our good works are gifts of the divine goodness' (*Catechism* 1994:434–7). What is anthropologically interesting is that the current Catholic Catechism seeks to define merit so much in terms of grace that it is relatively unclear as to why the language of merit is retained at all, except that it was firmly established by history and popular spirituality. Non-theologians might be forgiven for thinking that there is a degree of carefulness involved in this Catechism; indeed, it takes a particular degree of clarity to understand the statement that 'Even temporal goods like health and friendship can be merited in accordance with God's wisdom' (idem), without lapsing into the ordinary sense of meriting a good as a direct result of one's action.

An allied topic in the *Catechism of the Catholic Church* deals explicitly with Indulgences, defined as 'a remission before God of the temporal punishment due to sins whose guilt has already been forgiven', and set within both the context of earthly hardship and 'sufferings and trials of all kinds' and the purgation available after death (1994:331). Indulgences are also related to 'the communion of saints', those in heaven who are 'expiating their sins in purgatory and those who are still pilgrims on earth' (1994:332). Here, too, is described the 'Church's treasury' of 'infinite value, which can never be exhausted, which Christ's merits have before God'. It exists along with 'the prayers and the good works of the Blessed Virgin Mary' that are 'truly immense, unfathomable and even pristine in their value before God. In the treasury, too, are the prayers and good works of all the saints.' These individuals also co-operate 'in saving their brothers in the unity of the Mystical Body' (ibid.). It is the Church that is charged with the authority to open 'the treasury of the merits of Christ and the saints to obtain from the Father of mercies the remission of the temporal punishment due for their sins' (1994:333). The logic of the interlinking of the living and the dead within the fellowship of the Church is such that the living can help the dead if they 'obtain indulgences for them, so that the temporal punishments due for their sins may be remitted' (ibid.).

Mary, Mystics, Martyrs and Money

Historically, many have felt involved in gaining merit during life through obedience to God, not least the martyrs, who demonstrated ultimate obedience in death and whose merits entered the treasury of the Church and made their deaths purposeful. Indeed, a feature of merit is to make sense of human deprivation. Though, in terms of religious merit, acts are performed intentionally, they can also be located within a broader category of events including accident and disaster, for there is something about 'loss' that demands moral explanation and seeks some ultimate benefit, as I have shown for the sociology of disasters (2000c:404–17).

Although self-sacrifice can be discussed in near-monetary terms and is open to analysis on the simple model of reciprocity, it is not exhausted by them. For, while a martyr's death may benefit spiritually less well-endowed brothers and sisters, martyrs themselves cannot be sold. Martyrs are not slaves. Their very death indicates a quality transcending exchange: they could not be 'bought', and the same applies, but with even greater force, to Christ. Indeed, that is what makes the irony of his betrayal for 'thirty pieces of silver' doubly ironic (Matt. 26:15). I highlight this feature in relation both to Mauss's 'fourth obligation', mentioned at the beginning of this chapter, and to Godelier's development of it that will follow in Chapter 8, though here I simply state the proposition that the martyr, like the figure of Christ, belongs to the 'inalienable' and not to the 'alienable' property of the Church. And to them I would also add the mystic. For there is a sense in which both the self-sacrificed life and the life of united love with the 'other' reflect the depth of the value-laden self, on which most religions depend.

Mystics are unlike martyrs, in that they are not prime merit-generators; but they are responsible for a presence of 'power' within a Church. The martyr's life is lost in demonstration of the reality of God, the mystic's life is lived to the same end. And Churches benefit from each, for they demonstrate the ultimate value of the institution. Even though many priests, clerical bureaucrats and time-serving employees may be less than holy, all is not lost as long as there are some real witnesses, some clear embodiments of the truth within the broad membership at large.

Mary the mother of Jesus is also a major contributor to the treasury of merit. The Western Catholic tradition increasingly emphasized her sinlessness during the fifteenth and sixteenth centuries, and officially promulgated it as the dogma of the Immaculate Conception in 1854. She even came to be spoken of as a co-redemptress and, as late as 1950, the Catholic Church propounded the doctrine of her bodily assumption into heaven after death. Eastern Orthodoxy had long spoken of her as the Mother of God, the one who bore God (*Theotokos*), a doctrine that had been proclaimed officially by the Council of Ephesus in 431 AD. What makes these historical points germane is the way in which Mary seems to express something of the mystical aspect of the faith, as a complement to the more authoritarian role of the ascended Christ or of the even more potentially distant Father, and perhaps even of the Pope as their earthly representative.

Mary's role in Catholicism is not unlike that of women in those societies in which women are guardians of the 'inalienable' goods of a culture (Godelier 1999:34), a point adding a degree of sophistication to the otherwise starker complementarity of a gender distinction between female and male. If indeed it is the case that, as Godelier intimates and as Needham's work clearly implies, political power needs to be legitimated by a symbol that participates actively in the sacred domain, then the role of the Virgin Mary in Catholic thought becomes plain. Legal and mystical authority are symbolized and embodied in the Pope and the Blessed virgin.

We can now, in part, answer the question posed at the outset of this chapter over the 'real meaning' of Christmas, for we have exposed the paradoxical relationship between, on the one hand, the influence of reciprocal relations in determining human worth and the potential of reciprocity to become an all-pervading presence in human relationships and, on the other, the force expressed in grace, love and mysticism. It is the encounter of these two domains, one of rational exchange and the other of non-rational commitment, that creates confusion over 'gifts', and it is this confusion of the 'alienable' and the 'inalienable' that makes religious leaders anxious over Christmas. This issue of gifts, their status and use is so basic to human life and action that it now passes into the next chapter and its consideration of sacrifice.

–4–

Sacrifice, Body and Spirit

This chapter explores the ritual consumption of holy food as a form of sacrifice conferring its own kind of embodied knowledge within Christian spirituality. It also takes up the closely related themes of ritual purity, the Holy Spirit and the life-transcendence fostered by ritual events and expressed in selected biblical texts.

We begin historically with William Robertson Smith (1846–1894), who linked theology and anthropology over the topic of sacrifice. He was friends with Sir James Frazer in England, then a force in anthropological studies, with J. F. McClennan in Scotland, then developing anthropological ideas on marriage, and with Wellhausen in Germany, whose theory of the Pentateuch he popularized in Britain. As Hebraist, Arabicist and editor of *Encyclopaedia Britannica* Smith was influential in comparative religion, sociology and anthropology. Despite accusations of heresy, Smith the theologian was also a believer.

Smith's *Religion of The Semites* (1894 [1889]) described how members of a particular totemic group periodically killed and ate their totemic animal with a sense of joyous optimism and of union with their ancestor-gods. Smith concluded that early sacrifice worked not for the salvation of souls but for the well-being of society. Malinowski, who also considered the function of magic was 'to ritualise man's optimism, to enhance his faith in the victory of hope over fear', acknowledged Smith as a 'pioneer of religious anthropology' (1974:21, 90). Mary Douglas, too, singled him out as a theologian contributing significantly to the founding of anthropology (1966:10), while a congress at Aberdeen in 1994, the centenary of his death, celebrated his influence in theology, anthropology and Arabic (Johnstone 1995). Doubtless, he will attract biblical scholars for some time yet (cf. Bediako 1997). Certainly, *The Religion of The Semites* influenced Durkheim, who unlike Smith, was no believer and, unlike Malinowski, stressed society over individuals. Accordingly, it was within Smith's account of the social power of community collaboration that Durkheim discerned a foundation for his secular sociology of religion depicted in his *Elementary Forms of the Religious Life* (1915). Smith also triggered Freud's fertile mind to generate the myth of a primal horde killing its possessive father before deifying him in heavenly paternalism. Other anthropologies of sacrifice include Tylor's gift, homage and abnegation theories (1958:448ff.), Hubert and Mauss's communication theory (1964) and Firth's analysis of economic factors accompanying the personal act of 'giving the self or part of the self' in an event that is 'a critical act for a human personality' (1996:108–9). More psychologically, Girard pursued Freud's theme of violence in sacrifice (1977). Theologians and anthropologists have debated sacrifice together (cf. Bourdillon and Fortes 1980), and much could be said either on the biblical background (Davies 1977; Leach 1976, 1985), or on the anthropological possibility of sacrifice's emerging in the historical shift from hunting to pastoralism that might bear upon issues of monetary value and alienable and inalienable gifts as discussed in Chapters 2 and 8 (cf. Ingold 1986:243–76). Literary-philosophical reflections on whether religion is imaginable without sacrifice and prayer might also be explored (Derrida 1998:52); but amidst these possibilities our focus remains more narrowly upon embodiment, the consumption of sacred food and the consummation of religious ideas in relation to the Eucharist.

The Supper of the Lord

Our example, the Eucharist in the Church of England, begins with Archbishop Thomas Cranmer's *Treatise on The Lord's Supper*, itself a subtle exploration of the power of symbols within the life of faith (1907). He strives to find just the right expression of ideas, aware that statements such as 'this is my body' are 'figurative speeches', and that 'a thing that signifieth' is called by the name 'of the thing that is signified thereby', yet he seems to lack suitable categories for handling the relation between metaphor and sensation (1907:122, 129, 138). He strives for clarity over 'similitudes, mysteries, representations, significations, sacraments, figures, and signs' that all carry the same basic meaning of the bread and wine, before speaking of the Lord's Supper as the event in which 'the great benefit of Christ the faithful man earnestly considereth in his mind, cheweth and digesteth it with the stomach of his heart, spiritually receiving Christ wholly into him' (1907:202).

'Stomach of the Heart'

This highly evocative phrase, 'stomach of the heart', integrates Cranmer's theology of spirituality and materiality. His materialism could not accept the Catholic doctrine of transubstantiation, formalized at the Lateran Council of 1215 and developed by Thomas Aquinas using Aristotelian ideas. That argued that divine action, through the ritual of the Mass, transformed the very 'substance' or essential nature of bread into the very nature of the flesh of Christ, while the 'accidents' or the appearance to the senses remained those of bread. So, too, with the wine as the blood of Christ. But, for Cranmer, the bread still remains bread, in essence and appearance, and the wine. It is the process of eating and drinking that he adopts to express what takes place as far as the participating believer is concerned. Digestion becomes his model for spiritual knowing, as in the Collect for the Second Sunday in Advent, where the faithful ask that they may so 'hear, read, mark, learn, and inwardly digest' Holy Scriptures that the hope of everlasting life might be theirs. Inward digestion becomes the basic idiom for dealing with the relation of believer and God. Cranmer posits, as had John Calvin's Protestant theology of the Lord's Supper, that Christ's body is in heaven and not in the elements; yet to call the bread 'body' remains a vital part of the means whereby the spiritual task of engaging with the supernatural body of Christ is achieved. Cranmer strives to use metaphor to do justice both to human experience and to theological belief.

Alimentary Forms of the Religious Life

Holy food is eaten by devotees of many religions. Audrey Hayley's study of food offerings in Assam shows how eating holy things assists the thinking of holy thoughts within the total framework of piety, with the human alimentary system serving as a model of ritual interaction (1980). Food offerings provided by Vaishnavite devotees create a commensal relation between the deity and believer, with material offerings as vehicles of a devotional state of mind. To speak the names of Krishna is to engage with words that are 'nectarine juice' and that 'can be regarded as a form of verbal food', in contexts where 'speech substitutes for digestion' (1980:117). Hayley interprets the changes in holy food resulting from its being offered to the gods as internal changes taking place in the minds of the devotees. The ways in which people speak of their devotional acts reflect their awareness of attitudinal changes within themselves, echoing Cranmer's 'stomach of the heart'.

Babb analyses the contemporary Radhasoami Movement in India, where the divine is so enshrined in the physical person of living gurus that their very washing-water, and some other body products, are perceived as divine nectar. 'What is filth to the world is nectar to the awakened', conveying a powerful energy to the believer, and evoking an inner disposition on the part of the devotee (Babb 1983:310). In a complex interplay the devotee is, both ideologically and ritually, associated with the deity, who is the cosmic digester of evil. The supreme being is the universal alimentary actor, and worship a physiocosmological drama separating evil from good during the course of pietistic union. The devotee's identity is 'made sensible through enactment', and 'by means of a highly significant form of action his belief becomes an experience. Its validation is finally more affective than cognitive; for what is required of the devotee is not so much an understanding as feeling' (1983:312). Adoration and worship are completed in the act of eating and drinking materials intimately connected with the divine guru. Theology is fulfilled through action. Knowledge and certainty are the outcome of implementing beliefs through the consumption of divine food. Veena Das's analysis of Vedic sacrifice also relates the performative nature of words to the act of eating (Das 1983). Other, more contemporary tribal examples include Roy Willis's account of the African Lele people, who treat and eat the small or tree pangolin (*Manis tricuspis*) as a sacred animal (1974). As a carrier of symbolic meaning the pangolin helps those who partake of it to resolve at non-conceptual levels of life their perceived paradoxes of existence.

In terms of embodiment Lambek showed how the literary tradition of Islam interacts with indigenous religious traditions of spirit possession (1995:259). The Qur'an enshrines the truth of Islam and is accessed by being read aloud and not silently. This verbal power of truth can then be 'materialised' if the holy words, written in ink, are dissolved into 'medicine' and drunk by individuals assailed by evil. In the local tradition studied, sacred power comes from spirits manifested by speaking through people in trance states. Lambek interprets a case in which a possessed women 'chokes' on the 'medicine' as demonstrating the cultural conflict between Islam and traditional religion. Choking becomes an act of embodiment.

Faith-eating

So it is that sacred materials feed the religious sense and are not simply biological foods. Abstract doctrines and emotional dynamics of religion become integrated in ways largely avoided by traditional theology, though sacramental theology is beginning to appreciate the power of human bodies in ritual and spirituality. Even so, most theologians, despite their personal involvement in church ritual, pursue issues of experience mostly in terms of the philosophy of religion, which lacks any established discourse for expressing that 'knowing through eating', or 'knowing through singing' that typifies practical religion. Bodily activities possess a degree of authenticity and finality different from the outcome of theological debates that seldom reach any conclusion. The very terms 'reflection' and 'exploration', cherished by many theologians, reflect ongoingness. To wait for theological-philosophical certainty is to wait a long time; but ritual engagement with doctrine soon yields results, albeit not of the same logical type. The ordinary use of food by congregations is also open to an analogous analysis, as in Daniel Sack's study of congregations in the USA (1999:201ff.).

Divisive Words, Uniting Food

The distinction between philosophical argument and embodied engagement with ideas is significant for societies where religious opinions and experience vary considerably. While some believers enjoy that peculiar pleasure of hearing their own value system rehearsed and expounded in the company of like-minded people, many others find dogmatic pronouncements largely unacceptable. This makes the Eucharist particularly valuable, as its sweep of ideas in liturgical prayers, readings and hymns, with a low emphasis upon the sermon, allows individuals freedom to engage with their own needs and preferences whilst still providing the unified action of eating and drinking. Here the interface of theological and existential ideas is not an argument, but an act.

Music Unites

Music also unites diverse individuals, with many rites embedded in music, and choral Eucharists becoming normative in many denominations (Gribben 2000:185ff.). Even if groups favouring propositional forms of theology surround the eating-rite with solemn silence, with their leaders emphasizing words over tunes, other music will unite them as a group (Sloboda 2000:111ff.). Music can integrate otherwise divided aspects of an individual, framing inner-otherness and conducing to satisfaction as texts are rendered as chant and song. Underlying sung words is an energy derived from the bodily actions of breathing, singing and collaborative endeavour that adds value to simple texts. Texts that are read and texts that are sung belong to different categories of human action, a factor often ignored by textual scholars. Here we anticipate Sperber's argument in Chapter 7 over smell as the most fundamental way in which an idea, especially in the form of a memory, comes to concrete expression. Something similar happens with words and music, for to 'think' an idea is not the same as to 'sing' an idea. Even the kind of thought that engages with an idea through the interior dialogue of the self with the self, the dialogue of inner-otherness, differs from the kind of thought that takes place when someone sings. Songs tends to remove the dialectical aspect of the inner dialogue, they proclaim but do not interrogate; but this theme involves a philosophical sociology, resembling Kieran Flanagan's important analysis of contemporary Catholic liturgy, that lies beyond the immediate scope of this book (1991:250ff.).

Evil and Action

Another form of action is also basic to what theologians, echoing Liebniz, regularly call theodicy, or in other words the problem of evil, which seeks the justification of the goodness of divine nature in the face of human experience of evil. But Christianity possesses no satisfactory theology of the problem of evil. Its best response lies in the passion of God's Son, offered to frame the pain of today's believer. In theological, especially Lutheran, terms it is the theology of the cross, of the passion and suffering of Christ, rather than the theology of glory – of the splendour of God – that marks much of pastoral theology. The divine answer is an action; and while reasoned comfort seldom comforts, the active presence of another can comfort greatly. This is not to disparage systematic-philosophical theology, but to encourage its consideration of embodiment. From at least the 1980s increasing attention has been paid to the embodied aspects of life, often as a result of feminist and liberation theologies and the burgeoning field of Christian Ethics, as in the work of Stanley Hauerwas (Hauerwas and Willimon 1989). Liturgists have also increasingly responded to people's contexts, as in the Church of England's *Book of Common Worship*, launched in the year 2000 with multiple varieties of rites to match varied circumstances.

Eucharistic Rebounding Vitality

The Eucharistic rite's popularity lies in its appropriateness as an arena of interaction between ordinary believers, God and the symbolically attractive person of Jesus. It speaks of human failure, sin, misfortune, illness and the death of other people, all in relation to Jesus. He is spoken of as having been betrayed, killed and raised to new life and as benefiting believers through his death and resurrection. These experiences bring us to one of the key themes of this book, that of rebounding vitality.

The Eucharist interprets Jesus's crucifixion by combining sacrificial aspects of sin-removing temple-sacrifice, the covenantal domestic rite of Passover and the Last Supper, the exemplary suffering servant of God and the divine bond of Father and beloved Son. Together these give participants a new sense of power for life. Bloch's notion of rebounding violence, introduced in Chapter 1, is applicable to these features, as the Eucharist revitalizes the changed nature established by baptism. Transformed human nature, ascribed to contact with supernatural power gained in baptism, and revitalized in the Eucharist, is set to conquer the old nature wherever it may now be found.

That old, fallen, nature is acknowledged in a penitential phase confessing sin and wrongdoing. The Ten Commandments may be rehearsed, along with a confessional response. During Lent, the preparatory period leading to Easter, penitence is emphatic, and may include a Litany highlighting 'pride, vanity, hypocrisy, envy, hatred, malice, sloth, worldliness, love of money, hardness of heart, sins of body and mind, deceits of the world, the flesh and the devil' (*CW* 2000:111). The 1662 *Book of Common Prayer* regularly includes a prayer before receiving the bread and wine in which believers describe themselves as 'not worthy so much as to gather up the crumbs under thy Table'.

While the devout are left in no doubt that basic human nature is a miserable thing, they are not abandoned to it, for the priest absolves them. There follows a period of prayer, affirmation of the doctrines of faith and the reading of scriptures, with Old Testament preceding the Epistles, which themselves precede the Gospel reading with its focus on Jesus. In sacramentally focused Churches a Gospel-procession moves from the altar within its sanctuary space to a point amidst the people. The bible is carried, preceded by a cross and attended by candles and, on festive occasions, honoured with incense. People stand, facing the book and the priest, even if this means turning their back upon the altar which, otherwise, is the focal point. The priest reads or chants the text, holds the book high and may kiss it, announcing a formula to the effect that 'this is the gospel of Christ'. A sermon then often follows.

Then the emphasis moves to the altar, as the Prayer of Consecration rehearses the story of salvation. With bread and wine brought to the altar-table the prayer recalls how Jesus, on the same night that he was betrayed, had taken, blessed and given bread and wine to his disciples, telling them that they should remember him when they repeat this rite in the future. In more Protestant traditions the tale is simply told, and bread and wine distributed. Sacramental traditions also invoke the power of the Holy Spirit to enable believers to participate in the body and blood of Christ. Some rites make it dramatically clear that the very words of consecration, such as 'This is my body which is given for you', transform the elements, as taught in the doctrine of transubstantiation outlined earlier. Other traditions avoid that direct doctrine by simply juxtaposing ideas of bread and body and of personal engagement with each. This is intelligible in terms of the association of ideas and experience that the act of ritual eating brings about. A bell, the Sanctus Bell, may be rung to surround this moment of mystery with a suitable aural note. A brief silence may also be kept. Many denominations have increasingly emphasized the breaking of the bread as a separate moment from the prayer of consecration, reflecting the strong dual significance accorded to the bread. In the prayer of consecration the prime reference is directly to the bread as the body of Christ, in the 'breaking of the bread' the emphasis is upon the congregation as the body of Christ.

The priest exhorts the people to come and receive the elements. The traditional Anglican formula told them to eat and drink 'in remembrance that' Christ had died for them and his blood had been shed for them, and to 'feed on him your hearts by faith with thanksgiving'. This juxtaposition of actions and doctrines enables the faithful to engage with Christ. This already personal act has became increasingly personal, in the sense that whereas Catholic traditionalism had the priest place the sacred wafer upon the recipient's tongue, while someone held a vessel to catch any crumbs, the priest now places it into the hands of individuals, who 'feed' themselves. The priest still uses either a brief formula, 'the body of Christ', or a longer version expressing the ideas of feeding on Christ in one's heart by faith and with thanksgiving. Many traditions then observe a brief period of silent personal devotion.

At this phase of the ritual, analytically speaking, the old nature is overcome and the new experienced. Theologically, this reflects the belief that it was in Christ that the old Adam was replaced by the new, old humanity by new humanity, and that believers now share in Christ's life, with all that entails concerning the new humanity. A constant feature of this part of the rite is language of being 'fulfilled' with such things as 'grace and heavenly benediction', or of partaking in a holy communion. With this dual interplay of ideas of physical food filling the body and divine food filling the spiritual dimension of life the rite moves into praise, prompted by the new state of spirit-empowered life.

One of the liturgical gems that emerged in the Church of England's 1980 *Alternative Service Book* and was retained in the subsequent

Common Worship is a prayer after communion that not only reflects this heightened sense of the Spirit empowering the faithful through the Eucharist but also describes the basic structure of the entire Eucharist. It is a remarkably potent liturgical text, theologically complex and fruitful when analysed in terms of rebounding vitality. It runs:

> Father of all,
> we give you thanks and praise,
> that when we were still far off
> you met us in your Son and brought us home.
> Dying and living, he declared your love,
> gave us grace, and opened the gate of glory.
> May we who share Christ's body live his risen life;
> we who drink his cup bring life to others;
> we whom the Spirit lights give light to the world.
> Keep us firm in the hope you have set before us,
> so we and all your children shall be free,
> and the whole earth live to praise your name:
> through Christ our Lord.
> Amen (*CW* 2000:265).

The reference to Jesus as 'dying and living' involves a sharp reversal of the usual 'living and dying' description of life, and reflects Bloch's notion that processes of rebounding conquest usually start with a symbolic death before moving into a new form of life. In this prayer Jesus as the Christ has given grace to believers and 'opened the gate of glory'. In describing the new order of existence the prayer becomes theologically multivocal, adding idea to idea in a kaleidoscope of faith-inducing images. To 'Christ's body' and his 'risen life' are added grace and the gate of glory and then 'his cup' polysemically embraces his passion in the Garden of Gethsemane, with its dual prayer that if at all possible the destiny awaiting him might be removed or else that God's will be done. 'The cup' also embraces the vessel employed at the Last Supper and the chalice that has just been used in the contemporary Eucharist memorial of that Last Supper. The prayer asks that all the benefits of this cup may 'bring life to others' through the believers who have just, themselves, drunk of it. The Spirit is invoked as the believer's source of enlightenment and God is asked that these spirit-lit Christians might henceforth 'give light to the world'. Here devotees shift from being enslaved by their old nature to having it conquered as they desire to conquer others still living the enslaved life. Those met by the Son must themselves go into the far country to bring home the lost, a powerful image of Christian mission in contemporary cultures self-aware of lostness, wandering and cultural nomadism. This prayer is also multivocal in its threefold form of reference to Father, Son and Holy Spirit as representing the Christian doctrine of the Holy Trinity, itself the summative affirmation of Christian doctrine. And it is with the Trinitarian mode of 'blessing' that the Eucharist draws to its close

The blessing is a standard feature at the close of many services within sacramental traditions. Structurally speaking, it is the formal equivalent of the absolution given by the priest to the people at the commencement of the Eucharist. Absolution and blessing, along with the key prayer of consecration over the bread and wine, are three parts of the Eucharistic rite that demand priestly ordination. Priesthood marks the power of the words, 'the blessing of God almighty, the Father, the Son, and the Holy Spirit, be among you and remain with you always'. The significance of this blessing is enhanced by the words that immediately precede them: 'The peace of God, which passes all understanding, keep your hearts and minds in the knowledge and love of God and of his Son Jesus Christ our Lord'. In terms of rebounding vitality this formulation is telling, for it reflects the new sense of self attained through the service. The guilt-aware penitent becomes the peace-embraced devotee, whose peace 'that passeth all understanding' alludes to the sensory awareness of worshippers, to the state achieved in the rite.

Identity

This 'peace' also echoes the sense of mystery about self and its identity within the total community of faith. It is this awareness of affect, the knowledge of having entered into some form of transcendence, that impresses the individual; theological explanations of it are secondary. Psychological reasons are also possible in Barbara Lex's suggestion that concepts like 'mana, faith, and power', when used in contexts associated with sensations of integrated wholeness, are indicative of a state of mind generated by the right cerebral hemisphere of the brain (1979:128). The theme of brain laterality, concerning rational and symbolic modes of thought, is basic to ritual behaviour as discussed in Chapter 7; here we simply stress the symbolic integration of imaginative and intuitive processes in yielding a powerful sense of direction and relatedness (cf. Batson and Ventis 1982). The idea of fulfilment is itself an expression of direction and relatedness framed as wholeness and integration. It touches the notion of 'the total man', for whom, as Mauss so clearly put it, symbols 'bring into play not just the aesthetic or imaginative faculties of man but his whole body' (1979:27). The eucharistic rite conduces to such unity by moving the combined theological ideas and liturgical words from penitence through relatedness to Christ on to a sense of freedom and desire for service. In terms of rebounding vitality, transcendence emerges as the sinner is forgiven, shares in the merit of Christ, and sets out to live the new nature by the power of the Spirit.

Spirit as Conquest

Concern for that Spirit grew from the later 1960s, with increasing numbers of Charismatic groups practising the Spirit 'gifts' of glossolalia, visions, dreams, inspired utterances, and healing. Charismatic groups of this kind exist in the majority of mainstream denominations as well as in the more traditional and established forms of Charismatic religion in the Pentecostal Churches. The enormous growth of Pentecostal Churches in South America, for example, is one of the most distinctive features of religious life at the commencement of the twenty-first century.

One Charismatic version that typified the 1990s was 'The Toronto Blessing', mentioned earlier and named after its parent Canadian church. During communal worship and prayer individuals are 'slain in the Spirit': standing or kneeling before a leaders in a state of passivity or of slight passive resistance the devotee is pushed slightly with a hand movement to the forehead and falls backwards into the supporting arms of attendants. Then, lying on the floor silently or laughing, growling or barking like an animal, believers reckon to experience a sense of release, peace and unity within the group. But the very expression of being 'slain in the Spirit' tells its own tale of the idiom of conquest and holds its own consequences of redirection of identity.

The Spirit also came to prominence within the normative flow of liturgical life, especially in the Eucharist. Again the 1980 English rite is fairly typical, beginning with the assertion, 'The Lord is here', answered by the people, 'His Spirit is with us'. Unlike the 1662 *Book of Common Prayer* with its deeply solemn prayer addressed, immediately, to 'Almighty God', the 1980 community strikes a more familiar note. The liturgical arrangement of the people as worshippers is also different. In the traditional format the priest stood at the east end of the church in the sanctuary and faced east, with his back to the people. By the 1980s, the altar, or at least an additional altar table, was likely to have been set up in the nave of the church, allowing the priest to stand behind it and face the people. A centrally located altar with people gathered around was even more preferable. Not only so, but the congregation was now likely to be standing with eyes open and not, as hitherto, kneeling with eyes shut. The visual sense of community matched the changed theology.

Spirit and Life-power

These changes reflected wider social shifts from hierarchy to community, for which the symbol of the Holy Spirit was potently appropriate at the congregational level, combining a sense of the divine presence with communal fellowship. While the ideas of God as father or of Jesus as the divine son are both open to visual expression in pictorial art, flooding the historical culture of most Christian Churches, the Spirit – even though being iconographically depicted as a dove – does not occupy a dove-like position within popular religious awareness. The very freedom from iconographic representation makes the Spirit readily available for use.

Theologically, the Spirit provides the dynamism of Christians, with the notion of the 'power' of the Spirit being explicitly fostered both in Charismatic groups and in non-charismatic traditions, not least in healing services, one of the most significant British ritual developments starting from the late 1980s. These periodic events take the form of prayer and laying on of hands, with or without the anointing with oil, and it is unlikely that they would have developed without the high profile of the Holy Spirit within contemporary Christendom. Healing services often engender a sense of emotional support and mutual encouragement, aiming more at some form of deeper integration of individuals than at dramatic healings.

The ascending profile of the Spirit can also be assessed by comparing the 1662 and 2000 eucharistic rites of the Church of England. The 1662 Prayer of Consecration makes absolutely no reference to the Holy Spirit in connection with the bread and wine. This is perfectly consonant with the Anglican Reformation debates over transubstantiation, with their emphasis upon faith and memorial rather than upon any divinely caused change in the elements themselves. By the year 2000, growth in historical liturgical study led to an affirmation of the Holy Spirit's role and, in all eight alternative prayers of consecration, the Holy Spirit is invoked. The first prayer typifies the rest, announcing that, through Christ, God has sent upon the congregation his 'holy and life-giving Spirit', and petitions God that 'by the power of your Holy Spirit these gifts of bread and wine may be to us his body and his blood'. The further petition, 'renew us by your Spirit' is included before the prayer ends.

Baptism and Confirmation have always referred to the Holy Spirit as crucial for entry into, and confirmation in, the faith. Confusion emerges when these rites are separated since, theologically, Confirmation should follow Baptism rather closely, with the symbol of the coming Holy Spirit following the washing away of sin and identification with Christ in his death and resurrection. The symbolic watery death and resurrection is followed by the coming of the Spirit. For historical reasons the major sacramentally focused Christian traditions came to baptize babies and to confirm them as older children or younger adults. Liturgical language reflects this confusion, even though, by the 1980 rite, Baptism, Confirmation and Eucharist are brought together whenever possible. The characteristic prayer at Confirmation affirms that it is 'by the power' of the Spirit that God gives to faithful people 'new life in the waters of baptism' and through that 'same Spirit' people are 'born again'. When the bishop lays hands upon heads at confirmation, he prays that God may defend the candidates and asks that they may, 'daily increase in your Holy Spirit more and more'.

Vitality and the Spirit

The Holy Spirit's designated role in Christian spirituality can be described anthropologically through Bloch's rebounding conquest model. Human nature is transcended, becoming invested with a spiritual life as reflected in the ritual language of being born again, washed from sin and transferred from darkness to light. The Spirit is the symbol of this new life, and is necessary because, as the rite says, 'we who are born of earthly parents need to be born again'. Baptism and confirmation together furnish the mode of entry into the eucharistic life of the Christian community, with the Spirit at its sacrificial core as the theological means of explaining how believers experience the effects of this sacrifice, just as grace explains their participation in Christ's merit.

Spiritual Warfare

Indeed, there would be little point in any symbolism of the Spirit or doctrines of grace if nothing was experienced by individuals. One index of the rise of Charismatic influence is the Alpha scheme, originating in a London Anglican church in 1979. With its ten-week educational programme conducted in small groups it had grown to 14,200 local courses of 1,556,570 individuals by 1999. By the close of the year 2000 it numbered 17,000 local meetings. At the turn of 2000–2001 *Alpha News* reported a conference with group leaders from 44 different countries including, for example, 1,524 courses in Australia, 1,240 in Canada, 31 in France, 2 in Honduras, 134 in Russia, 248 in Sweden, 2,363 in the

USA, 132 in Zimbabwe (*Alpha News* Nov. 2000–Feb. 2001, p.15). It even attracted a ten-week documentary television programme in Britain in the summer of 2001. Not all Churches employing this method are Charismatic, involving 'slaying in the Spirit'; but they would be likely to emphasize the presence of the Spirit as part of a renewal of life. Indeed, from the 1960s many Charismatically influenced groups were described as part of a 'renewal movement', with the understanding that it was the Holy Spirit achieving the renewal.

This dynamic Spirit is closely linked with orthodox Christian belief in Christ's sinlessness and its consequent merit now made available to believers. In practical terms this is demonstrated as valid – audibly and visibly – through speaking in tongues, visions and healing and in group fellowship and mutual concern. The regular worship of charismatically inspired groups is typified by a creative outpouring of new music and distinctive songs, often with arms raised in postures of adoration. Charismatic life is also impelled into mission. While this takes one form in the educational-style evangelism of the Alpha course, it can also be more explicitly outwardly directed in what is called 'spiritual warfare', including 'marches for Jesus' or meetings for prayer in particular locations regarded as strongholds of the devil or of evil spirits (Davies and Guest 2000:14).

Such spiritual warfare mirrors exorcism, itself a feature of this style of spirituality. The old nature of the Charismatic is not simply described in traditional Christian terms of the Fall of Mankind, a Fall corrected in Christ and restored through Baptism, but as actively influenced by evil, perhaps personified by the devil or evil spirits in general. Indeed, there is a relatively strong tendency in both Pentecostal and Charismatic groups to speak of a double process of Christian development, involving an initial conversion and the coming of the Holy Spirit, followed by a second influence of the Spirit or of a gift of the Spirit advancing individual spirituality, as in earlier Holiness Movements and Methodism, with its promise of 'perfect love'. Just as believers may be slain in the Spirit in the positive process of conquest so, too, evil spirits may now be cast out or controlled by the Spirit-slain and Spirit-empowered person. Whether in sacramental eating or Charismatic events the Holy Spirit is the motif of rebounding conquest.

Modes of Thought

If some find it conceptually difficult to accept that eating can be a form of 'knowing', they may find it equally hard to accept the power of being slain in the Spirit as, also a form of awareness. Yet both are true from the perspective of embodiment theory. Part of the difficulty lies in the much broader area of theological discourse, where truth and myth, literalism and analogy jostle each other for primacy of place. What is at stake is a world-view. Behind any theology lies some principle of interpretation and words have long constituted the matter for interpretation. A prime example in social anthropology is Rodney Needham's relentless argument that expressions of belief and states of experience or emotion simply cannot be positively correlated, so that language itself ultimately produces a conceptual disease or instability (1972:235). When theology follows suit, wedded to propositional data and literal texts, it too becomes progressively useless outside academic circles, and this is probably the reason why Liberation, Black, Feminist and Gay Theologies made their appearance to answer needs of dynamic life-contexts.

Still, theologians often remained committed to the study of language, with philosophical theology exploring its limits. While some found promise in, for example, J. L. Austin's notion of the 'performative utterance' they often ignored Austin's reference to the 'force' of these terms which gave them significance (1961:238). Their 'meaning' lay more in the force attached to them than in the verbal significance. This is a useful idea, and can be applied not just to speech-acts but to numerous acts of embodiment, such as the eating and drinking of sacred things or in exorcism.

Sacrifice and Embodiment

This reflection on embodiment allows us to see that sacrifices denote a particular quality of relationship between agents, engendering a transcending quality of knowledge by drawing heavily upon symbols of embodiment, including food, blood, speech, life and death. Sacrifices need not be interpreted as conveying only one particular message, but as making possible a wide variety of ends reached by similar processual means. In one sense this means disagreeing with Leach's view that the central problem of sacrifice lies in 'the metaphor of death'; even though it often seems to involve that metaphor (1976:81). The performative force assists the transmission of many kinds of message, while its cultural and liturgical contexts determine the message announced, as Stephen Sykes recognized in evaluating New Testament sacrifice (1980:63). Within any differentiated tradition there emerge distinctive grammars of sacrificial discourse. If theology is to find any interpretative help from anthropology it will be in terms of general categories applicable to a variety of specific meanings. Two terms – participation and substitution – are particularly helpful as far as embodiment is concerned. Lévy-Bruhl's stress on participation was an attempt to show how 'primitive' people perceived themselves as inextricably related to their natural environment and, despite his unfortunate discussions of pre-logicality, this remains valuable, since participation concerns the way an individual or group senses itself to be related to or caught up in the existence of other persons, objects, or events.

In the sense that participation belongs to the same logical class of terms as substitution, one of its clearest discussions is that of Evans-Pritchard in his classic study *Nuer Religion* (1956:322). Observing the complexity of these Sudanese sacrificial ideas, he considered 'substitution' to be the best expression of the relation between what Nuer do in their external sacrificial offering and what goes on in their minds. Ignoring any specific religious emotion, he stresses the broad relation between inner states and outward actions; and underlying all this is the fact that substitution possesses its force only because of the pre-existing degree of participation between Nuer and the cattle used in sacrifices. Substitution of cattle for people is possible because of the prior degree of Nuer participation in cattle, both practical and conceptual.

Much of this also applies to Christian contexts, where the identity of the participant is related to the use of symbolic objects as one means of self-reflection. One of the inescapable aspects of theology in relation to anthropology is that human beings often require some 'external' means of self-reflection. The analogies and metaphors surrounding ritual resemble totems in being just such a mirror of self. In this sense there is a real and vital part played by the process of projection, as people 'see' themselves in things and gain a degree of distance from themselves through symbol, myth and story. Here we can extend Sykes's argument that there are two interlinked stories, one about God and one about the man Jesus, which together account for the relationship between deity and humanity in connection with sacrifice in the New Testament (1980: 66). So it is that the relation between human embodiment and Divine Incarnation comes to fulfilment in the eucharistic meal. Soteriological ideas are consummated as sacramental symbols are consumed. Here the technical distinction of Christian traditions between doctrine believed (*fides quae creditur*), and the trusting attitude in which the doctrine is apprehended (*fides qua creditur*) becomes ritually apparent. It is the latter that human embodiment ultimately demands, and the former that makes the demand possible.

One consequence of 'the stomach of the heart', once it has been satisfied, is the desire for self-sacrifice or the ethic of responsive love.

The assimilation into self of the sacrificed Christ involves a change in self-image, producing an altered sense of embodiment. For embodiment is neither unchanging nor unchangeable. This is what Paul means in saying that it is no longer he who lives, but Christ who lives in him (Gal.2:20). Here the idea of the Christian as a 'living sacrifice' and of the ethical life framing that sacrifice is an expression of rebounding vitality. It concerns the mode of engagement between old and new 'natures'. One traditionally distinctive way of discussing this interface has been through the topic of ritual purity.

Ritual Purity and Power

Although ritual purity is regularly discussed in both theological and anthropological accounts of sacrifice, religious life and death, the concept is far from transparent. Mary Douglas's influence has been great, but has, perhaps, tended to create an over-attention to boundary maintenance to the ignoring of other potential directions of thought, as in Malina's otherwise useful biblical reflections (2001: 161–97). At the outset it is important to distinguish between the notion of ritual purity as an abstract anthropological model seeking to explain human behaviour and indigenous theology and practices that simply utilize explicit notions of purity and impurity.

Ritual purity concerns power, not only as an abstract concept but also as affect. While abstract analyses dwell upon issues of boundaries, boundary marking and boundary maintenance, the practical domain of experience should not be ignored, because it is within the sensed awareness of bodily life that the restrictions of ritual purity come into play. 'Power' underlies not only the truth claimed by groups but also the experience echoing truth claims within daily life, as Van der Leeuw's notion of 'power' as the essential feature in a tremendous diversity of religious phenomena demonstrated (1967/1933). Embodiment adds the dynamic dimension of felt experience to formal classifications of the world and boundaries.

Purity and Impurity as Religious Ideas

Within the Judaeo-Christian tradition notions of purity and impurity are closely aligned with the concept of holiness, itself an attribute of deity and related to supernatural presence. Holiness enshrines honour and respect and controls the behaviour deemed appropriate for encountering the divine; but it is also a term used, albeit rarely, to describe religious believers who express a distinctive form of dedication to the 'higher' life that pertains to deity. By contrast, ritual purity, rather than holiness, denotes the status of individuals able to perform rites associated with the cult of the deity. One aspect of purity concerns the condition of the human body as the agent for ritual performance, and is especially applicable to priests. In ancient Israel priests' bodies were not to be marked by physical deformity, but they could be rendered impure for limited periods through seminal emissions or contact with menstruating women. Similarly, women were rendered impure by menstruation and childbirth, an important field of its own that cannot be pursued here (cf. Buckley and Gottlieb 1988). Both sexes were rendered impure by dead bodies. Impurity could apply to the temple or to the house, making the religious rules an intimate part of experience, not least through food and marriage rules. These notions were framed by the idea of Israel as a divinely chosen people in a covenant with God, a relationship controlled by purity codes, with circumcision as pivotal. Circumcision rendered boy babies ritually pure, and purity was maintained both in the daily life of individuals and families and in the major festivals focused on the day of atonement. Purity also came to be associated with ethical concerns expressing the notion of the righteousness of God.

Early Christianity, as a sect of Judaism, was confronted by this scheme of purity, especially rules concerning circumcision, food and marriage, as highlighted in *The Acts of the Apostles*. Here I draw attention to 'purity' through the conversions of the apostles Paul and Peter. I describe Peter's vision or dream as a 'conversion' because it marks the rebounding conquest of his old and new orientations.

Peter, Paul and Purity

The transition from Judaism to Christianity was made within the life experience of individuals and not by formal dictat. While academic traditions often handle the history of ideas as the development and transformation of abstract formulations, the reality of practical life is that major changes occur through the commitment and conviction of individuals. And this is especially true in religion. Starkly put, Christianity's emergence is focused through the life of an Orthodox Jew, through one whose identity had been forged and maintained by means of the boundary defining rules of ritual purity. And such was Saul of Tarsus. Early Christianity involved dramatic shifts in notions of community and of the notions of purity that bounded community, and this is exemplified in the shift of personal identity of Saul re-identified as Paul. When Paul speaks of a necessary renewal of mind in Christian conversion he reflects his own transformation. His conversion is starkly portrayed as an encounter with the supernatural, resurrected Christ, with a falling into blindness and in a restoration of sight once he had been, quite literally, led into the new Christian community. It results in his belief that circumcision is no longer necessary for Christians, that Jewish food rules need not be maintained, and that the new community is inclusive and not exclusive, with its membership grounded in experiencing grace and faith. Experientially, grace is encountered as a creative act of divine love and forgiveness within a community, and faith is its sensed response. Gender differences of status no longer hold the sway they once did, and the New Testament ignores menstrual or seminal impurity, an absence that should not simply be taken for granted.

This new religious movement and the ritual purity of its cultural matrix is explicitly marked in the text of the *Acts of the Apostles* at the Council of Jerusalem (Acts 15: 4–28). Triggered by pressure groups, including believing Pharisees, it argued for the continuation of circumcision for Christians (Acts 15:5). But Peter notes that God had given the Holy Spirit to Gentiles and had 'cleansed their hearts by faith', just as in the case of believing Jews, and requests that no yoke be placed upon Gentile necks that even his fellow Jews had found hard to bear. The outcome is interesting. Circumcision, the topic that occasioned the council, is not required of gentile converts, but they are requested to abstain from things sacrificed to idols, from blood and from things strangled and from fornication (Acts 15:20,29). Food regulations and sexual control now overshadow circumcision. But the food rules are not the Jewish dietary laws, in that no named beasts are forbidden: the scene has shifted to the Hellenistic world of pagan temples and their sacrifices, which were also items of ordinary food. Part of the logic of Hebrew food rules is maintained, but within a new symbolic and social field. Gentile believers are asked not to live in a way that others might construe as acknowledging pagan gods.

Circumcision

The inescapable feature of these debates is the Spirit, group identity and salvation. It is difficult to change belief without also changing the behaviour that is its vehicle. Here philosophical and systematic theology must appreciate that for many devotees 'belief' involves the sensation of wearing particular clothes, or adopting particular postures, as much as or even more than holding certain doctrines. To change 'belief' necessarily involves changing behaviour.

This perspective adds a dimension to forms of symbolic analysis reflected, for example, in Leonie Archer's theological study of the Jewish rite of circumcision, which she sets within the traditional anthropological distinction between nature and culture, a distinction she regards as universal (1990:40). The essence of her argument, unfortunately, reflects an earlier anthropological assumption that while women 'make' boys, only men 'make' men (Strathern 1988: 209ff.). Accordingly, circumcision becomes a 'rite of cultural rebirth' with the 'blood of circumcision' serving as 'a symbolic surrogate for the blood of childbirth', blood that was shed 'in a voluntarily and controlled manner' (Archer 1990: 53). While that may well be an accurate observation as far as it goes, it leaves untouched the entire issue of what circumcision meant to Jewish men of that period, of what it 'felt like' as an aspect of embodiment. This is a difficult topic for, while anachronism always terrorizes historical interpretation, there is today a considerable discussion of circumcision's disadvantages and benefits within both Jewish and non-Jewish groups.

Ignoring these emotional issues, it may, with Archer in mind, be better to talk less in terms of nature and culture and more of the transcendence of nature when it comes to circumcision. Indeed, more than one form of transcending takes place. If Israel's mythical-history set Jews apart from Gentiles through circumcision's covenant mark, it makes perfect sense to see that another form of transcendence will, in turn, demand its own 'mark'. This suggests why the *Acts of the Apostles* spends so much of its time reflecting upon what we might call the marks of the Spirit, including glossolalia. While Paul reflected upon circumcision as something that had become an 'interior' mark, arguing that 'real circumcision is a matter of the heart' (Rom. 2: 29), his prime focus was upon 'life in the Spirit' (Rom.8:2–27). Whereas the 'life' had once been in the blood, it was now in the Spirit.

Archer speaks tellingly of the distinction in Israel between the intergenerational aspect of blood related to birth and to the further 'cultural rebirth' involving 'a network or brotherhood of blood which transcended generations' (1990: 53). With the emergence of Christianity the brotherhood of blood itself becomes transcended in the brotherhood of Spirit. But now it is no longer simply a 'brotherhood' dependent upon outward circumcision, but a community including women who, equally with men, experienced the Holy Spirit in a public and audible and visible form. Indeed, while the emphasis upon the Holy Spirit in *Acts* is obvious from its first chapter, it is still relatively easy to sideline the 'language event'

(Acts 2:4–18, 33); yet this it is vital for the apostles' evaluation of divine activity (Acts 15:8). To see this mark of the Spirit as foundational for understanding changing notions of identity is to establish a firm foundation for dealing with the issue of ritual purity in early Christianity.

Interpreting Impurity

Following Mary Douglas's anthropological interpretation at the outset of her explorations in the Old Testament, the Christian leaders at Jerusalem were seeking to perpetuate a commitment to the one God in the practice of gentile Christians (Douglas 1966). The prohibition on blood and things strangled is a reference to the mode of slaughter of animals, and reinforces the call not to eat animals slaughtered at or through modes patronized by pagans. The request to avoid things sacrificed to idols applies the Jewish notion of monotheism to the social context of Hellenistic life, with its numerous temples, deities and cultic acts. Gentile Christians are asked to live without reference to the reality or influence of any other 'deity'. Paul is very clear not only on the food issue but also regarding marriage. In his first letter to the Corinthians, Chapters 7 and 8 are, respectively, devoted to marriage and idol-food, and are distinctive in avoiding rule-based prescription. Purity rules related to boundary maintenance have given way to internal relationships between members of the Christian community. Rules once serving to separate insider from outsider now became principles for intra-community life. Elsewhere, he describes Christians as constituting the body of Christ or as being a Temple for the Holy Spirit, terms expressing their own form of embodiment theory. This important aspect of the sociology of the earliest Christianity contrasts Jewish purity rules, as highly formalized priestly idealizations of cultural practices, with New Testament texts produced by young and vibrant new religious movements concerned primarily with the internal dynamics of their growing membership and, secondarily, with their break away from parent and surrounding groups.

Absent from these texts are food rules for natural types of animals, prohibitions related to menstrual or seminal body fluids, and death pollution. By contrast, much is said about faith and the communal bonding of 'brothers and sisters', whose spiritual kinship derives from their commitment to Jesus as the Christ and Jesus as Lord. Positive affirmation largely replaces negation. A form of ritual purity rather than ritual impurity preoccupies the texts, as evidenced at the Council of Jerusalem, with Peter speaking of God as having cleansed Gentile hearts by faith and as having given to them the Holy Spirit (Acts 15:8,9). This debate flows throughout many of the epistles, highlighting the inadequacy of the Jewish purity rules and of the Law in general to ensure salvation. The dominant forces driving the internal life of Christian groups appear as grace, faith, love and the fellowship that binds the members of the new community together, while the frame integrating them is constituted from both the death and resurrection of Jesus as the Christ of Jewish expectation and the power of the Holy Spirit, which also added an outwardly directed mission. It would take time and new contexts before new purity rules would emerge, flourishing for example in the monasticism of the Middle Ages as pursued by Talal Asad's analysis of bodily control and the will to obey in medieval monasticism (1993:125–67). Further developments would be associated with pastoral disciplines associated with the confessional in Roman Catholic life and with forms of the Protestant work ethic.

Purity and Death

By distinguishing between living and dead things ritual purity also marks the transition between 'ordinary' and 'transcendent' forms of life, and blood is one of the readiest symbols of this divide, especially when shed in slaughter. For pastoralists the familiar throat-slitting showed life flowing away with the blood. Blood also served as a symbolic medium in Jewish circumcision, where it must flow; so if a baby does not bleed when circumcised it needs to be slightly cut so that blood does flow; and contemporary traditionalist practice forbids the use of surgical clamps lest no blood 'of the covenant' flows.

The link between ritual purity and life and death is important in the Jewish tradition, where a *Cohen,* one reckoned to be of priestly status, should avoid dead bodies and any roof or cover over corpses, such as hospitals or trees overarching graves. But the life–death distinction can also be extended to apply to the divide between ritual death and ritual rebirth, allowing Bloch's process of rebounding conquest to furnish new examples of ritual purity. The divide between the old nature that has been conquered in the rite of initiation and the new nature is likely to be marked in terms of ritual purity. This perspective explains why menstruation and seminal discharge so often cause ritual impurity, for they are distinctly symbolic of the natural order, of the 'old' basic human nature that is to be conquered in the 'new' servants of God. This is also why sexual relations are so often forbidden at times when particularly important rituals are to be performed. Those rites pertain to the 'higher' realms of power, and should not be confused with the 'lower' and former order of things. It was this very idea of 'confusion' that Mary Douglas developed to good effect in her early work on the Abominations of Leviticus. Ritual purity prevents confusion of categories and maintains the power inherent in orderly systems. The animals that symbolize good order are 'clean', but those that confuse categories are 'unclean'.

Humans may also express both impurity and purity, as with lepers in the Hebrew Bible, whose physical condition involves the death of body parts, while the High Priest has to be a physically perfect individual able to engage in contact with Yahweh as the very source of life. But to stress only negative aspects of category confusion is to ignore John Davis's important anthropological suggestion that, 'the imperfection of classes may be an opportunity, giving people room for manoeuvre, scope for inventiveness and creativity' (1992:54). The Incarnation may be just such a case, for the idea that Jesus was God in human flesh whilst also being entirely human does present an anomaly, a potential confusion of categories. This anomaly has prompted two thousand years of inter-pretative theology, alongside a focus for worship as the embodied response to something perceived as holy. The forbidden and the desired lie close in the phenomenon of holiness.

Purity and Holiness

For some Christian devotees 'holiness' has denoted a form of spirituality in which individuals seek lives that mirror the moral perfection of God, longing to embody and express the ideal. This desire exemplifies the rebounding conquest hypothesis, as it seeks to replace fallen human nature with a renewed personal style of life invoking images of self-sacrifice. While examples are legion, two will suffice, one in a person and the other from hymnody.

Jonathan Edwards

Jonathan Edwards (1703–1758), American theologian and revivalist, speaks of himself as a young man for whom 'holiness . . . brought . . . an inexpressible purity, brightness, peace and mad ravishment of the soul'. His 'heart panted after this – to lie low before God, as in the dust: that I might be nothing, and that God, might be ALL (*sic*)' (Edwards 1966:87–8.). He could weep a flood of tears and fall into deep dwelling upon the wonders of Christ at the hearing of a single word of reminder. 'Groanings that cannot be uttered' attended his longing 'to be emptied' of himself, an infinitely wicked self, and to be 'swallowed up in Christ': these feelings could only be tolerated through the Holy Spirit, who purifies the individual

(1966:93). This self-loathing, with its desire or 'thirsting' for purity, portrays an ideal-type of spirituality that longs for transformation of identity. Here the human drive for meaning assumes a moral path, with intellect and emotion uniting in a theological language that shaped emotion. That 'inner-otherness' of Chapter 2 makes the individual aware of self as a negative force and destructive evil – 'the bottomless depths of secret corruption and deceit' – that lies contrary to the real desire of the self (1966:86). Inner-otherness is characterized as fragmented. In this context it is no accident that it is the 'Third Person in the Trinity . . . God in the communications of his holy spirit' that comes to the fore and to the aid of inner-otherness (Edwards 1966:93). Nor is it accidental that these experiences were associated with Edwards's coming to admire and love watching dramatic thunder and lightning storms, whereas once he had hated and feared them. It is as though the *Sturm und Drang* of his spiritual life were symbolized in the hated thunder, yet conquered in the love of the heavenly manifestations: thus is nature doubly transformed by divine power.

Hymns of Holiness

Nor is it accidental that Edwards refers to prayer and devotion, often out of doors, as involving a form of singing. He 'often used to sit and view the moon for a long time . . . in the meantime singing forth, with a low voice, my contemplations of the creator and Redeemer' (1966:85). His low singing gave pleasure, allowing him to express that sense of unity and perfection so desired in the longed-for holiness of faith.

In public worship hymns have also united holiness texts with harmonies expressive of longing. *Sacred Songs and Solos* (1873), associated with Ira D. Sankey and D. L. Moody's evangelistic campaigns in the USA and Great Britain, devotes sections to 'Desires after Holiness' and to 'Consecration', with its fifty hymns of 'consecration' directly expressing notions of self-sacrifice. 'Whiter than the Snow', by J. Nicholson asks that Jesus 'look down from his throne in the skies, and help me to make a complete sacrifice'. Others ask why their soul is not satisfied? Satisfaction becomes a prized goal in the pursuit of holiness, evident in the undercurrent of a process of change from an earlier stage of Christian understanding to a higher or more developed form typified by resting and peace and, often, by a new 'melody' within the heart. Change comes from the insight of faith, resulting from the work of Christ or of the Holy Spirit. Edith Cherry's hymn, 'The Heavenly Secret', tells how even in 'life's glad music there was always that which jarred' until the hand of Christ took the 'harp of life' and struck it with the 'keynote of love' so that she 'heard the music change . . . the music change'.

Death and Blood

What is clear from many similar hymns is the sense of conquest through blood, death and life, all irrevocably tied to the body. Death and blood are seldom neutral entities, often coming to be invested with moral significance. In Christianity's international culture and global symbolism blood and death have combined to provide a means of transcending selected negative aspects of life. Whether focused in the Eucharist or in preaching, teaching and hymnody, the blood of Christ has been made to speak of his death and of the life it brings to others.

The use of the image of blood in the Christian Eucharist is remarkable within the total field of Judaic-Christian symbolism. Despite the earliest Christian exhortation to abstain from blood, over time Christians began to associate the wine of the Eucharist with the blood of Christ. The eucharistic act using the express words 'this is my blood that is shed for you. Drink this . . .' can be read as the final symbolic barrier dividing Christianity and Judaism. This distinction becomes all the clearer when ritual purity is understood in terms of rebounding vitality. The distinction between impurity and purity is a symbolic representation of a distinction between two domains, two orders of existence, that are qualitatively distinguished from each other. Impurity ensues from engaging in the negative order, it detracts from the sense of power and its associated status of the positive order. Ritual impurity denies and ritual purity affirms transcendence. Impurity comes from dealing with the old nature or with features reflecting the old nature, including death, for death is frequently identified with the nature that is to be transcended. It is no accident that Pauline theology speaks of death as the logical outcome of human disobedience. Paul sets up a symbolic contrast between the old and the new human nature in terms of the distinction between 'flesh' and 'spirit'. To be a Christian is to live according to the spirit, and converted Jews, too, must live according to the spirit, and not according to human tradition, even the tradition of God's chosen people.

Like its offspring, Christianity, Judaism was founded on a ritual system of blood underlying covenant, including circumcision, Passover lambs and animal sacrifice at the temple. It was precisely because of the close association of blood with life itself and as a vehicle for covenant relationships with the deity that ordinary Jews were forbidden to ingest this highly charged symbolic medium. Jewish tradition brought considerable power to what was, already, a potent human substance. The annual Passover sacrifice and meal institutionalized the reminder of being saved through blood and established eating as a form of memory, with the meal embodying this mythical history. Christianity integrated Passover meal and temple sacrifice to furnish the medium for blood symbolism in the New Testament, for the synoptic gospels and the *Acts of the Apostles* hardly refer to blood in connection with the crucifixion of Jesus, while the *Gospel of John*, regarded by many scholars as a relatively late document, does so in a dramatically marked episode (John 19:34). In the *Acts of the Apostles* the numerous set speeches and sermons that argue for the Messiahship of Jesus and that establish him as the saviour figure do not use blood language at all. It is only towards the close of the *Acts*, when Paul addresses Christian leaders – whether Jew or Gentile – and not outsiders that he briefly alludes to believers as the 'church of the Lord which he obtained with his own blood' (Acts 20:28). In the *First Epistle to the Corinthians* it is in a reference to the special communion meal of disciples that Paul speaks of a 'participation in the blood of Christ' (I. Cor. 10:16), before going on to remind the Corinthians that he had passed on to them what he had received from the Lord: 'that the Lord Jesus on the night when he was betrayed' had said 'this cup is the new covenant in my blood' (I. Cor. 11:25). When the author of *I Corinthians* furnishes a set-piece of Paul's message concerning salvation it makes no reference to sacrificial blood at all (I. Cor. 15:1–58). When in *II Corinthians* there is a direct reference to a new covenant it is said to be written, not in the blood of Christ, as one might expect, but in 'the Spirit' (II Cor. 3.6) – indeed there is no reference to blood at all in that second epistle.

Spirit Replaces Blood

As was intimated earlier, Spirit replaces blood in the embodied spirituality of the earliest Christianity. This does not mean that the purity–impurity distinction disappears, but that it now operates through the grammar of discourse of spirit and not of blood. The case of Ananias and Sapphira in *Acts* expresses this schema, and makes greater sense if discussed in terms of 'blasphemy' against, lying to or tempting the Spirit, as in our final chapter (Acts 5: 3, 9). Blasphemy against the Spirit becomes a direct symbolic equivalent of ritual impurity involving blood or death. The Old Testament motif that 'the life is in the blood', and as such is the dynamic force by which the body is empowered, is replaced by the Holy Spirit, which is the power that engenders the identity of Christians. New life is in the Spirit. Contact with the life-force, whether of blood or spirit, is to be circumscribed in order to affirm its significance.

The creative feature of early Christianity lies in the interfusion of ideas of blood and of spirit in Jesus. His death is the sacrificial medium of atonement, and his resurrection the catalyst for the Holy Spirit's advent. Blood conducts Jewish believers from the cult of the temple to the cult of Christianity, into which they are inducted through the power of the Holy Spirit. This is the crucial reason why circumcision came to prominence in the critical debates amongst the first generations of Jewish Christians, as witnessed by the presence of a 'circumcision party' in the dissension between Paul and Peter (Gal. 2:12–21) and in debates on food proscriptions (Col. 2:20–1). Circumcision was the mark of the covenant people, and demanded the shedding of human blood, just as the temple rites demanded the shedding of animal blood. But the experience creating the earliest Christian groups was interpreted as the Holy Spirit manifested in such a phenomenon as glossolalia, or speaking in tongues (Acts 11:15–18), a form of linguistic activity expressing experiential shifts within individuals.

Blood, atonement, Holy Spirit and Christian identity are all involved in this transformation, especially in the Epistles, where Christ's death as a blood sacrifice for sin becomes the source of life for believers (Rom 5:9). But references to blood are limited, with *Galatians, Philippians, I and II Thessalonians*, and *James* simply not mentioning it. When mentioned blood remains significant, with *Ephesians* speaking of redemption being accomplished 'in his blood' (1:7), which also brings believers nearer to God (2:2). Colossians speaks of reconciliation and peace made 'by the blood of his cross' (1: 20). Similarly the *First Epistle of Peter* describes Christians as having been 'sprinkled with his blood' and ransomed with 'the precious blood of Christ' (1:2,18). The *First Epistle of John* similarly refers to the 'blood of Jesus' that 'cleanses from all sin' (1:7), and of Jesus being identified as one who came 'by water and blood' and of whom there are three witnesses, Spirit, water and blood (5:6,8).

The two documents that stand out in their emphasis upon blood are the *Epistle to the Hebrews* and *The Book of Revelation*. *Hebrews* likens Jesus to the High Priest of the Jewish Temple, but deploying his own blood and not that of animals (9:7, 12–25) when entering the sacred sacrificial space (10:19, 29. cf. 11:28) He is, in fact, the mediator of the new covenant (12:24), suffering to 'sanctify the people through his blood' (13:12), which is the 'blood of the eternal covenant' (13:20). The *Apocalypse* adopts a similar position, with his blood freeing believers from their sins (1:5), and ransoming 'men for God' (5:9), who, in turn (7:14) wash their robes in the blood of the lamb and conquer by his blood (12:11). The death of believers – defined as martyrs – is also expressed in terms of their loss of blood (17:6, 18:24, 19:13).

In terms of the rebounding conquest image the overall transition from an old to a new order is completed in the image of the Christian community as the 'body of Christ'. In fact this is the prime Christian mystery, that the Gentiles are fellow heirs and members of the same body (Eph. 3:4). Christianity requires that the old nature of believers 'be renewed in spirit of your mind' (Eph. 4:23). Indeed, in this new body there is 'neither Jew nor Greek' (Gal. 3:28). Even the image of washing in the process of renewal is to be accomplished through the Holy Spirit (Titus 3:5).

In the Gospels, generally believed to have been written after most of the Epistles, much attention focuses on the night before Jesus died, when he is believed to have used the traditional Jewish Passover meal as a means for his disciples to remember him in the future. Given the primacy of place of the traditional Passover account of Israel's delivery from Egypt and the destroying angel passing over houses marked with animal blood it was almost inevitable that blood would become part of the symbolic grammar of discourse of the new group. Given that a theological ident-ification came to be made between the death of Jesus and the sacrificial atonement for sin, it is all the more remarkable that blood comes to occupy a secondary place to spirit in many of the Epistles, as sketched above. It was in subsequent eras of Christian development that the blood motif resurged, as the rite of eating and drinking assumed an increasingly formal status – one that, in the fullness of time, would be interpreted sacra-mentally; but that history of the return of blood lies beyond this book.

Corpses, Pure and Glorious

But what of the dead? Although many cultures have regarded their dead as ritually impure, this is not the prime thrust of most Christian traditions. This is unusual and merits fuller treatment than is possible here, for not only was the dead body of Jesus not described in terms of impurity, but its ongoing iconic representation increased its sacred status and that of the corpses of ordinary believers. The bodies of early Christian martyrs were honoured and respected and given burial sites that became found-ational as places of worship, as Augustine observed (Augustine 1945: 252ff.). He also strikes a positive Christian attitude towards living bodies, reminding Christians that their 'bodies are not to be despised', not least because the bodies of the righteous and faithful have been used by the Holy Spirit 'as organs and instruments unto all good works' (1945:17). Here we see a clear association of the Holy Spirit with the body, echoing the argument just made about the significance of the Holy Spirit in the dynamic of Christian identity. The growth of rites associated with the relics of the Saints witnesses to this positive valuation of the remains of the Christian dead from the earliest centuries.

The doctrine of the Resurrection also enhanced the status accorded to the body, for God would, in the fullness of time, provide a new body in and through the process of resurrection. This transformed or 'spiritual body' contrasts with the physical body that is 'sown' in death, and affords a powerful cameo of the contrasting old and new natures that underlies the rebounding conquest motif of this book (I Cor. 15:44). The kind of conquest involved in Christ's resurrection is, itself, echoed in the New Testament text that describes him as being 'put to death in the flesh but being made alive in the spirit' and then going into the realm of the dead, described as being in prison, to 'preach to them' (I Peter 3:18).

–5–

Ritual and Experience

Ritual and symbolism are closely united aspects of human behaviour, and are treated separately here and in Chapter 7 only for the sake of convenience. Tylor's early division of ritual into performance and communication remains valuable, with rites being 'expressive and symbolic', the 'gesture language of theology' and 'directly practical' as a 'means of intercourse with and influence upon spiritual beings' (1958 [1871]:448). These assumptions remain important, despite more sophisticated developments.

Ritual is as important to anthropology as to theology, and its historical matrix in theology was a major catalyst in the emergence of the anthropology of religion, as was shown in the preceding chapter for Robertson Smith's influence on Durkheim. But the word 'ritual' often carries strong religious values within different traditions. Catholicism, Orthodoxy, Lutheranism and Anglicanism see 'ritual', along with 'liturgy' and 'ceremonial', in a positive light, with Greek and Russian Orthodoxy identifying the 'liturgy' as the prime work of the Eucharist, carrying tradition forward and bringing faith to life, while in Catholicism the ritual of the Mass is of the essence of the mystery of the faith. In Protestantism the idea of 'ritual' is more negative, hinting at inauthenticity of faith, with conservative Protestants tending not to see their own religious behaviour as 'ritual': 'ritual' is for those who lack the real essence of faith. At least one anthropologist has criticized his colleagues for tending 'to characterise ritual action in quasi-theological terms' (Boyer 1994:219). Still, in anthropology at large, ritual has often been the primary mode of access to the symbolic worlds of other people, as anthropologists created their own texts in the form of ethnographies, studies that describe and interpret the lives of a people or group. Towards the end of the twentieth century, however, under the intellectual trend towards reflexivity and the pressure to consider their personal agendas anthropologists also became increasingly self-conscious about ethnographies.

Theologians, by contrast, have tended to ground their work in the texts of their own religion. Texts that are, at their simplest, believed to represent a formal expression of the faith of their authors and, at their most affirmative, to be the very voice of God. Most theologians have taken for granted the ritual life of the Churches to which they belong, viewing rites as but a formal expression of doctrine. Only in the later twentieth century did theology generally take an interest in ritual as a distinctive form of human activity. Martin Stringer, whose research on British church worship adds significantly to this field, has provided a summary of theological borrowings from anthropology in liturgy and worship (1999:21ff.).

Ritual Reflections

My concern is narrower than his, offering no systematic consideration of ritual, either historically or methodologically. Lawson and McCauley (1990), Pascal Boyer (1994), Catherine Bell (1997), Roy Rappaport (1999) and many others furnish excellent accounts, and there is even a field of ritual studies associated with Ronald Grimes (1990). My intention grows out of Chapter 2, and concerns the way in which ritual processes embodied values. In particular, it explores the difference between viewing ritual either as a kind of language with a code that may be cracked to discover its meaning, or as a non-language-like phenomenon.

Communicative Simplicity

One key aspect of ritual observable in much contemporary Christian liturgy lies in its communicative simplicity, with the content of the information passed within the ritual event remaining virtually constant in each performance. Churches of a sacramental tradition following a liturgical calendar and lectionary of biblical texts do possess one constant element of change from week to week, as the theological themes pass through a scheme of thought focused largely on the redemption of the world. Advent and Christmas emphasize the redemptive work of God in the coming of Jesus as the Messiah and the Saviour of the world. His life and teaching are explored before the period of Lent, whose sense of Christian discipline and self-denial prepares for the suffering and passion of Christ leading into Good Friday. Then follows the resurrection motif of Easter Sunday, Jesus's subsequent Ascension and the coming of the Holy Spirit, leading, finally, to the affirmation of God as divine Trinity. Readings and prayers illustrate these themes, embedded within a liturgy that otherwise is the same. But these prayers and readings are also cyclical, and conduce to a ritual repetition within the ongoing religious life.

While each liturgy reflects a condensation of many historical and doctrinal themes, these appear in the ritual as fixed forms, rehearsed rather than intellectually explored. And this is what constitutes liturgy's communicative simplicity. But this simplicity of cognition is complemented by a communicative complexity of emotion. People often speak of the depth of significance of the Eucharist in their experience; and one way of doing justice to their comments is to pose the specific question of whether ritual is a language.

Ritual as language

My answer to this question will be both affirmative and negative, depending upon the definition of language as an encoded structure of communication. Is language a code that needs to be cracked in order for its meaning to become apparent? If ritual is regarded as a coded 'language' in need of decoding before its meaning becomes apparent then I propose that religious ritual is not a language-like phenomenon as far as most participants are concerned. To adopt the alternative possibility is to see ritual behaviour as an end in itself. Its meaning lies in the very act of performance. I specifically mention the majority of practitioners, because many religious leaders – as ritual specialists – will tend to view ritual as a form of language, seeing encoded within it the historical doctrine of their Church. It is for theoretical purposes that this distinction between ritual as language and ritual as a 'performative end in itself' is drawn, for these models are complementary and relate to particular contexts, even though anthropologists often divide over the issue. Scholars like Edmund Leach did tend to see ritual and symbolism as crackable codes for, as Leach said, 'we engage in ritual in order to transmit collective messages to ourselves.' (1976:45). This has, probably, been the dominant view both in anthropology and, certainly, within the wider field of the history of religion, especially in the nineteenth and early twentieth centuries, when scholars argued over the priority of ritual and myth.

Here I opt for ritual as an end in itself rather than a decodable language, for two, interconnected, reasons. One concerns the historical significance of theological debates and controversies in European religious history, and the other affects contemporary clergy and those who lead religious ceremonial.

History and Ritual

Every culture presents itself to new members in some historical form, not least through conventions of liturgical dress that are as marked by controversy as they are adorned by revelatory style. Christian history is distinctive in possessing one, determinative, ritual at its heart, the eucharistic rite of bread and wine or, in shorthand, the bread-rite. Having already described this in its historical Anglican forms in the preceding chapter I now give it this more theologically neutral name, because ecclesiastical names betoken distinctive interpretations. This ritual originated in the biblical account of the Last Supper of Jesus, which was a Jewish Passover meal, itself symbolizing the deliverance of the Jews as God's people from their captivity in Egypt. At the Last Supper Jesus added his own gloss to the effect that the bread was his body and the wine was his blood. This gloss then provided a text that subsequent generations used as a focus for expressing their own theories of his death and of the nature of his ongoing relationship with the Christian community. In the Catholic and sacramental traditions of Lutheranism and Anglicanism it helped define the nature of the priesthood, while for more explicit Protestant and Reformed traditions, including parts of Anglicanism, it helped define their own theological beliefs against those of Rome. To this day the ritual of bread and wine, which is theologically reckoned to be the prime moment of union between God and Christian believers as well as of union between believers, is the prime sign of division between Catholics and Protestants, for they cannot share in this rite. The rite of communion is, *par excellence*, the rite of division.

History furnishes innumerable examples of detailed debates over this rite, demonstrating how concepts of sign, symbol, metaphor, trope, and other interpretative notions became increasingly formalized when making explicit the implicit sensations of religious experience, as with Cranmer's reflections upon eating eucharistic bread in the previous chapter. Long before the Reformation, the Catholic Church also had its own internal debates on the topic (Dimock 1895); but after the Reformation's growth in diversity in theological opinion concern with ritual became more explicit than ever before. Practically overnight, Churches across Europe now possessed a different version of the bread-rite, often in the mother-tongue and not Latin, and during the reign of Edward VI and Elizabeth I the Church of England even published sermons to be used by clergy caught up in these changing theological interpretations. These addresses on Common Prayer and Sacraments, on The Right Use of The Church and on the Peril of Idolatry gave firm direction in interpreting ritual within changing religious worlds (Griffiths 1914: 163ff.).

Liturgical Debate and Ritual Interpretation

Not only have Church leaders approached the bread-rite through extensive interpretation, but this theological attitude was generalized to much other church ritual under the implicit assumption that ritual is a coded language. I suspect that this ecclesiastical view of ritual extended into the wider intellectual world, including anthropology, so that by 'cultural instinct', or at least by an implicit cultural convention, ritual is viewed as an encoded language open to code-cracking and the consequent discovery of meaning. Incidentally, this cultural assumption prepared Western intellectuals for Freud's view of dreams as a realm ripe for code-cracking. As with the interpretation of ritual, dreams are not allowed to be ends in themselves, but only vehicles for therapeutic interpretation. The 1960s acceptance of the notion of 'body-language' also followed this pattern.

Ritual Non-linguistic

To set a non-linguistic model alongside this dominant language-like model of ritual opens up greater possibilities of approaching ritual in a complementarity reminiscent of Paul Ricoeur's philosophical approach to hermeneutics in his *Interpretation Theory*, where he speaks of the 'non-semantic moment of a symbol' in contrast to the 'semantic moment of a symbol' (1976:54, 57). The anthropologist Gilbert Lewis also advises us not to presume ritual is essentially a form of communication, because such a presumption can lead both 'to a search for meaning that actors do not have' and to 'a contrived intellectualism' (1970:117). Certainly it is possible to seek forms of meaning where it cannot be found, and to generate interpretation piled upon interpretation. Here it is essential to differentiate between propositional meaning and that meaning or significance related to emotions and embedded in action or performance. Propositional meaning is easily explained in terms of the formal ideas lying behind actions; but emotional forms of meaning are not so self-evident. The latter express the satisfaction gained from doing something – from a specific performance of some definite act. For example, people may kneel, sit or stand to pray. All three forms might even be employed in one church during one service. It is perfectly possible for theologians or anthropologists to interpret these postures propositionally; but, equally, they may simply be something that people do and benefit from, without being able to give any ideological explanation of why they do this.

Jack Goody drew attention to the fact that it may be 'intrinsic to the nature of ritual' to have 'superficial meaning in explicit and rational terms'

(1977:31). Here 'superficial' does not mean irrelevant or redundant, but refers to explicit and rational aspect of formal belief statements. There still remains the entire realm of the sense gained from having performed an act, as concisely emphasized by Rodney Needham: *'It may well be that the purpose and meaning and effect of a rite will consist in no more than the performance of the rite itself. Ritual can be self-sufficient, self-sustaining, and self-justifying. Considered in its most characteristic features, it is a kind of activity – like speech or dancing – that man as a 'ceremonial animal' happens naturally to perform'* (1985:177).

This anthropological caution is timely, given some tendencies to romanticize ritual and to forget how ritual relates to ordinariness, a point stressed by Michael Aune when affirming the relationship between ritual, liturgy and mundane life and expressing a growing consensus interpreting ritual as a 'way of acting and speaking' that 'provides a way to know the world and to act on such a world' (1996:142, 143).

Music and Poetry

One medium that fosters 'knowing and acting' is music, a regular presence in much ritual whose 'meaning' is not always immediately apparent. Indeed, to pose the question, 'what is the meaning of music?' is soon to appreciate that it is, quintessentially, more an end in itself than a code to be cracked for propositional meaning. In one of the most enduring reflections on the nature of music Susanne Langer considered how music affords 'not communication but insight' (1951[1942]:244). In a slightly confusing word, she accounts for music as an 'unconsummated symbol', one whose 'real power lies in its . . . ambivalence of content', able to embrace opposite emotions at the same time (1951[1942]:240). This 'unconsummated' nature refers to the fact that music cannot be spelled out, its meaning cannot be explicated as can the meaning of a sentence. It is a slightly unfortunate adjective, since she did not wish to imply imperfection, but benefit. To draw an analogy between music and smell will reinforce Langer's account of music as one of those feelings or moods that have to be described in terms of their causes or effects, as when we say that we feel 'like running away'. Langer's account resembles Dan Sperber's observation, made decades later, that cultures do not possess classifications of smell as they do of colour (1975). Smells do not exist in a spectrum or in a classification with names of their own: they are described more in terms of something else, they smell 'like a rose' or the like. This concept of smell is radically instructive, in that we should no more speak of musical experience as a 'language of feeling' than of our olfactory experiences as 'a language of smell'. Both smell and music can be viewed as modes of embodiment caused to exist by external stimuli that leave a mood-memory with the embodied individual. Having said that, particular musical forms and idioms can assume distinctive signif- icance within a culture, not least within religious groups, where aspects of musical expression and religious expression may coincide to a point of merging. The potential of music to foster a sense not only of such inner unity but also of being acted upon by an external source cannot be ignored when interpreting religious behaviour (cf. Storr 1992:96).

Anthropology, especially ethnomusicology, and to a lesser extent theology have both seen that music is fundamentally important to human culture. Alan Merriam's extensive and useful anthropological study of music, first published in 1964, was unconcerned with theoretical issues of embodiment even when considering the human body and its physical responses to music. Ten years later, however, John Blacking's autobio- graphical little book *How Musical is Man?* reveals an inevitable interest in cognitive processes, the human body and cultural environments (1974:89). Others have described how the very shape of the body influences the structure of musical instruments and, therefore, of the music made (Baily 1977:275ff.), or the way in which the body moves during musical activity (Kunik 1977:260ff.), including a formal notation to describe body movements (Benesh and Benesh 1977: 331ff.) Similarly, the anthropology of dance affords another clear example of the deep relationship between embodiment and social values, including those of different social classes (Lange 1977:242ff.; Spencer 1985). The use of music in relation to trance states has long been acknowledged in the history of religions, especially for Shamanism (Rouget 1977:233ff.).

Still, serious theological concerns with the nature of music are still in their relative infancy. The Swedish theologian Mattias Martinson, for example, has indicated something of music's complexity and opportunity in relation to different kinds of theology, albeit in terms of philosophical analysis (2000). Less abstractly some have sought to analyse musical forms in relation to theological ideas (cf. Begbie 2000:45–75). What is of fundamental importance to the study of religion is the fact that musical 'knowing' affords an end in itself and is not a means to an end and, in that sense, music is not like a coded language referring to some other, explicable, meaning. This interpretation of music poses a theoretical problem for those seeking to use musical form as the vehicle for proposit- ional theological meaning, for within most Christian contexts music takes the form of song or chant in which music and words yield their combined significance to the devotee. The extensive Protestant development of hymn-singing witnesses to this distinctive form of religious activity of 'meaning-making through action', which carries its own significance for individual and group integration (Slough 1996:183).

Language in its poetic forms reinforces a similar point. This is, of course, a complex question, given the great variety of established styles of poetic composition that exist; but in the ritual context poetic word-forms often function as summations of sentiment rather than as questions for detailed consideration. There is a power in language itself to hint at completion, at perfection of meaning and understanding, though but few words are used. To take but one example from the Bengali poet Rabindranath Tagore (1924:82):

> When I stand before thee at the day's end thou shalt see my scars
> and know that I had my wounds and also my healing.

These twenty-five words, neither poem nor prose, say all there is to say, even though they could be used as the basis for an extensive existential text on anything from suffering to intimacy, from destiny to eschatology. The force of the few words provides mental satisfaction, a sense that individuals may, after all, know the depths of each other. This capacity to summate and satisfy is regularly found in the ritual use of verbal formulae, and reverses the capacity of words found in philosophical texts or analytic discourse. In this sense worship almost reverses philosophical theology. The power of words to disclose the truths of humanity to itself is such that it is easy to grasp 'the high degree of overlap between poet and prophet' (Friedrich 1997:193). Examples drawn from any liturgy and many a play would show how their verbal formulae achieve dramatically what volumes of formal theology or philosophy of religion seek to achieve critically.

The Ritual Solution

This power is captured in Eugene d'Aquili's bold conclusion that ritual might be one of the few means available to humanity to 'solve the ultimate problems and paradoxes of human existence' (Aquili, Laughlin and McManus 1979:179). This is almost unintelligible without an appreciation of embodiment and a recognition that formal systems of thought play but a limited part in very many people's understanding of life. Philosophy may be important to philosophers and theology to theologians, but for many people philosophical fragments and clusters of belief will not only suffice but may even be more useful, as they confer a degree of freedom for response to novel situations. It is the very fixity of some systematic theologies, set at specific times and in specific circumstances, that often frustrates inter-Church activities, ecumenism or union, under later and changed circumstances.

Even in ritual performances formal theological ideas are 'simply not used in the deductive manner theologians would take for granted' (Boyer 1994:222). As was argued in Chapter 2, to approach human life in terms of embodiment is to underplay mind–body distinctions or the exclusively logical nature of verbal propositions. Few systematic theologians and philosophers actually live solely in terms of some system of thought. Realistically, individuals hold opinions, beliefs and values that are partial, fragmentary, and changing and that interfuse with activities, rites and the manifold endeavours of life. This means that, for example, 'going to church' is an intriguing activity as far as the anthropologist is concerned.

'Going to Church'

In British Christianity this phrase, 'going to church', can be highly illustrative of the nature of ritual and its interpretation. For some 'going to church' is synonymous with 'churchgoing' and 'nominal churchgoers', designating those whose church attendance means little and is in some sense insincere because of its habitual or customary form and because it does not spring from some deep and active commitment to core religious beliefs. This is especially true when the expression is used to describe people who attend church infrequently, especially those who only come at major festivals. This idea is reinforced when the linguistic theory of ritual deems liturgy to be doctrine-filled and to demand regular involvement for its fuller personal realization. This perspective reflects a prevalent form of modern Christianity in which active church life is seen as a major focus of identity in which doctrine, the study of the bible, formal teaching sessions through sermons, study groups, the use of tape-recorded talks and the like combine with active involvement in acts of worship to undergird the rest of life in its daily forms of family, work and play. This is a classical outworking of the more sectarian style of religion that may, today, be found in ordinary congregations of Protestant and Catholic Churches, not least those influenced by Charismatic spirituality. But, it is perfectly possible that many occasional attenders do find a degree of satisfaction from the very fact of having been to a place of worship and having engaged in prayer and worship and met with other people; and to press such attendances for every drop of explicit and formal meaning would be to ignore the significance and the very 'meaning' of doing something.

Dual and Multi-purpose Rites

Leaders of ritual often regard the event as attracting common assent from participants, especially when shared words and actions are reckoned to unite all together to achieve a common goal, be it baptism, marriage, funeral or Eucharist. But this assumed unity should not be too easily accepted, for there are cases in which leader and participants engage in a rite for different ideological reasons, even though the pragmatic goal is jointly achieved.

One illuminating study by Chris Binns involved the rise of ritual in the former Soviet Union and showed how the desired goal of new rituals, introduced by state authorities, was not in fact attained even though people found many of these constructed rituals appealing and used them freely. Their popularity pleased officialdom as a mark of success in replacing religious with secular ceremonial marking rites of passage and nature festivals. But, when people were asked what they got from the rites their answers were at odds with the official intention. Binns did note the inadequacy of the Soviet surveys on which he bases his final evaluation of the failure of these rites, at least as far as their formal intention was concerned, and we need to remember the academic caution he expresses (1979–80:183). Even so, is there not sufficient material here to raise a theoretical point for Christian rituals in which authority figures and participants engage in the same rites but with quite varied intentions? To deal with such contents I speak of 'dual-purpose' rites, though one might, equally, speak of 'multi-purpose' ritual. Dual-purpose ritual serves both the ideals of the sponsoring body and the intentions of the utilizing agent. In the above reference Binns said of some Soviet ritual that 'What people like about these events are meeting friends, being the object of attention and concern, festivity, colour and variety. Ideological content, Marxist-Leninist ideals, patriotism etc., is completely absent from the replies, even from the dislikes : it appears to be virtually ignored. Only those familiar with Soviet reality can appreciate the ability of Soviet citizens to "switch off" to the constant ideological barrage.' The application to Christian usage is not hard to see.

Sociologists of religion have tended to view ritual in developed societies in the light of secularization or, especially in the USA, as a form of civil religion, but they also rather presume that they are dealing with a single, homogeneous, entity (Bellah 1970). Our contention is that some rites that fall squarely within the religious domain may yet possess what might loosely be called secular goals, since the clergy involved in acts of civil religion may also have their own interpretation of what is going on, which differs quite significantly from the intentions of other participants. It is but rarely that a clash of diverse intentions is clearly made public. One such case of a very public nature in Great Britain was the service or ceremony organized in the wake of the 1982 Falklands Crisis, or the 'Falklands War' as it was later to be called. This involved a degree of disagreement between some ecclesiastical and political authorities over whether the event celebrated a victory or gave thanks for peace and commemorated the dead of both armies. This is all the more telling given that the Church of England, the host and conductor of the rite, is a State Church, by law appointed. Apart from the annual Remembrance Sunday Services, Royal Weddings and major funerals, as in the funeral of Diana, the Princess of Wales, most encounter ritual as a personal or family affair in baptism, confirmation, marriage and death. Infant baptism and funerals well exemplify the issues involved.

Infant Baptism

Infant baptism clearly exemplifies dual-purpose rites through the explicit concern of some clergy over the 'indiscriminate baptism' of babies irrespective of the religious commitment of their parents. Clerical unease over accepting all comers reflects their sense that the rite is not being used for the purpose intended by the Church. They think it necessary that parents and godparents should attend instruction classes to ensure that they know what the Church intends by the ceremony, since this cannot be presumed in a relatively unchurched society. Amongst popular motivations is a sense of natural gratitude for a new child, not least in the contemporary world, where many parents have but few children and the child has come to be more of a prized person than ever before. There is also a desire to mark this new addition to the family in terms of its acknowledgement both by other kinsfolk and by wider circles of friends. The party following the church service can also be seen as a crucial aspect of the lay or popular purpose of the dual-purpose rite. In one sense the party is a lay-led mirroring of the priestly baptism. It is a thanksgiving and a welcoming recognition of the new member of the group and of the new parents. For family and friends the total event includes the service and the party while, for the priest, only the liturgical facts are germane.

It is understandable that Church leaders want to foster official beliefs whenever possible; and they are able to do that as far as regular Church members are concerned, or at least they have every expectation of so doing. Since most Churches seldom test active members on belief, leaders tend to assume an orthodoxy that may seldom be present. Often it is the fact of activity rather than beliefs that underlies clerical perceptions, and this can be misleading, as we demonstrate below for funerals and afterlife beliefs. When diversity is acknowledged, the exclusivist type of priest seeks to purify the motives of those present through prior instruction and by making meaning as explicit as possible in the rite itself. The inclusivist accepts the welter of mixed beliefs and opinions of people at large whilst seeking to turn some of them in a more established Christian direction.

In terms of ritual studies the infant baptism of a child of parents who seldom or never attend church poses intriguing questions. The people might desire priests to have a broader sense of popular expectation and not simply expect dogmatic compliance. Contrariwise, priests want to use the event as an opportunity to further their doctrinal cause. Alongside these doctrinal and attitudinal factors come powerful and complementary aspects of the ritual itself. Here I take the simple question of ways in which people may feel themselves to be included or excluded from the ritual event, despite their obvious presence. One aspect relates to whether the clergy insist on baptism's being performed during the Sunday congregational service, usually the Eucharist. The theological reason for doing this would be to express the nature of the Church as a community, often viewed as the family of God or the 'body of Christ', and of the child's now being incorporated into that family and body. The rite may involve a formal ritual welcome of the child as a fellow member in the company of the faithful. Where, however, the child's natural family are very peripheral members of a congregation, or may not be active members at all, this very proper symbolism of entry into the family of God may actually serve the purpose of making these particular people feel strangely alien. If what the minister seeks is some sort of pastoral context in which a rapport may be established with the people that may lead to future contact, then a more private form of baptism might better express that intention. But, practically speaking, some clergy find relatively intimate contact with a small group of relative strangers more disturbing than dealing with them formally within the wider comfort of the regular congregation.

Funerals and Marriage

Funerals and marriages furnish further examples of dual-purpose rites in which the clergy comply more fully with the requests of people almost irrespective of their belief. One major difference between infant baptism on the one hand and marriage and funerary rites on the other relates to the explicit goal of marrying and burying, which is clearly achieved through the rite. As performative acts they are visibly attained, a goal that is not so easily visible in baptism, with its possible outcome of the child's not being brought up in a Christian way. This element of uncertainty introduces a feature absent from the other cases.

Types of ritual

From these broad accounts of church-based rites we turn first to rites of passage in Arnold van Gennep, who originated the idea, and then to its development by Victor Turner and Maurice Bloch, whose form of analysis becomes deeply significant for theology in this context.

Rites of passage

When van Gennep (1873–1957) published his original study in 1909 he thought he had discovered something quite new, viz., that beneath the great diversity of human ritual there was a basic threefold scheme of separation (*séparation*), segregation (*marge*) and incorporation (*agregation*). First, individuals were separated from things associated with their former status, to undergo a period of seclusion during which truths and the values of new commitments were taught, before being finally incorporated into the new status in the mainstream of social life. Society takes the individual in hand and assists his or her transition from status to status. Transition is the key term and, as he said, van Gennep might easily have called these phenomena 'rites of transition'. The combined ritual activity of many people helps forge a new sense of purpose and duty. Although all three phases are usually part of any transition ritual, one of them tends to be stressed, depending on the ultimate purpose of the particular rite. In funerals, for example, he argued that transition was the major feature, both the transition of the dead and that of the surviving mourners. In marriage, by contrast, incorporation can be stressed for the bride in contexts where she moves into the groom's family circle.

Van Gennep also described the threefold passage in terms of pre-liminal, liminal and post-liminal phases, rooted in the Latin *limen* or 'threshold'. Spatiality and locality are highly significant in this regard, not only because he acknowledged the influence of place upon personal identity, but also because the very idea of the 'magico-religious aspect of crossing frontiers' absorbed him. Unlike Durkheim, who distinguished between the personal goals of magic and the public good sought in religion, van Gennep took religion to mean doctrine or abstracted thinking and magic as ritual action. Accordingly, 'magico-religious' is his description of religious action, and in rites of passage there is a kind of 'pivoting of sacredness' centred on the liminal stage. This centrality can, sometimes, be overshadowed when 'liminal' is, wrongly, replaced by 'marginal'. Van Gennep's use of the French *marge* to account for individuals being on the border or edge of mainstream social life should not be confused with the English notion of 'marginality', which carries the rather different connotation of a permanent position in isolation from the main flow of life, whereas in Van Gennep the isolation is temporary.

Victor Turner's Developed Liminality

In speaking of society as a house with many rooms and of status transition as the movement from one to another through various thresholds van Gennep set the scene for Victor Turner's work on liminality some fifty years later. Turner analysed the distinctive features of periods of liminality by developing the notion of *communitas* as the experience of those in the state of liminality. There is more than mere jargon involved in what Turner has to say, for his perspective opens up the possibility of some creative theological analysis.

As a historical aside it is of some interest to observe that the Church of England's *Alternative Service Book* of 1980 introduced an Index containing an entry for 'Initiation Services', reflecting a growing interest in rites of passage. This was twenty years after the first English translation of *Les rites de Passage* (Vizedom and Caffee 1960), and marks a major change, for van Gennep's ideas had gained relatively little ground during his lifetime. Indeed, Rodney Needham incisively judged his treatment at the hands of the sociological establishment of Paris as 'an academic disgrace' (1967:xi). Van Gennep ended his life in relative impoverishment. From the 1960s, however, the notion of rites of passage made its own rapid passage from the narrower confines of anthropology into the intellectual world at large, influencing by 1980 the Church of England, which included in this category Thanksgiving for the Birth of a Child, Baptism, and Confirmation, but not Marriage or Funerary rites, nor rites of Ordination. Van Gennep would, of course, have included all these within the form of rites of passage: indeed, Ordination is almost an ideal type case of a transition ritual, for the ordinand – the priest in training – occupies a liminal period, neither fully in lay status as far as most other laypeople are concerned, nor yet a Deacon in Holy Orders. In a somewhat similar way the Deacon is in a transitional phase too, not quite Lay and not a Priest.

Some caution is necessary when using 'rites of passage', for there are cases when people are more marginalized than being truly liminal. Some unemployed and bereaved people can easily come to stand between fixed social statuses devoid of communal unity. One feature of contemporary British culture, for example, lies in the fact that many women find it hard to pass through the transitional stage of bereavement, precisely because there is no formal rite of reincorporation into society as a widow. When is a widow a widow? On the day of her husband's death? On the day of his funeral? But society is ever adaptive, and one feature of the later twentieth century lay in the emergence of support groups for many categories of bereaved people, groups in which a degree of *communitas* can be experienced.

Communitas

Turner tells how he became interested in *communitas* – relationships of immediate, direct, heart-to-heart experiences – during the Second World War when serving as a non-combatant soldier in a bomb-disposal unit. In his later African fieldwork he thought he could see similar conditions emerging during ritual performances of transition rites, (1975:21). But Turner's argument begins by presupposing that societies are not, generally, egalitarian, but are hierarchically divided into statuses of ordered rank. Rites of passage move individuals from status to status within this hierarchy of positions but, and this is a very important qualification, there are moments when hierarchy, rank and class marks disappear, and in this liminality *communitas* is sensed. In two different books Turner analysed various situations in which different forms of *communitas* emerged. In *The Ritual Process* (1969) African rites are set alongside reflections on St Francis and the Franciscans, Gandhi and the schooling of Charles, Prince of Wales. Far from being a miscellany, this is a systematic reflection on the nature of human nature in relation to class-, caste-, and rank-divided societies, and furnishes a classification of kinds of *communitas*.

Existential-spontaneous Communitas

Existential or spontaneous *communitas* breaks out amongst people who feel bonded together in a profound unity standing in stark contrast to the barriers between them in normal life. The obvious New Testament experience of Pentecost provides a type case, in which a sense of fellowship is associated with the apostolic teaching, the breaking of bread, of being together and having everything in common (Acts 2:42–7). The text reflects the later description of the early community, telling how all the believers were one, both in heart and soul (Acts 4:32). Even property was taken to be held in common.

Normative and Ideological Communitas

Normative *communitas* emerges when a degree of control is required to achieve new-found goals. A degree of organization develops as both the initial enthusiastic *communitas* and the original charisma of leaders are 'routinized'. Finally, he uses the term 'ideological *communitas*' to speak of those rather utopian groups that set out to generate a style of life in which community and a total lack of ranked barriers surround human life.

In illustrating these latter forms of *communitas* much eucharistic liturgy could be seen to express normative *communitas*. The 'exchange of the peace', for example, is a formal symbol of the belief that the Church is intrinsically a deep fellowship of believers. This rite occurs before the act of eating and drinking and expresses the formal unity of the group as it shares in the peace Christ brings to believers. Because some congregations, or at least certain members of them, have experienced something of an existential *communitas* in Charismatic groups they also anticipate a vital bonding to be repeated whenever possible in Church life, and want 'The Peace' to break with formal ritualism, allowing real heart-to-heart exchange in physical hugging or handshaking. Most congregations, however, simply shake hands in a more or less friendly fashion.

Koinonia and Communitas

Theologically, the liturgy tends to express normative rather than existential *communitas*, and this keeps the flow between the ideal and the actual relatively realistic. Still, some groups not only see the Acts of the Apostles as an ideal of Christian fellowship, but also seek to realize it in their contemporary groups. Here the link between anthropological and theological considerations of this sense of unity, whether idealized or routinized, can be brought to sharp focus by aligning *communitas* as a technical (Latin) term of anthropology with (the Greek) *koinonia* as a technical term of theology. As such, *koinonia* means communion amongst people or between believers and the Holy Spirit (e.g. Acts 2:42; Gal.2:9; Phil. 2:1.). In many respects it becomes a defining attribute of the earliest Christian groups whose integrity is grounded in the mutual fellowship of believers (I John 1: 3–7).

In *Dramas, Fields and Metaphors* (1974) Turner identified *communitas* with specific processes within religious traditions, including pilgrimage which he later elaborated in *Image and Pilgrimage in Christian Culture* (Turner and Turner 1978). He subsequently pursued the relation between moments of freedom from customary hierarchy and worship in *From Ritual to Theatre* (1982). These studies raise interesting theological questions, even though care is needed when relating key concepts to contemporary life. Appreciating the inherent problems of applying concepts originating in analyses of tribal materials to modern groups, he developed the notion of the 'liminoid' to account for festive, leisure, or holiday celebrations in modern society (1985). Generally speaking, the idea of *communitas*, whether experienced liminally or in liminoid contexts, is useful when discussing aspects of religious community. There is much in Turner's belief that '*communitas* is the primal ground, the *urgrund* of social structure' (1975:23). Liminal periods can often be highly educative when people are open to learning truths not only of a rational and formal type, but also of a more direct, emotional kind. Here *communitas* and *koinonia* reveal their deep rooting in embodiment.

In congregational life periods of intense religious or social activity can produce a sense of *communitas* amongst members who may have been on retreat, mission or some special venture together, when the formalities of everyday life gave way in the desired unity of purpose. When such intense periods end a redirection of zeal can be highly productive. It was Turner's conviction that the total flow of social existence moved between *communitas* and hierarchy and back again, and it is precisely the alternations between fixity and flux, between hierarchy and *communitas*, that give power to each state. Hierarchy would not be possible unless people sensed that all men and women were intrinsically the same, and on the other hand the sense of sameness would be relatively worthless without the usual structure of rank. It is the interplay, the dialectic, the process of movement between the one condition and the other that yields the total process that is social life itself.

It is impossible to maintain a perpetual liminality and still live in the ordinary world, though it sometimes happens, for example, that young people who have found extremely rewarding intimacy with other believers in their university Christian group then find it odd that local churches seldom match that ideal. But one potentially enduring aspect of such *communitas* is the strong sense of the power and truth of the gospel message. This reflects the educative power of liminal contexts and relates to the 'rebounding' dynamics of Bloch's approach, to which we return below, but only after some consideration of how Turner's key notions might furnish a medium for some theological reflection.

Theological Interlude

A conversation between theology and anthropology implies that the ideas of the one may appeal to the thoughts of the other, bringing new light simply through the use of unfamiliar expressions. Such is he case of *communitas* and Incarnation, of interpreting the life of Jesus as a form of liminality. The theological idea that in Christ God assumes human nature can be viewed as an act of *communitas*. Oneness, solidarity, and the opposition to hierarchy all betoken the love expressed in Jesus. Status and rank, beloved of the world at large, is deemed inappropriate amongst his disciples. Since the Master washes feet, they too should gladly accept the prize of humility. Yet this is just the place where a *communitas* model of the Incarnation almost becomes a test of different styles of Christian theology.

Theologians following Karl Barth's view of God could not accept that Jesus as the Incarnate Son of God adopted only a temporary form of humility for his earthly ministry, which was different from the Son's eternal being within the Holy Trinity. In other words, one cannot contrast the *communitas* of his earthly life with some hierarchical life in the Godhead. That option would be to follow the pattern of Christology which is often expressed in kenotic or self-emptying theories, and which matches many popular views of God expressed, for example, in Christmas carols telling how he who was once 'rich beyond all measure' now for love's sake becomes poor. By contrast, the Barthian view would see the Incarnation as but an expression in time of the eternal nature of humility (Barth 1956:181). The Incarnation becomes the embodiment of humility, and its nature is to enter into a fellowship of love.

Doctrine and practice often reflect each other, and, in terms of strict theological discussion, it could be argued that if the Incarnation is viewed as a narrowing of the power of life in God's Son and if the Incarnation is taken as an act of asceticism on God's part then the pattern of piety that is likely to be adopted by the believer will also espouse asceticism. Indeed, kenotic Christologies easily foster that way of thinking and living. The alternative approach takes the Incarnation as a continuation of that same Godly fullness that at first made the universe, and sees the *communitas* of love as itself a fullness of moral existence. It is then an expression of human fallenness that such overflowing community is possible only for short periods, even though the desire for such is deep.

Priests and Communitas

From that abstract theological reflection we move to a more practical consideration of the relation between priests and the sense of *communitas* associated with ordinary rites of passage. In the face of joy, sorrow, celebration and grief people come to share in their unity as human beings with the capacity of empowering others in need. The joy of a new baby amongst family and friends is one such cause for unity, especially in the modern context where babies are relatively rare. At weddings, too, the couple elicit basic hopes of all present that things will go well with them and, certainly, funerals evoke mutual succour and primal optimism in the face of death.

In all such moments of *communitas* priests may recognize the power of mutuality in human co-operation. It is as creatures of God, made in the divine social image, that people and priest reach out to help one another. For many the ritual goal is precisely that of attaining a degree of mutual succour, finding it, perhaps, more in the Christening Party, Wedding Breakfast or Funeral Tea than in the religious ceremonial, which is one reason why the priest does well to enter into the spirit of those occasions, fostering *koinonia* amidst *communitas*.

Natural priesthood

While religions the world over have always produced priests and ritual experts of whom a degree of competence is expected by their communities, there is a strain within many traditions, not least in Christianity, that stands in opposition to aspects of what might be called natural priesthood (cf. Davies 1985a). Not only does this element of dissonance touch on the judgemental and prophetic aspect of faith in relation to the givenness of society, but it also embraces a proper element of what might be called 'spiritual incompetence'. Whilst Christian priests, for example, cannot speak with any substantial knowledge of life after death, they can foster trust, and trust typifies both *communitas* and *koinonia*. Perhaps the remarkable thing is how similar rather than how different these phenomena are. This is why the Christian Minister is called to be aware of the power inherent in human fellowship and of the perspective grace affords in the awareness of the processes in life where God is creatively present in a kind of social sacrament. For, theologically speaking, *koinonia* is a sacrament of Trinitarian love, and *communitas* a natural sacrament of *koinonia*.

Sacred and Secular Unity

To what extent, however, can ideas of liminality really be applied within contemporary societies, whether to religious or other contexts? Turner developed his analysis in terms of the distinction between pre-industrial and industrial societies, with the Industrial Revolution as a turning-point in forms of social organization and in relation to the topics of work, leisure, play and worship. In *From Ritual to Theatre* he develops most fully his distinction between the liminal and the liminoid (1982:20–60). Sub-titled 'The Human Seriousness of Play', this distinguishes between liminal events perceived as times of work or of play and designated liminoid features as occurring during play or leisure. Indirectly, Turner raises the issue of whether worship in pre-industrial society was work? The implication is that worship as a form of work is a concept quite out of keeping with industrial and probably also post-industrial societies. Many sociologists, and probably many clergymen, would view the ritual happenings of a Sunday as taking place in leisure time, and therefore as being leisure activities. If that is the case, it raises some quite fundamental theological questions about the classification of worship in relation to work, creativity, re-creation, and recreation, and suggests that, for example, sport and the Eucharist share certain liminoid dimensions.

Sporting Fellowship

The twenty-first century witnesses a remarkable growth in sport and leisure activity in which many find a degree of freedom, release, pleasure, relaxation and company. Through sports clubs, leisure and health clubs and gymnasia a great deal of active sport takes place outside the work domain. In this liminoid space sport fosters a high degree of positive emotional and sensual awareness. It is possible to see this development in more than one way.

In terms of health and physical activity many leading sedentary professional lives see sport as a desired means of attaining health. This is theologically interesting, since the notion of health is one element in the total wholeness viewed by some as a state of salvation. The secular wish for fitness is not far removed from the religious desire for wholeness. In its attainment much social benefit derives from other participants. In terms of post-modernity, in the absence of large-scale shared values, the body becomes the focus of human concern, and values focused on bodily well-being can replace religious values, with sport and health clubs vying with Churches in the experience of significant minorities.

Another aspect of sporting culture concerns simplicity and well-being. Many find themselves saturated by information technology, the complexity of decision-making and the burden of responsibility. Business often involves a great deal of competition and rivalry, and the hierarchical nature of work is marked. Against that background sports offer two potentially significant benefits. First, they involve a very limited amount of information used to maximum effect: vigorous activity combines with minimal mental exertion. Sport, in other words, is a low-information-processing world, just as it is a highly physically demanding world; as such, it inverts the work-experience of many middle-class individuals. Second, sport demands a high degree of co-operation between players. In the team sports this is obvious; but even in the pair playing badminton or squash there is a necessary co-operation in making the game possible; even the competition should not detract from this fellowship in exertion. Beyond the game itself there is the whole social world of players being together after the event in the sports-club context. Sport is conducive to the 'restricted code' format of social events, to which we return below. There is probably some further significance in the fact that sports allow both male and, to a lesser degree, female groups to emerge among adults who otherwise would be constantly part of the gender-mixed family, work, leisure or religious group.

Sport fosters the sense of equality necessary for liminality: uniformity of dress and of possibility all lie within an arena where embodiment is more obviously sensed. Sport, fitness, and activity are bodily acts; but they are bodily acts of a corporate kind involving the mind in the tactics of the game, and such bodily acts follow into social discourse. The fact that much amateur sport takes place on a Sunday is in many senses quite proper from a theological standpoint, given its recreative capacity. Turner makes the interesting comment that 'ritual, unlike theatre does not distinguish between audience and performers' (1982:112): on that basis amateur sport is more like ritual, and professional sport like theatrical performance. This might go some way to explain elements of *communitas* in the former and hostility in the latter.

While the Eucharist also takes place in leisure time, the question of how to classify when it occurs is intriguing. Perhaps worship, as worship, should be ascribed a category of its own, and neither relegated simply to leisure time nor even to 'sacred' time. To slip easily into the work–leisure dichotomy may be inappropriate, even though church worship largely occurs on Sundays, social holidays or weekday evenings, and, as such, within liminoid periods beyond ordinary work.

Liminoid Duration

Many have drawn attention to ritual and changes in the quality of duration, of the experience of time passing. The notion of 'quality-time' popularized in the closing decades of the twentieth century reflects the appropriateness many find in distinguishing between time spent on different activities. One characteristic activity conducted in liminoid periods is celebration or festivity, something Turner explored at length and whose analysis could be pursued further with the observation that at 'the end of history', as Fukuyama once described aspects of contemporary social and political existence, there emerges celebration (E. Turner *et al.* 1992). If the Reformation magnified the doctrine of the priesthood of all believers within a Protestant work ethic, then Postmodernity glories in celebration framed by a consumerist hedonism managed by the self as a secularized priest.

Quality-time for Christian activity involves symbolic participation in the founding events of Christ's life enacted in contemporary worship, where the acts of God are related to the autobiography of each participant and to the church group. To unite history and the present the congregation takes a step out of time, and in this liminoid moment equality among believers is asserted as they claim to be the body of Christ. Rank and status have no place amongst these who are equally sinners and equally redeemed. A distinctive feature of much contemporary church life in numerous denominations is the stress on the Lord's presence by and through the Holy Spirit.

Flow-Spirit

One theoretical way of approaching this sense of the Spirit from an anthropological perspective is through the notion of 'flow', a concept that also possesses applications to embodiment, and designates a sense of achieved competence experienced by ritual participants. Victor Turner (1982) took the idea of 'flow' largely from Mihaly Csikszentmihalyi (1991[1974]) and related it to his own idea of *communitas*. Flow describes periods when action and awareness merge with attention focused on a limited stimulus to achieve a set goal. It may affect individuals acting alone or in a group. This sense of flow takes place in events that are reckoned to be ends in themselves and not means to some other end, echoing our earlier discussion of ritual. This notion applies to many activities, including sport, art and liturgy, and relates to psychological processes that affect mood, again rehearsing issues of embodiment. As

Turner expresses it, 'To flow is to be as happy as a human can be – the particular rules or stimuli that triggered the flow, whether chess or a prayer meeting, do not matter' (1982:58).

Flow and Liturgy

Applying 'flow' specifically to Christian worship three types have been singled out for analysis; they represent (i) the fixed liturgies of Churches of the Orthodox, Catholic, Anglican and Lutheran form; (ii) the partly fixed and partly open rites of many of the major denominations, such as those of the Baptists and Methodists; and (iii), finally, the open form of worship of some Charismatic groups. It is important to stress that we are looking at these as ideal-types, as formal and abstract descriptions of groups, realizing that, in practice, their concrete realities may well overlap.

Liturgical Type

The liturgical type employs fixed forms of worship enshrined in established liturgies, often contained in service books that, in time, come to assume a status of their own, as in the case of the Anglican *Book of Common Prayer* or the Roman *Missal*. Often associated with a liturgical calendar and with prayers and prescribed biblical passages for each day of the year, this type, ritually and symbolically, divides time into distinctive periods of varying theological significance, each related to distinctive moods. The music, hymns, and vestments worn by the clergy, along with church decoration, all reflect the total environment within which religious flow may take place.

Liturgical and Open Type

The liturgical and open type uses both a set form of worship and the opportunity for leaders to use prayers and readings of their own choice. The option between set readings or personally chosen passages allows for a sense of divine influence whilst also acknowledging that sense of individualism intrinsic to Protestantism. While most Protestant denominations mark the major Christian festivals of Christmas and Easter, they tend not to pay attention to saints' days and other holy days. Instead of organizing what might be called sacred time across the whole year each Sunday comes to be a major focus of religious activity in its own right, with its opportunity for 'flow' to occur.

Charismatic Type

In Charismatic Churches the power of the Holy Spirit is expected to intrude upon religious meetings to yield periods, easily interpreted as 'flow', that differ from the quality of experience and participation at other times. People may speak in tongues, receive revelatory messages, fall to the floor and produce a variety of sounds or engage in melodic singing. One distinctive feature of such periods lies in the expectancy of 'otherness'. There is a sense that something distinctive is taking place, something that does not belong to the ordinariness of everyday life.

Fixity and Diversity

Christians from traditions that do not use written liturgies express a degree of disapproval of those who do, on the assumption that fixed ritual will be associated with a rote mentality, a kind of vain repetition devoid of sincerity – a criticism that fails to appreciate that flow can emerge within set liturgies to which individuals bring their own commitment as easily as within any other context. Contrariwise, there is no guarantee that any rite, fixed or impromptu, will generate a sense of flow, and there are many occasions when rites do not 'work' in that sense. Still, they must serve an emotional end often enough to be supported, often over many centuries. So it is that 'flow' takes different forms, and can occur in contexts of both *communitas* and hierarchy, depending upon what we might call the code of the religious setting and cultural context.

Codes and flow

One theory of ritual shedding considerable light both on this issue of flow and upon Turner's sense of *communitas* can be derived from Basil Bernstein's work on the restricted and elaborated codes underlying patterns of speech and communication between groups of people whose patterns of relationship took different forms (1971). Now rather dated, it was controversial in its day, because political correctness objected to what he seemed to be saying about working-class and middle-class groups in Britain. Here we ignore those arguments, to give prominence to the intellectual significance of his main theory on how patterns of human relationship are reflected in forms of speech.

One type consists in relatively closed and tight-knit communities grounded in hierarchies of respect and kinship relation in which people are expected to know their place and remain in it. They do what they are told and respect their elders, and individuals are not expected to stand out over and against others when it comes to fundamental opinions. Much of their speech reflects this mutuality and operates, as Bernstein said, on a 'restricted code' base. The other type reflects groups prizing individuality and the distinctiveness of each member. Children are expected to have opinions about issues: they are given explanations for questions they ask rather than some authoritative statement on the acceptedness of things. All this is reflected in forms of speech. Bernstein thought that British working-class communities tended to operate on the first pattern of restricted codes, while middle-class groups operated on the elaborated code base, while also possessing their own form of restricted code when needed. To be able to switch codes was socially advantageous. Since the formal system of education then was, and largely to this day still is, grounded in an elaborated code structure, he suggested that working-class children were at something of a disadvantage in relation to middle-class children: and it was this conviction that was interpreted by some critics as his saying that working-class language and culture were, in some way, worse than middle-class forms: hence the controversy over his work.

The real import of his insight was, however, picked up by the anthropologist Mary Douglas, who related it to her developing theory of social control already mentioned in Chapter 2. I also utilized it for an earlier consideration of Charismatic religion to account for the differential significance of glossolalia amongst different groups of people, arguing that glossolalia in classical Pentecostalism amongst working-class groups in Britain in the early decades of the twentieth century differed from glossolalia in middle-class groups of the late twentieth–twenty-first century Charismatic movement (1984c). One feature of Charismatic activity is a collective sense of 'flow' related to the verbal and bodily activity of other participants, and intrinsic to its power is 'excitement'.

Flow and Excitement

Experiences motivate religious life, whether in the intensity of the divine presence impressing itself so forcefully that God seems more real than the devotee lost in adoration, or in a passing memory of the tradition witnessed in the faith of others. And excitement empowers much of this experience. For many young people, not least teenagers, there is an excitement in discovering the religious domain. The thought that God exists in a realm of power awaiting to be explored through group worship, in communal evangelism, and in the privacy of prayer, has an attraction all of its own and, as Western societies become increasingly secular, there are growing numbers coming to Christianity in adult life. With the onset of maturer adulthood, when relationships can crumble and the sense of certainty and security in the world begins to falter, the call of religious renewal can be highly appealing. The need to start afresh, the desire for a life that offers more than failure or tedium, is profoundly appealing. More than that, it is exciting. It is no accident that a characteristic feature of much religious activity in suburban populations over the turn of the millennium has taken the form of Charismatic Christianity, offering inclusion in relatively tightly-knit groups of fellow believers and a new depth of personal emotion.

Beyond the main denominations increasing numbers pursue alternative forms of spiritual involvement in New Age Movements, reflecting the additional power that alternative sources of excitement offer to people. As in Charismatic Christianity, there is an appeal derived from the framework of the search. For the Christians it lies in a God they have bypassed for much of their life, or hardly knew was there, while for New Age devotees it is often some specific manifestation of nature that is discovered for the first time. For both the body and experience stand to the fore, not least through the sense of 'flow'. Charismatic Christians may sing, sway, raise hands in the air, speak in tongues or laugh and roll on the floor when 'slain in the Spirit'. New Age devotees too may also dance, raise hands, and share with others in physical contact as rhythmic drumming encourages suburban shamanism, a spirituality of 'inner-journeys' to encounter spirit beings and returning to tell of new insight on life. For both the Charismatic Christian and the New Age devotee there is a renewed sense of freedom. Paul Heelas has explored the New Age complex of activity in terms of its celebration of the self in a form of 'self-religion' that also 'sacralizes' the contemporary world, all within a broad context of 'detraditionalization' (1996:22ff.). Life is transformed from a heavy weight of tradition into a world of personal opportunities. While the Charismatic context is one of community, often within the broad framework of the cultural tradition of Christianity, that of the New Ager is the natural world, with all its energies and hidden potentials hinted at by science. In all this, excitement predominates over traditional forms of authority.

Liturgical code

The ritual of major Christian denominations regularly operates upon a restricted code base within a group grounded in hierarchy and deeply influenced by tradition. There is an absolute minimum of variation in words used; even if leaders use informal words of welcome or direction, these also tend to become rapidly stylized. The behaviour of participants is also highly formalized and repeated. The form of restricted code underlying both the language and action helps integrate and unify an otherwise mixed group and fosters stability of formal doctrine. The more a Church focuses on a set liturgy as its prime activity the less likely it is to encounter major challenges to its doctrine. To embed doctrine in liturgy is to commit it to a safe place. Such a repeated ritual helps foster a sense of secure identity, reinforced weekly or even daily, and the significance of the daily Mass for priests in sacramentally focused Churches can hardly be over-emphasized. There is a form of 'flow' that is consonant with this scheme of ritual just as surely as there is a 'flow' that pertains to the Charismatic moment of ecstasy, for 'flow' as such is not restricted to any particular tradition.

Bloch

Through the notions of 'flow' and *communitas* Turner made it obvious that he was concerned not simply with changes in social status as established by van Gennep, but also with the experiential or existential dimension of life; and this emphasis has been taken further still in Maurice Bloch's work on rebounding conquest. Bloch sees van Gennep's emphasis upon social status in rites of passage as ignoring personal change that ritual involvement at least makes possible. The question is whether people are the same after major rites as before them? His basic answer is that they are not, for people change. This existential dimension cannot be ignored in any conversation between theology and anthropology.

Apart from his earlier studies as a Marxist anthropologist, Bloch has worked on death, as in his joint volume with Jonathan Parry, *Death and the Regeneration of Life* (1982). But, as I have stressed throughout this present study, I wish to emphasize the worth of his *Prey into Hunter* as a key text for the study of ritual of many sorts (1992a). Rather like van Gennep, Bloch thinks that he has discovered an 'irreducible core' of the ritual process; what is more, he thinks that it possesses a near-universal status, and almost apologizes for advancing such a notion in a post-modern age inimical to overarching explanatory schemes.

Through this existential dimension Bloch develops the relationship between status and experience to show the potential of ritual to transform people. For him, societies do not simply allow the facts of biological life to dominate their thinking about themselves. In other words, birth, maturity and death are not the sole facts of life, for societies transform them, not least in rituals of initiation. The phenomenon of death is especially important, since physical death is regularly taken and used symbolically, and if physical death is the great fact of biological life, then ritual death is the great fact of cultural life. In ritual nature is reversed. Instead of life ending in death, a ritual death becomes the beginning of a new life. Initiates, in particular, are said to be killed or to die through ritual. This is their ritual death. But they are then said to be reborn or to come alive as a new form of being, with new powers as well as with new responsibilities. And this transformation is possible, for ritual brings them into contact with a transcendent power, a power beyond the mere power of nature. It is through contact with the ancestors, spirits or deity that this power comes. In their newness of power, usually involving a new social status, they now set out to overcome their old or former nature. This may be through some actual social act such as warfare or hunting, where the animal hunted is a symbolic representation of the old nature. This is why Bloch calls his book, *Prey into Hunter*.

This model has wide application in the realm of theology. It reflects, for example, the negative evaluation of 'ordinary' life compared with the 'spiritual' life entered through contact with the Holy Spirit and by means of divine grace. The Pauline distinction between the 'flesh' and the 'spirit' or between the 'old Adam' and the 'new Adam' also echoes this distinction. The symbolic theology of baptism as involving a death to sin and its Adamic nature and a rebirth to a life of righteousness in Christ is a perfect example of Bloch's scheme. In more Protestant and Evangelical Christian traditions the theology of death and rebirth is strongly linked with personal conversion, as we show in the next chapter. But, whether in conversionist or sacramental traditions, it is the subsequent phase of 'rebounding conquest', as Bloch calls it, that is of paramount significance. Other aspects of spirituality also express the conquest aspect of this overall process, as in the tradition involving the conquest of human desire and of the 'flesh' on the part of the faithful. For, while it is easy to argue on the conversionist model that once people's old nature has been conquered by the new, spiritual, nature they then set about converting that old nature in other people, that is not the only case worth pondering. For, in most Christian traditions, the spiritual nature is not complete in this life, but is set within an ongoing process of transformation directed towards the self within the religious community.

Rites of Intensification

This is precisely where the ritual of the Eucharist comes to be related to that of Baptism. For, if baptism is the symbolic rite of initiation, involving the death of the old self and the birth of the new through contact with the divine Spirit, then the Eucharist is the prime rite of intensification, in which the process of conquest continues in two directions. One covers the ongoing conquest of the self by the Spirit, and the other the conquest of 'the old' within social life. The preoccupation that most theologians, and anthropologists for that matter, have had with the anthropological notion of rites of passage has tended to overshadow the significance of rites of intensification; but they are of considerable importance. This preoccupation is unfortunate, since Chapple and Coon have firmly identified rites of intensification as more significant in the 'development of complex religious institutions' than rites of passage (1942:410). They also showed how Christian institutions, including priests, could be discussed alongside 'primitive' religious practices, since rites of intens-ification both strengthened relationships amongst people after they had been apart or had been engaged in different activities and, more psycho-logically, also reinforced individuals in their patterns of behaviour. While Chapple and Coon were influenced by psychological ideas of conditioned responses, I am accentuating rites of intensification more in terms of embodiment, stressing the additional moral force such rites bring to community values. It is precisely because values are embodied within members of a community that their presence can be periodically rein-forced.

Within some Christian traditions, for example, the rite of baptism can be both a rite of passage and a rite of intensification. For the candidate it is a rite of passage, one in which status changes and, under appropriate circumstances of age and preparation, one in which the individual may also be affected existentially. For the baptized also present at the rite it may also be an occasion for them to recommit themselves to the essentials of their religion. This can be expressed more formally in a specific rite of Renewal of Baptismal Vows. Similar rites deal with ordination and marriage vows.

Other rites of intensification in religious groups include conferences, houseparties or retreats at which people focus their attention upon their religious lives and values and often reckon to come away 'refreshed' or with a heightened commitment to their faith; and specific hymn-singing events and festivals can achieve a similar purpose (Slough 1996:181). If the hymn allows the Protestant to 'travel' to a source of revitalization, then the pilgrimage allows the same within more Catholic traditions, even if, for example, someone who regularly visited Lourdes as a pilgrim found that the event led her to pray more regularly after the visit, though 'the effect always wore off a few months later' (Fulton 2000b:142).

In a much more ordinary sense the regular services of religious groups serve a basic purpose of intensification of religious beliefs through their pattern of confession, absolution, worship and prayer. Very many hymns are vehicles for the intensification of religious experience and belief. A distinctive feature of rites of intensification lies in the experience of 'flow' that brings to many individuals a sense of having achieved a purpose through participation in rites. While it is customary in the social anthropology of religion to dwell, very largely, upon group ritual, the place of the private rites of believers should not be ignored in relation to rites of intensification.

Few studies, anthropological or theological, match Durkheim's *Elementary Forms* for its breadth of vision in grasping the power of faith to inspire the believer. Despite writing as an unbeliever, he aptly describes the 'confidence, courage and boldness' of the believer who 'feels the regard of his god turned graciously towards him' (1915:211). Although Durkheim is adamant that the 'force' underlying religion is, basically, a force of society, and that it is vitally important that group rites recur, periodically, to recharge this force, he also speaks of the presence of this force within individuals. Certainly, he underplays the autonomous possibility of the religious creativity of the individual, something for which Malinowski not only furnished appropriate criticism, but which he also counter-balanced with his emphasis upon the powerful effect of the 'outstanding personality', his own term for what Weber termed 'charisma' (Malinowski 1974:59, 83). Certainly Durkheim could not account for the 'prophet' figure, as Robertson Smith, Malinowski and Weber did; yet the potential of the individual remains, because, ultimately, Durkheim cannot sever the individual and society and cannot conceive of either without the other. It is for that reason that *The Elementary Forms* reads in many parts like a text on rites of intensification.

Private Power

Much religious behaviour is private and passes unstudied, yet many private rites serve the precise function of intensification in the sense of fostering the group goals of faith. Christian traditions advocate and practise such ends through private prayer on a daily basis. Some use set prayers or set biblical passages that link the individual with thousands of others similarly engaged. Other forms of devotion also empower individuals, as in the widespread availability of personal music systems, computers and the internet. Even private prayer can, for example, be infused with the devotional music of the group. Individual Charismatic Christians might, for example, avail themselves of a musical background while engaging in the practice of glossolalia during their private prayer. This is a clear example of an intensification of belief and emotion, as the social realm of music, with all its evocation of the congregational setting, provides a background for individual piety. Another aspect of private rites involves the phenomenon of the inner-dialogue, which is related to the notion of inner-otherness introduced in Chapter 2 and concerns that activity often described loosely as 'talking to myself', which takes place silently but may, occasionally, turn into actual speech. This inner-dialogue is a complex process, and has not been the subject of widespread study as far as prayer is concerned; yet the distinction between an inner-dialogue of the self with itself and of the self with God designated as a real 'other' is pregnant with possibility.

Ritual Arenas and Ruins

Corporate ritual often takes place in a particular setting, which often proves important for memory and mood, for ritual processes set within particular places lead to a form of sedimentation of sentiment, of experience associated with particular embodied acts. The sights and sounds of distinctive places come to bear a weight of significance. But times change, and some ritual arenas fall into disuse as memorable ruins. Though nothing has been said in this book about the extensive sociological debates on secularization, it is at least worth noting Rappaport's anthropological reflections on what he sees as 'serious damage' inflicted upon ritual, which, in itself, he sees as 'an instrument for establishing the foundation of human worlds' (1999:451). His extensive anthropology of religion is, at the same time, a form of natural philosophy, and one of its crucial emphases lies on the human condition of having to live in a world grounded in humanly devised meaning amidst a world 'devoid of intrinsic meaning' (ibid.). He brings to sharp focus the divide I discussed early in this book between revelation and projection, which he sees as 'epistemologies of discovery' coming to be set against those 'fabrications of meaning' that have constituted the heartland of religious doctrine and mythology. Rappaport's important contribution to philosophical anthropology lies in his conviction that the natural laws of the world have been respected during the history of mankind. Religious beliefs and rites have served as a kind of adaptive arena in which human reflection has encountered physical nature in a drive to survive. Interestingly, Rappaport cites Simmel's sociology of money in a way that also echoes Marcel Mauss's nostalgic sadness in seeing a market economy taking over the rationale of human activity. Money, says Rappaport, 'dissolves the distinctions between qualitatively unlike things' . . . 'Monetary epistemology' is dangerous and can reinforce 'Idolatry' and the 'Diabolical Lie' (1999:454–5). Here he invokes Tillich's theological idea of idolatry as the process in which non-ultimate things are credited with ultimacy – indeed, Tillich recurs throughout Rappaport's study.

Rappaport desires new formulations, new descriptions of the world that can serve to mobilize people in ritual-like ways that elicit commitment. He utilizes the traditional theological idea of 'logos' to describe such existentially vital accounts of the world, taking the term 'eco-system' as one such new case. The human need is for people to 'realise, participate in, maintain, correct, transform and not merely observe' ecological problems, in other words there is need for a 'high and explicit sanctification' of concepts of this kind if there is to be a 'preservation of the world's wholeness in the face of fragmenting and dissolving forces': there is a need to ritualize 'eco-systems' (1999:459, 460). A great deal more could be said about Rappaport's study; indeed, it merits an entire volume in response. In certain respects it accords to humanity the kind of status that Durkheim accorded to society, except that it sees humanity as more integrally related to the realm of nature, for humanity 'is that part of the world through which the world as a whole can think about itself' (1999:461). And when he says that he closely resembles Teilhard de Chardin's meditative theology on the evolution of love.

When Rituals End

From this holistic framing of the world, ritualizing its meaning and ethically responding to its demands, we close this chapter with a brief sketch of the liturgical act of 'blessing', the rite of bringing a ritual event to an end. When rituals end participants often view themselves as having gained a benefit, and the fact that rituals often end with some kind of formal 'blessing' is not insignificant, for blessing is the process that consummates an event of intensified embodiment. The use of words and action – often a lifting of the hand or hands, perhaps making the sign of the cross whilst so doing – brings an event to its conclusion in a blessing that is an end in itself.

In its traditional Christian form the priest brings together one verbal and one manual symbol to achieve an embodied summation. The verbal emphasis lies upon the Holy Trinity and manually upon the Cross, two of the most potent symbols in the entire Christian repertoire. Liturgically they are not explained. No rational reflection is given. They are simply practised. Just as bread and wine are ends in themselves when received at the Eucharist so is the Blessing at the conclusion of the service. Some liturgical words may follow the blessing, as in the traditional exhortation telling the congregation to go because the Eucharist is ended or, in some contemporary rites, commanding the people to go and 'love and serve the Lord'. But these are statements of re-entry into ordinary time, for the blessing is the verbal and manual closure of acts performed within sacred time. One feature of the blessing, as of the bread and wine, that does demand attention concerns 'conceptual mystery', an idea that will only be developed in the next chapter. For the moment we remain with the performed blessing, marking, as it does, the identity of a Christian as an embodied individual and as a member of the body of the faithful. Its presence at the close of 'ordinary' ritual events affords another example of intensification, for blessings will have accompanied every key moment in the ritual life of Christians in the major sacramental traditions, while similar forms of emphatic prayer will also have done so in less sacramental streams of Protestantism. People are blessed at their baptism, confirmation and marriage. They can be blessed when they are sick and when approaching death. Baptism is basic to and for Christian identity, as is demonstrably apparent in the giving of a Christian name to the individual at the time of baptism. As the most condensed symbol of all, the blessing is the symbol of salvation as an expression of divine generosity or grace. It is no accident that in hierarchically structured sacramental Churches it is the most senior person present who pronounces the blessing, a fact that leads us into the following chapter and to the relationship between identity and salvation.

– 6 –

From Meaning to Salvation

This chapter asks how the human sense of meaning becomes a sense of salvation? It resolves this key question by combining the notion of 'super-plausibility' derived from the sociology of knowledge with that of 'conceptual mystery' alluded to when ending the previous chapter.

Salvation

The fact that there never has been one exclusive Christian doctrine of salvation qualifies 'Salvation' as a term that is more a 'conceptual mystery' than an exclusive assertion of doctrine, exemplifying the process – described below – in which a higher-order 'frame' is placed around a group of related, mixed and potentially contradictory ideas, enabling them to be discussed in a relatively simple way. As such salvation involves a set of relations between God and mankind that creates a sense of purpose, direction and well-being. It engages reason just as it stimulates emotional moods.

In evaluative terms salvation describes a quality of identity. It involves a moral 'charge' of meaning added to, and becoming part of, ordinary identity, so that salvation emerges as a form of super-identity. In terms of sociology's plausibility theory we might equate super-identity with what I will call 'super-plausibility'. These sociological descriptors mirror the sense and notions enshrined in the theological motif of transcendence, of that sense of overcoming lesser things to attain unity with God. This sense of ultimacy lies at the heart of formal theological accounts of salvation, as in Tillich's conviction that religion is that which concerns us ultimately. Indeed, he speaks of the 'passionate longing for ultimate reality', which, given humanity's 'tragic estrangement from its own ground and depth', has led to separate institutions of religion amongst other aspects of life (1959:8). A similar ultimate point of fusion of intellectual and emotional desires is found in the Danish theologian often designated as the father of existentialism, Søren Kierkegaard. In one of his meditative prayers he expresses the desire, 'To Will One Thing'.

Amidst innumerable distractions he longs, intellectually and emotionally, to relate to God alone, asking that God might, 'give to the intellect wisdom to comprehend that one thing, to the heart sincerity to receive this understanding; to the will purity that wills only one thing' (LeFevre 1956: 23). Dwelling on the changing stages of life through which his single-hearted desire has failed he now longs for its restitution. Here there is a profound self-consciousness to live other than he lives, to live by what he called 'reduplication'. Reduplication is to live in and through the very categories of life that one accepts philosophically. This parallels our concern with embodiment, for 'reduplication' is 'being what one says; it is the opposite of pretending, of hypocrisy, of the double standard and the double life' (LeFevre 1956:189). This single prayer brings us to consider the nature of that power that enables 'reduplication' and facilitates a desired state of embodiment.

Power and Spirit

'Power' is the fundamental existential theme implicated in salvation. When John Beattie writes anthropologically about sacrifice, for example, he thinks it 'correct to say that almost always sacrifice is seen as being, mostly about power, or powers', (1980:37). He is right to suggest that power, force, energy, and other descriptions of this desired resource are basic to all human cultures. Epstein, too, is correct in advocating a 'social anthropology of affect' to interpret such phenomena, in which 'the emotional dimension of human behaviours comes to be given no less weight than the social and intellectual ones' (1978: xv). An anthropology of affect grounded in a grammar of discourse integrating social and intellectual factors by embedding them in mood, experience, and sense becomes an anthropology of embodiment. And that is attractive to theology

The phenomenology of religion partly deals with this kind of approach, as in the much ignored work of Gerardus van der Leeuw, who wrote explicitly on salvation as 'power experienced as Good' (1967[1933]:101). He acknowledges the broad and vague nature of power, and suggests that perhaps Rudolph Otto chose the concept of the numinous for use in religious debate 'because this expression says nothing at all' (1967:681). Less sceptically, he discusses power as embracing the idea of meaning, much as Paul Tillich described religion as that which concerns us ultimately. 'Power' is, then, a necessarily vague term, because it embraces the sense of private awareness intimately involved in salvation.

'Power' is almost limitless in its significance, having dominated intel-lectualism from political philosophy to theology. It is open to many kinds of analysis in studies of religion. When Eliade considered power as a means of approaching the sacred as *Homo religiosus* he cited Luther's influence upon Otto, illustrating the religious tradition that grounds power in the dynamic experience of God. Eliade showed how Otto's notion of God as totally distinct and 'other' can nevertheless be related to human forms of knowing (1970:123 ff.). Yet, for many devotees, the power of God in worship may impress them as a reality more profound than their own existence. Again, divine power may also be encountered through the priest or minister of a congregation with a sense of worth, significance, succour and strength, emerging through personal contact. One influential ethical trend in theology grounds such power in the divine humility, thereby acknowledging a trans-valuation of values demanded by the life of Christ in the will to service. When Henri Nouwen spoke of the minister as a 'wounded healer' (cf. T. S. Eliot, *Four Quartets*, 'East Coker', Part IV, ab init., for the 'wounded surgeon/healer') he touched a very real nerve in the lives of many priests (1972:83). But the important theological fact is not simply that someone who has undergone pain is the better enabled to help those currently suffering pain, but that the minister is symbolic of the ministry of Christ as the wounded Saviour. Nouwen's notion of the wounded healer is a category well known to ethnic and natural religions in the figure of the shaman. As a ritual specialist and healer, the shaman is very often a person who has undergone some sort of disability and has come through the trial to become a help for others in his or her community (Ohnuki-Tierney 1981). In this sense the wounded healer is a species of natural-priest in line with our earlier discussion of natural priesthood.

Historically, ministers bear a power because of the continuity of tradition they represent. When post-modern selves lack firm rooting in society and selfhood there is some succour to be gained from another person who stands within a distinctive fellowship of continuity, mediating the power of the sacramental, public, moment into the private areas of life. Similarly, just as eucharistic ritual gives the priest a power for later use that is hard to define, and that will probably be interpreted in terms of wisdom or insight, so the preacher can be viewed as one knowing God's ways. When pastoral care is set within this kind of total ritual context its significance is heightened, as Thomas Oden argued for the influence of the overarching life of Christian congregationalism (1984). This gives Christian pastoral care an advantage over secular therapies, which seldom come with a sense of community power.

Power and Worth

The theological picture emerging here sees power as an increase in self-worth on the part of an individual within a community, guided by an ethic of humility. This relational element of power comes to prominence in and through the doctrine of Salvation. Worth is asserted by God in and through humanity's redemption. The worth of men and women, fallen and flawed as the Christian tradition asserts them to be, is proclaimed through divine humility, while the answering faith of mankind is itself found to be of the same kind as the merciful endeavour of God. In this sense a servant Church is the only appropriate marriage partner for the suffering servant, theological motifs that have their counterpart in our discussion of gifts and grace in Chapters 3 and 8.

But this sense of 'power' is predicated upon Christian tradition. It is no accident that during the 1970s there was an upsurge of what has been called 'Narrative Theology' or the 'Theology of Story'. One of its telling features witnessed the older nineteenth-century theological notion of salvation history, which dealt with sweeps of history and divine action, being transformed into the more individualist and small-group preoccupations of the 1960s. Theologies of Story also adopted less respectable notions of mythical forms of thought, and baptized them into more traditionally acceptable forms of reflection. During the first half of the twentieth century some sought refuge in the myths of Freud, Jung, or Marx, treated either as history or as an aspect of psychology; towards its close Narrative Theology took self-reflection away from myth and psychology to link it with God's self-expression in scriptural narrative, disclosed through the contemporary lives of congregations (cf. Doctrine Commission of the Church of England 1981:79–107). Among the key metaphors of this style of theologizing are journey and story. The journey motif invests bodily and spatial dimensions of life with moral values, as expressed in themes such as 'home-coming' (Navone 1977:89; Winquist 1978). Within mainstream Christianity, too, the later twentieth century came to emphasize self-discovery, as a brief analysis of the Eucharist in the 1662 *Book of Common Prayer* and the 1980 *Alternative Service Book* will show.

We approach these through Mary Douglas's (1970) distinction between positional and personal types of group, a distinction grounded in Bernstein's work as discussed in Chapter 5. The positional type sets store by the hierarchical nature of life, on roles played and on discipline and authority grounded in hierarchy. The personal type, by contrast, prizes the personality and sensitive awareness of individuals. The former stresses what people do and the latter who a person is. I drew on that work some time ago to differentiate between forms of evil, arguing that positional types define evil as sin, rooted in acts of disobedience to authority, as in the case of Anselm's idea that God was an offended overlord whose outraged honour required satisfaction through an appropriate ransom (Davies 1981). Such feudal theology presupposed a hierarchical view of divine verities as well as a structured view of ordinary social life. Personal forms of evil dwell more on love in the form of grief and remorse, and are found in exemplarist notions of atonement rather than in theories of substitutionary atonement. Abelard and Leonard Hodgson would be interesting examples drawn from the twelfth and twentieth centuries (Hodgson 1928). In addition, personal forms of evil focus it as internal to individuals, while positional patterns tend to focus evil on the devil as an actual entity within a hierarchy of created things.

The *Book of Common Prayer* was the product of a positional social type. The monarch's earthly throne patterned a worldly realm, just as God is King of Kings and Lord of Lords upon His heavenly throne. Salvation comes through the relation which the Father has with the Son in a saving act of mercy to mankind. Men and women approach God the Father as His humble and obedient servants. The power that comes to them through eating the holy bread is a power born of the divine hierarchy. Worth comes to each person as a servant of God; the love of God is revealed through His Son, it is a boon, a merciful expression of God's good will. Whatever significance accrues to the servant of God does so in a way that sets that believer in a broad and all-embracing world under the divine rule. The power gained by the individual at the Holy Table is extended through the power of the magistrates and judiciary and monarch to the whole world. In other words, the external and obvious life of the world is assumed to be Christian. The *Alternative Service Book* exists in quite a different world. Its motif is not the Lord of Hosts upon His throne, but as immediately present, as in the expression: 'The Lord is here, His Spirit is with us.' The major theological shift is from the Father and Son to the Spirit and the Son. The gathered community replaces an entire cosmos of Christian obedience. The personal model replaces the model of hierarchy. Persons replace roles. Being replaces doing. The power gained by the individual at the Holy Table is a power of fellowship and community. In the 1662 rite the external pattern of social life is replicated within the ritual; in the 1980 form the congregational pattern inverts life outside in the world. Though hierarchy may exist without, fellowship exists within. There is possibility of both *communitas* and *koinonia* in the 1980 form, but not in the 1662 form. Whether or not the 1980 liturgical reformers were socialized in a personal way and therefore ill-disposed towards hierarchical forms or not we cannot say. What can be said is that the pattern of rites facilitates the expression of personal ideals of human relationship. Similarly, in the marriage service the words accompanying the exchange of rings bring out the sensitive ideal of person-to-person relation: 'all that I am I give to you, and all that I have I share with you'. The bride and groom are instructed to face each other during these rites, unlike the prior tradition of their standing side by side facing forwards.

Embodied Power

This personal approach is apt for many English middle-class people, who constitute the majority of Anglican congregations, while many working and upper-middle-class groups might well favour more positional ritual forms. The degree of fit between patterns of liturgy and theology and of the life lived by people is likely to influence the success or failure of Church ventures. The rise of the Charismatic Movement from the later 1960s exemplifies the way in which a middle-class, personal style of spirituality marries life and message. I have argued elsewhere that the Charismatic ethic reflects the post-industrial concern with people and servicing people, and would add that the sense of power bred by the emphasis upon the Spirit is perfectly in accord with such a stress (1984b).

One application of this approach to identity, power and society lies in what came, throughout the 1970s in the Church of England, to be called the Non-Stipendiary Ministry. Unlike the parish priests, who have traditionally been set in a hierarchical and positional realm where their duty was clear and their professionalism obvious, the Non-Stipendiaries were supposed to work out ways in which their priestly identity could be expressed in relation to their ordinary jobs in the workaday world. Here we see a clear shift from priesthood as a transitive phenomenon – priesthood as 'doing' – to the intransitive phenomenon of priesthood as 'being'. Here, role-theory becomes an inappropriate form of analysis. The power of priesthood, traditionally understood to consist in the historical authority of the episcopate, the biblical task of preaching and the celebration of the sacraments, now moves, becoming a sense of presence amongst others. The difference between these models of priesthood is quite striking, and it is not hard to see why some found it difficult to sustain, since, ultimately, priesthood exists for action and not appreciation. This is obvious in terms of rites of passage managed by priests as representatives of official bodies.

Humanizing Priesthood

Priesthood often appears to make people more rather than less human, for the longer priests serve the more frequently do they function within liminal positions sharing a great variety of human experiences. Early years of ministry necessitate a learning how to cope with these degrees of emotion, moving from a funeral to a wedding and so on without carrying a shadow of overlapping emotion. This depth of liminal feeling and shared fellowship in joy and sorrow is not granted to many people in our culture. In terms of priestly identity this aspect of liminality, with its *communitas* and *koinonia* depth of sentiment, is of deep significance. There is a sense in which a priest's identity involves a permanent liminality. But another aspect of priestly ritual performance is that they must ensure that the rite proceeds smoothly and, to achieve this, priests often remain pragmatic and rationally minded, whilst the congregation of the faithful may be set in a worshipful, intuitive, and more mystical mode. The leader may serve as a symbol of religious experience without actually experiencing any personal emotional shift. This makes it all the more important for ritual celebrants to know what may be going on in the entire process of the growth of their own priestly identity, as also in the worship of the people.

Deifying Humanity

A final point remains as far as identity and power are concerned, not of priests but of Jesus. This derives from Hans Mol's seminal study of the process in which those things that confer identity upon an individual tend to be invested with deep respect by that individual (1976). This respect exists on a continuum that includes the sacred. It was, for example, as Christianity emerged as a distinct group from its parent Judaism that the doctrines of the deity of Jesus as the Christ grew in strength.

The more the group derived its identity from a single source, the more that source would be likely to be defined as ultimate – a significant feature in the growth of many religious movements. This is the clearest example of the way in which superplausibility emerges from plausibility in relation to identity. This might lead one to see how Jesus of Nazareth could move from the status of a Jewish prophet to becoming that of a Gentile God in direct relation to the rise of a Hellenistic Church separate from the synagogue. The more the Christian group separated itself from its Jewish base the more its defining focus, the person of Jesus, would be accorded increased status. The increasingly clear identity of being a Christian then matches the increasing status of its founder. One aspect of this transition involves the attribution of deity to Jesus, as explored by the biblical scholar Maurice Casey (1991). This approach has the benefit of a dual and parallel description of change in individuals and in the group to which they belong. For the convert the process of change not only heightens self-awareness and self-attribution of distinctive characteristics, such as being a new-person, or belonging to a community in which status hierarchies are overcome, but also involves a criticism of the pre-existing form of life. This disjunction within life helps fuel the ethical system of the new faith. While some theologians see the point of this kind of analysis (cf. Kee 1980), others would question such a reductionist explanation. Yet, even theologically speaking, people do have a capacity, perhaps even a tendency, to place above all contradiction those persons, places, and beliefs that have given them some special sense of purpose and existence.

To be aware of such psychological and sociological processes of identity-conferring and respect- or sacredness-investing response is also to be alert to pathologies of this human procedure. When people come to faith and new identity through a particular kind of tradition, they may invest that pattern of religion with an unquestionable authority. Those who have found in Jesus of Nazareth the Christ who is God with us may also invest him with statuses and images of the highest order that actually prevent the human element in his nature from emerging. It may be a human temptation to make Jesus of Nazareth more divine, after human ideals of godhood, than he might have wished to be. Ironically, the Incarnation as a dynamic doctrine that gives an identity of salvation to men and women can, also, rob them of certain images of God. The omnipotent and alien god standing unmoved in eternity is impossible for the kind of Christian thought rooted in notions of the divine humility mentioned above. The power disclosed in the humble Incarnation opposes the mighty notions of despotic omnipotence, and the appropriate human response involves both sacrifice and self-sacrifice. This is where theological ideas engage with the emergence of a new sense of identity as part of what, theologically speaking, is a process of salvation.

Super-plausibility

Theoretically speaking, this sense of salvation-identity emerges from our earlier consideration of embodiment; but, under the impact of the rebounding conquest thesis, it begins with the human drive for meaning. From the outset children explore and categorize the environment, developing their discovered world in relation to their personal needs, desires and imagination, all under prevailing cultural constraints. Society makes available a layered set of meaningful worlds, from the concrete location of territory and its physical boundaries to the language-bearing logic of poetry, philosophy and mathematics. Some of these forms of meaning are endued with high levels of emotion, while others gain their strength from a purely rational explication of things. These anthropological views of identity are paralleled by theological perspectives of humanity viewed as creatures in a created world, engaging with it and exploring it as a God-provided and not as an alien habitat, even when it is harsh and problematic. Whether as a locale of wonder or of bare survival, the world evokes a sense of response and involvement.

One characteristic feature of religious life involves a heightening of ordinary processes of meaning-construction and human awareness, and, for convenience, I will call it super-plausibility. Super-plausibility is an ongoing consequence of human intelligence and, theoretically speaking, is an extension of the notion of plausibility pursued by phenomenologists and sociologists of knowledge. In an earlier study I began to show how notions of plausibility might be related to religious ideas of salvation; here I am able to press this argument much further (Davies 1984a: 29ff.). A similar idea appears in Paul Ricoeur's account of the 'surplus of meaning' that comes in and through the act of interpretation: that 'process by which disclosure of new modes of being gives to the subject a new capacity for knowing himself' (1976:94). Here we are not only concerned with the inevitable construction of meaning in life, but also with ventures that conduce to 'new modes of being'.

Individuals are constantly socialized into pre-existing cultural under-standing of the nature of things in their 'everyday life-world' as phen-omenologists describe it. While accepted world-views regularly undergo modification and only occasionally encounter radical change, religions regularly assert the inadequacy of every ordinariness of life. Religions specialize in the double process of pinpointing the flaws in the human condition and positing modes of redress. And it is these affirmations that constitute schemes of super-plausibility, in which a higher-order claim of meaning transcends the lower-order realm of failed plausibility in the everyday life-world.

'Conceptual Mysteries' and Superplausibility

Both in my earlier study of plausibility and in the brief text on pastoral theology and social anthropology that presaged this volume (1984a, 1986 respectively) the notion of plausibility was grounded in the sociological theory of knowledge, but with some recognition also paid to psychological aspects of religion, especially to aspects of brain research informing studies of symbolism (cf. Davies 1984a:158ff.; 1986:25ff.). Subsequent research, especially in cognitive psychology, has much more to contribute to forms of human knowing, as has already been indicated in Chapter 2. Here I pinpoint but one element derived from that seminal perspective, encapsulated in Sperber's phrase 'conceptual mystery' as cited by Scott Atran in his own exploratory theory of religion, and derived from cognitive studies (1993:62). Essentially these evolutionary arguments witness to the fact that human beings possess certain dispositions of thought that organize information in particular ways and, because of their success in fostering human survival, have become established modes of mental operation. Not only do children, for example, seem able to classify different sorts of animals and plants into broad groups in relation to their grasp of what constitutes a human, but they do so in such a way that well-established social scientific theories about social learning, training and cultural development are called into question. Starkly put, there is something about our make-up that makes us make up the world in a particular way.

This kind of hypothesis and research is guaranteed to divide anthropologists as much as other social scientists, not to mention theologians, because each possesses many vested intellectual interests in the definition of humanity. Despite the weight of anthropological information on different cultures and the way they manifestly organize their ways of life it seems judicious to remain open to the rapidly developing information of cognitive research, as to research in genetics. Here we focus on the way some cognitive researchers describe those human thought processes engaged in perceiving the world and arranging its classifications into an increasingly more abstract order of values. In other words, we think about thinking by produce meta-representations. And it is this capacity for producing higher-order schemes of thought that attracted both Sperber and Boyer. Boyer's argument is that these meta-representations allow us to play with ideas and to explore their various possibilities. Speculation becomes possible only when we move from the immediately available information to ideas about that information. One advantage of forming ideas about ideas is that to give a firm frame to something we only half understand enables us to play with that half-idea in ways that may lead to a firmer grasp of the remainder. Dan Sperber argued in this way when considering not only how people can 'hold as beliefs incompletely understood ideas' but also how we can 'process information . . . which exceeds our conceptual capacities' (1982:51, 53). A slightly similar point was made by Ohnuki-Tierney in her study of Ainu Shamanism, when she described what she called a 'phenomenon of vagueness' in which she thought that the greater the 'intellectual and psychological' content of a cultural idea 'the less articulated are the concepts involved' (1981: 146). She interpreted this 'phenomenon of vagueness' as due to the many individual beliefs that come to be associated with prime religious ideas, and she thought that it might also apply to the Christian idea of God, references to whose capacity are more general, whereas references to particular saints and their functions are more specific. Her case might be even better made by distinguishing between references to 'God' and to the individual persons of the Trinity.

Linguists have long seen the wisdom of locating forms of language at the appropriate level of abstraction to assess their full significance, with poetry, for example, provoking 'a shift in attention to the form of the message' (Leavitt 1997: 158–9). George Hagan's account of Christian trance states in Ghana expressed something similar when he likened the 'compelling speculative ascent to higher, more abstract levels of thought' in dealing with philosophical paradoxes and dilemmas to the 'ascent to levels of existence that transcend the realm of the sensed' when searching for solutions 'to existential paradoxes' (1988:155). At the beginning of the twentieth century Georg Simmel had observed much the same in his sociology of religion when arguing that certain types of social relationship become 'detached from their social context and raised to the transcendental dimension' to constitute religion as a 'self-contained sphere' (1997: 158). Once more the movement in religious thinking is ever towards what, in one sense, is more abstract and in another is more unified. For Atran science, too, engages in meta-representations in a way that 'allows the construction of conceptual stages towards a full understanding' (1993: 62). But religion, though it begins from the same starting-point, takes a different direction. It, too, constructs meta-representations, it places frames around issues and then talks about that frame in relation to other frames that have been placed around other, half-understood, issues. And it is here that Atran borrows Sperber's description of the process as creating 'the possibilities for conceptual mysteries, which no amount of processing could ever clarify, to invade human minds' (Sperber 1975:84). Five basic examples will not only exemplify this notion but will also further our consideration of superplausibility.

The Problem of Evil

To reflect upon meta-representations of experiences brings us directly both to systematic theology and to that clustered experience of daily life already discussed in Chapter 2. The topic of the 'problem of evil' provides a valuable example of a 'frame' that systematic theologians place around the many complexities of human experience. In fact 'the problem of evil' is a particularly good example of a meta-representation of half-understood ideas. Situations of misfortune, suffering and disaster often seem to have no rhyme or reason to them yet, as we saw in Chapter 3, the moral aspect of human meaning-making often drives the 'why me?' question in response to them. Christian theology does not answer the question posed by peril, but creates a category that gives a name to it. Accordingly, 'The Problem of Evil' constitutes an inevitable entry on the syllabus of practically any course in systematic or philosophical theology (cf. Hick 1966). By possessing this named framework theologians can, to a degree, ignore inconsistencies of argument that might be marshalled for each of its constituent elements. This frame then allows a debate to take place with other such frames, such as, for example, The Incarnation, or Providence, or The Love of God.

The Holy Trinity and Christology

The Holy Trinity and Christology are two powerful frames for problematic experience. The Holy Trinity is a name for a doctrinal complex of ideas that seeks to relate Jewish Monotheism with the developing Christian sense that Jesus of Nazareth was no ordinary man and that the experience of changed lives and community-grounded inspiration seemed to demand supernatural explanation in the concept of the Holy Spirit (itself a subframe that dealt with experience). For Jews, Christians are polytheists of some sort, despite firm disavowals. In practice it is likely that many Christians are oblivious as to whether they are related to God the Father, to Jesus as the Son or to the Holy Spirit when engaged in worship or the like. Often one takes precedence within particular groups and yet, doctrinally, The Holy Trinity is the defining norm of and for orthodoxy.

Much the same could be said for Christology, the formal doctrine that 'frames' the many aspects of the life of Jesus and affirms him as being both human and divine. Many would lose friends to defend this 'frame' while not being able to explain the complex categories used in the first four centuries of Christian history to describe the relationship between the human and divine natures of this one man. Realistically speaking, an extremely small percentage of active Christians, and probably of clergy too, would be able to give any lengthy account of the idea of Jesus being 'of one substance with the Father', as one of the Creeds affirms. Within Christology we might also, for example, identify 'The Incarnation' as another meta-representational frame that deals with this notion of the interplay between deity and humanity. Here an extensive discussion is possible between anthropology and theology if we started, for example, from Atran's brief description of the way in which people seek to 'unify phenomenologically diverse sorts of experience, including the integration of fundamental ontological domains that manifest *prima facie* differences', along with the tendency to 'use people as a model' (1993:63). We touch on this subject in the next chapter when dealing with symbolic bodies; but, certainly, the human body of Jesus has offered a potent symbolic bridge for integrating the human and the divine.

Resurrection and Soul

The Resurrection is another doctrinal meta-representation of mixed human experience; it is also one that is part of, a sub-frame of, the Christological scheme. 'The Resurrection' is an extremely important category in providing a focused means of discussing diverse and potentially problematic, if not contradictory, issues. Some theologians argue that Jesus's physical body was transformed into a 'resurrection body'; others stress 'the empty tomb'; yet others see the Resurrection as an experience convincing believers that Christ is a power to be reckoned with in their own lives. Quite a different view interprets Resurrection 'appearances' in terms of group hallucination caused by grief (Kent 1999:35). But, whatever is the case, all these people can talk about 'something' when they talk about 'The Resurrection'. When people at large discuss survival after death they tend to opt for language of the 'soul' and its immortality, which matches Catholic theological thought but contradicts several influential Protestant theologians, who emphasize 'resurrection' above all else (Davies 1997: 115–31). In practical terms theological discussion can become problematic when participants make the category mistake of linking what I am calling the 'frame' with any one of its constituent parts. This often happens with The Resurrection, as different groups assume that The Resurrection is, really, about the empty tomb, or the mutated body of Christ, or their own inner experience.

Symbolic Outrage

In relation to this kind of situation Atran suggested that 'symbolism often aims to draw people ever deeper into unfathomable mysteries by pointedly outraging everyday experience' (1993:62). This process is highly positive, because 'symbolic analogies provide rich conduit metaphors for linking together diverse phenomena that would otherwise be lost to an uncompromisingly rational mental processor' (ibid.). The final advantage of this scheme of things is that the purpose of symbolism, 'unlike science, is not to resolve phenomenal paradoxes or increasingly to restrict the scope of interesting conceptual puzzles. Instead, cultural symbolism aims at eternal truth' (ibid.). I have used Atran's own words here to pinpoint his theory of religion and to highlight its stark conclusion in the unexpected phrase 'eternal truth'. The key, perhaps, lies in the verb, 'aims at', which emphasizes the ongoing process of engagement with some of the greatest of human problems rather than any immediate 'answer'.

While this cognitive approach is valuable, it remains important to stress that meta-representations of theology are also related to embodiment and religious practice as well as to the more obvious dynamics of super-plausibility. For Atran's talk of symbolism 'outraging' ordinary experience becomes all the more significant if we take the case of Christianity's affirmation of The Resurrection and see it employed not academically in seminars on Systematic Theology but directly in funerary rites or Pascal liturgy. There can be a sense of 'outrage', or at least of dissonance, when people look into a grave with its inevitability of decay while hearing the priest say that we bury 'in sure and certain hope of the resurrection'. It may well be that the doctrines of the Holy Trinity and Incarnation also share in this attribute of 'contradicting common sense'; yet, these too, have their festivals, liturgy and hymns that engage with the problems of life whilst affirming 'frames' that cope, 'frames' that are as ritually focused as they are philosophically grounded. Here there is a parallel to be drawn between 'awareness' and 'heightened-awareness', on the one hand, and plausibility and superplausibility on the other. In each case there is a transformation of levels, with the ordinariness of things being set into a higher-order through the cognitive processes and through the affective domains of ritual.

Transcending Plausibility: From Meaning to Salvation

This transformation of levels of experience and thought conduces to a new sense of identity, one that 'transcends plausibility' and with the property of 'salvation'. The theoretical background for this analysis obviously lies in its classical context of Durkheimian social facts, whose essence lay in their 'transcendence over individual minds' (1915:231), and in the ensuing tradition popularized by Berger (1969) and Berger and Luckmann (1966) in their accounts of plausibility and plausibility structures. Weber's concerns with both the drive for meaning and forms of salvation are also germane (1965). Also of advantage is the cognitive approach mentioned above, along with Bloch's idea of rebounding conquest.

The key factor lies in the transformation of ordinary forms of meaning into ultimate explanations that individuals encounter as a decisive period or moment. Lives alter and values shift as a new sense of reality breaks in upon them. This inevitably raises the question of conversion as a natural human process and of its consequences for our understanding of social life. Indeed, this may be one way of relating contemporary cognitive studies to conversion studies; but here we simply explore this change in terms of a transition from plausibility to superplausibility. This 'super' element is often described in terms of salvation, insight, release, or some other term of transition involving a sense of development. In a religious context plausibility is transcended when meaning passes into salvation for the devotee. Mysteries are encountered, other realms lying behind or beyond the mundane are entered, and there are shifts in the dynamics of inner-otherness. Mere life becomes eternal life, ordinariness becomes extraordinariness and so on. From the social scientific standpoint salvation describes that quality attributed to a universe of meaning that has transcended the plausibility of the everyday life-world. Far more than any simple transcendence of culture over nature, this involves a form of transcendence of culture to yield a new cultural form that overcomes earlier doubts and problems.

Here Geertz's description of the 'aura of factuality', essential to his definition of religion described in Chapter 1, is ambiguous in as far as it relates to our account of 'transcending plausibility'. When that factuality is strong there is no drive for any new apprehension of belief, and little likelihood of a new message being accepted. It is when a new message casts a shadow over a pre-existing 'aura of factuality' that its status may be questioned, be found wanting and be replaced in what becomes the process of transcendence. Sometimes this happens through particular prophets or reformers, and, in those cases, 'superplausibility' comes to relate to 'charisma', in that a charismatic leader fosters a sense of greater possibility and change amongst followers. A type of knowledge and a type of leader often interfuse.

Truth

One consequence is that the very notion of truth comes to be increasingly explicit and may, even, become important for people for the first time. The dynamics of change in identity raise the very question about the nature of things, not least about interpretations of life itself. Once a new world-view becomes an option, the nature of plausibility-provision becomes a question. The new-found plausibility has the effect of being of a higher order than that previously available. At the personal level, the erstwhile sense of identity now becomes a sense of salvation. At the social level, the ordinary world encounters the salvation-religion.

Conversion

This perspective also allows us to ask if the phenomena of salvation and conversion throw any light on the intrinsic nature of meaning-generating systems. It is not adequate to assume that salvation is simply one kind of plausibility available to members of a religious community, whether by birthright or conversion. It is interesting that the very notion of conversion became increasingly topical, in scholarly circles associated with religion, in the decade of the 1990s, a period when post-modernity highlighted the varied and optional nature of individual.

What, then, is conversion for? What does it indicate? I do not want to analyse here the important technical fact that while conversion is a singular noun it is not a single phenomenon. Rather like sacrifice, its simple singular form hides a complexity of content, and probably betokens its meta-representational status. Nor do I want to consider the variety of stage theories of conversion processes that have been advanced, important as they are (Rambo 1993; Heffner 1993). I want to suggest that conversion has some benefit, some positive adaptive significance for individuals and groups.

Contextual factors are radically important here, not least the oddity of the formal distinction between world-religions and other religions. Almost by accident, scholars divided religious phenomena into the world-religions, often called salvation-religions, and other religions, either graced with the generic name of Animism or simply as the religion of whichever tribe or group was ethnographically described. Much was, of course, implicit in this classification, including evolutionist notions of development in religion and ideas of empire and civilization. Any full account of that period of classification of religions would also have to take into account the complex political, philosophical and theological world from the late eighteenth until the early twentieth century, not least considering the impact of new religious movements in the USA and western Europe upon devotees, apologists and scholars alike. Even Tylor's influential formulation of Animism emerged while he was studying Spiritualist groups (Stocking 1971:89–91; Taves 1999:198ff.). Many were content to think that the world-religions of salvation were proper realms into which their native subjects could be initiated to gain salvation. The kingdom of God matched earthly kingdoms and, in one sense, expressed the modern society of over-arching meanings. As far as the British were concerned, the Kingdom of God and that of Queen Victoria often coincided.

In terms of plausibility theory something interesting underlay this scheme, as pre-existing religions – indigenous universes of meaning – were denatured. Missionaries and associated political authorities largely assumed there was no salvation in them. It was the incoming message that gave salvation. Knowledge thus became ranked in terms of its saving capacity to engender an ultimate identity. This could be discussed in terms of political economy, involving the relative power, prestige and material superiority of the salvation-religion's culture; it also often involved a moral judgement on social structure and organization. But, frequently, the contact between structures of meaning and of salvation tended to denature the pre-existing world-view, as Deng described for the Dinka of the Sudan (1988:157–69), though the missionary process can also bring new meaning to a traditional language, as also with the Dinka (Lienhardt 1982:81ff). And there certainly were cases where indigenous groups did not capitulate to the incoming religion or where, for example, the local practice of divination did not succumb to the 'literate religions', as in Yorubaland (Akinnaso 1995:234–57).

In terms of epistemology, new knowledge obtains a qualitative attribute. Truth triumphs over error, falsehood, and perhaps even over the works of the devil. Though, philosophically speaking, it cannot be assumed that such a use of religious doctrines for purposes of conquest does not, in fact, even denature aspects of that very teaching, an issue to which Philip Rieff drew attention as far as the Christian cross was concerned a generation ago (1966:203). Still, the very idea of truth tends to assume a distinctive form in this interaction between tradition and what is, often, deemed to be a revelatory innovation. Evolutionist influences also had their part to play when early social scientists began discussing primitive forms of thought in relation to Western intellectual ideals. Though salvation was not the moral charge attending the analysis, the difference between primitive mentality and enlightenment thinking echoes something of its perspective. It is only within that broad frame of enlightened thought that, for example, radically different systems of meaning and salvation may address each other as 'religions' without reckoning status differences between themselves. Inter-faith dialogue is a clear example. The very word dialogue not only expresses equality, but also hints at the removal of the relative moral value ascribed to a religion. In the process we can see how the very word 'religion' can serve as an example of Boyer's meta-representation, one that makes the engagement of several such 'frames' possible. So it is that the political and intellectual status of the universe of meaning helps define the moral value ascribed to a scheme of belief.

Conversion, Confidence and Adaptation

Part of the adaptive significance of conversion lies in challenging the prevailing social world. Conversion is not only a form of decision-making akin to the psychological process of problem-solving, as Batson and Ventis have shown (1982:71), but is also a form of exploration of moral and social possibilities: it is one means of fostering change, both personal and social. Of course, the conditions need to be right. David Martin has developed the point that 'people do need to be relatively independent before the prospect of individual conversion can become part of their horizon of hope', and, with reference to South America, he shows how Protestantism is of benefit to those 'above the lowest levels of indigence and with some independent resources of mind, money or skill' (1990:186, 202).

Martin's mentioning the 'horizon of hope' bears many ramifications. It was, for example, integral to the evolutionist belief of the theologian-anthropologist William Robertson Smith when he spoke of the 'joyous confidence in their God' expressed by his ancient Semites (1894:257). It was Smith's conviction that helped inspire Durkheim's affirmation of the 'happy confidence' lying at the heart of ritual activity (Durkheim 1915: 224). This outlook sees humanity as being made more content by religion, as it fosters positive attitudes to the world: religion was of positive adaptive significance. The Durkheimian field is rich here, in that his notion of transcendence represents a kind of conversion. It was a form of what we might call 'temporary conversion', for his analysis demands a repetition of ritual much in line with our discussion of rites of intensification in Chapter 5. Yet this notion of temporary change is well worth sociological consideration, since we all too readily accept the implicitly theological idea that conversion should be permanent. Malinowski, no friend of Durkheim's sociological theory of religion, and much more prepared to acknowledge the inner power of individuals in religion, also affirmed the positive sense of optimism at the heart of religion, convinced that 'religious faith establishes, fixes and enhances all valuable mental attitudes, such as reverence for tradition, harmony with environment, courage and confidence in the struggle with difficulties and at the prospect of death' (1974:89–90). He was also prepared to see these religious functions as conferring 'an immense biological value', and, had he lived another forty years, Malinowski might well have been classed within the broad socio-biological approach to humanity. Certainly, he was happy to talk positively of the 'biological function of religion' (1974:52). A. M. Hocart, an anthropological contemporary of Malinowski, also pressed the idea of ritual as helping to 'procure life' (1935:51), and gives the same sense of the dynamism of life at the heart of religion that is found-ational to Georg Simmel's conjoint sociology of religion and of the individual running up to the beginning of the First World War (1997:29–64). Certainly, Malinowski's phrase 'desire for life' summarizes a great deal of early anthropology in its appraisal of religion as being of positive adaptive significance to humanity as it faced many dangers and difficulties.

Conversion allows a relatively rapid response to a person's social environment, allowing new forms of meaning to emerge from familiar but unsatisfying territory. In saying this I am rehearsing my 1984 argument on plausibility theory as a basis for describing salvation in other than theological terms pertaining to any particular religion. Then, I simply described salvation as a state of sufficiency of durable plausibility such that no other was sought – implying that, for example, a traditional religion might serve a people well until a missionary religion arrived on the scene. The incoming religion would devalue the pre-existing cosmology and replace it with its own. As useful as that suggestion was at the time, it did not sufficiently emphasize the power inherent in the new condition. It talks about one plausibility replacing another, and not about the significance of the super-plus of meaning involved in the process of change. What is sociologically interesting about such a hypothetical scenario is that the higher order of salvation also introduced the convert into a larger society. Just as the traditional religion pertained to a relatively small tribe, the new religion confers a status as a member of the world-wide community of Christianity, or of Islam: identity is expanded, is given a wider field. This shift in spiritual demographics involved a kind of paradigm shift in the nature of religion. And all of that is contained within the individual sense of newness of what one historian described as 'the revolt of high seriousness combined with rapture' when accounting for the eighteenth century Methodist revival in Wales (Hughes 1983:5).

The emergence of superplausibility thus involves discovery, challenge and the reinterpretation of past identities. This is particularly important in religious movements that take preceding eras seriously and that accept some cultural direction underlying passing events. Here one cannot help but recall Wittgenstein's image of silver paper that, once crumpled, cannot be smoothed out again. This I borrow from Rodney Needham's (1985: 165) discussion of ritual to describe the loss of innocence and abandonment of naïveté involved once one religious scheme replaces another. Primitive accounts of the gods come to be as nothing when the dogma of the Church denatures them as mere myths. But, of course, this can lead to an ongoing set of denaturing critiques when, for example, dogma comes to suffer at the hands of historical-critical and social scientific analysis. For many devotees, however, it is the basic transformation that counts as an experience in the present, often interpreted as conversion.

Ritual Process and Superplausibility

Conversion is no simple act of mind, but an embodied process rooted in ritual, with Bloch's rebounding conquest motif being one valuable way of interpreting it. Rebounding conquest or rebounding violence is powerful in demonstrating not only how certain types of ritual engage in the symbolic death of one form of life and the symbolic rebirth of another, but also how symbolic power is generated in the process. Bloch's prime notion is that the culturally enacted death of the old nature rebounds in the new-life of its replacement through ritual contact with supernatural powers.

One significant difference between rituals of initiation within a traditional society and major periods of conversion of its members by an introduced form of religion from elsewhere is that the supernatural powers once deemed to be the most powerful are replaced. Here 'conversion' involves a degree of social change. The new 'God' is reckoned to be stronger than the old 'gods', and it is this heightened degree of power of contact that makes the conversion plausible. This is not to say that, in practice, a convert people will not still harbour interests in the old gods and their ways, but that the dominant social identity of the converts is marked in terms of the new deity.

Conversion becomes one manifestation of Bloch's quasi-universal process of rebounding violence. Central to the newly transformed identity is contact with supernatural power, and that contact can be all the greater when framed by contact with representatives of a politically powerful society. In the eighteenth and nineteenth centuries, for example, missionaries from several European monarchies evangelized within their own colonies and, in those contexts, it is difficult not to think of contact with 'supernatural powers' as involving more than a presumed contact with

God. In a similar way the last two decades or so of the twentieth century witnessed a tremendous growth in conversions in some South American countries, not least through North American missionaries, whether from mainstream Protestant Churches or, for example, from Mormon Churches (Gooren 1998). When the message of the 'power of God' comes in close liaison with the power-background of missionary agencies it is not hard for the two forms of power to co-mix. I have already extended Bloch's argument in close relation to Stanley Tambiah's idea of ethical vitality in Chapter 3 and to eucharistic sacrifice in Chapter 4; here I draw on that discussion, because conversion often makes use of available merit, derived from saviours, prophets or reformers, to transform identity by locating it within a state of salvation and revitalizing it through eucharistic or other forms of worship. The essential feature is that superplausibility is achieved through rebounding vitality.

Dimensions of Superplausibility as Rebounding Vitality

The following examples of superplausibility are all interpreted through the notion of rebounding vitality. Though they are described briefly, it would be possible to expand each into a small monograph, so extensive are the associated implications.

Calling: Beruf

Luther's notion of *Beruf* expressed a distinctive attitude towards work as a vocation or 'calling'. For Weber, 'calling' represented the Protestant replacement of Catholic life, with his analysis of the Protestant Ethic demonstrating the transition from one sort of traditional society to another or, perhaps, even a step towards modernity (1965:79). The Reformation heralded a sense of self that stimulated a great deal of religious life, including factionalism, with the sectarian creativity of Protestantism furnishing a variety of religious mutations capable of colonizing new social worlds. While many failed, others survived, some becoming central to mainstream political and economic organization. New identities felt free for exploration to those empowered by a sensed intimacy with God, reflected in the doctrine of the priesthood of all believers and devoid of liturgical intermediaries. In terms of this chapter, one plausible life-world was replaced by a super-plausibility, living by calling, existence by vocation: a Protestant rebounding conquest over things Catholic.

Grace

Behind the 'calling' of believers, and the doctrinal core of Protestantism, stood grace. Grace refers both to an idea and to an experience. Ideologically, grace is divine generosity, a creativity of love that transforms the recipient; experientially, it is the individual awareness of transformation. Its theological impact is through the doctrine of justification by faith alone through grace alone, often used to explain conversion. Understood through rebounding vitality, grace is the awareness of a quality of life that has overtaken and transformed an individual and is experienced as a transcendent power.

Dispensations and Prophets

The experience of grace and the sense of vocation are often described through a particular view of time. An underlying rationale of Christianity differentiates between the Old and The New Testaments and, within each, between various eras and dispensations, with their distinctive attributes and expectations. This reflexive form of religious understanding accentuates the superplus of meaning that comes with Christianity, as it contextualizes as inferior that which preceded it.

This model of succession took on deeper significance through the Reformation, when the old world of Catholicism was deemed inferior to the new world of the Reformed Churches. But the Reformation triggered a chain-reaction, as reformers, prophets, *illuminati* and sectarians in general reckoned their message supplanted its predecessors. With prophetic figures, the most recent tends to be the most true, and once the prophetic ideal is established within the epistemology of a tradition it functions in a repetitive way. This is very largely the case in Protestant Christianity, in which new sects are usually founded by individuals deemed to be prophets. To a degree it is also the case in Islam, as in the relationship between Islam and, for example, the Bahá'i movement, with its founding prophets.

Conversionist Groups

Conversion in contemporary society often involves new membership in a relatively tight-knit community with its own interpretation of time and history. Whatever meaning life held before, the convert now experiences a higher quality of meaning understood as salvation. Meaning becomes salvation in and through the process of comparing former and current experience. This element of comparison of experience within an interpretation of time is crucial for the meaning–salvation metamorphosis. One excellent example is portrayed in *Believing Identity* (1997), Nicole Toulis's excellent study on Pentecostalism and Jamaican ethnicity and gender, focused on that 'crisis of presence' when individuals no longer feel in control of their lives. Conversion brings a degree of control, a 'sense of presence'. This kind of description of a sense of presence or absence of 'self' is highly reminiscent of Simmel's early sociological analysis of the nature of trust and of 'belief in oneself' that individuals may extend to others, to society at large and to God (1997: 168–9). Many groups provide strong social support for convert members, as well as providing opportunities when they may testify to the change they have experienced. Testimony, as such, becomes a prime medium for describing and enhancing the biography of salvation within the group's account of cosmic salvation in time and beyond.

Authenticity and Superplausibility

Within groups valuing salvation-experience considerable emphasis is placed upon personal authenticity. Epistemologically it is clearly focused on the source and validity of knowledge, and exemplified in the contrast between 'book-learning' and 'inspiration'. Examples of Southern American evangelical groups demonstrate the value of the immediacy of God through the Holy Spirit to inspire those preaching or praying. Their group status is validated by that inspiration, while as individuals they sense the immediate truthfulness of the message and the proximity of the divine. The contrast between the human tradition that underlies years of theological study or 'book-learning' and the direct inspiration of the Spirit is clear and direct (Sutton 1988). This distinction is related to the fact that the Spirit's presence is a 'felt' presence, it is embodied as believers speak in tongues or directs their bodily movements. Learning, by contrast, seems such an abstract and almost disembodied activity and, as such, is not the outcome of Spirit activity.

Charismatic Movements

Charismatic Christian groups exemplify this shift into superplausibility over the turn of the twentieth–twenty-first centuries, and there is something to be gained by approaching their example in a slightly indirect way. Serge Moscovici's stimulating volume, *The Invention of Society*

(1993), takes money as the key for understanding human relationships and social representations. In effect, he engages in a major analysis of secularization without using the word once. In passing, he describes how institutions become represented by letters and are depersonalized in the process. The North Atlantic Treaty Organization becomes N.A.T.O. and then, full stops removed, NATO: it is depersonalized and abstracted, with language trivialized in the process (1993:316). In parallel he speaks of the hunger for relationships emerging in towns, where there is a 'wearing away of character' as he puts it in his extensive gloss on Simmel's sociology (1993:319). This is reminiscent not only of the Church of England, so often abbreviated as the C. of E., where letters replace a name, language trivialized and character worn away, but also of a movement originating within that Church called 'Alpha'. Here the first letter of the Greek alphabet echoes the symbol for Christ as 'the Alpha and the Omega', and designates a religious learning event. The Alpha Course in basic Christian knowledge and discipleship emerged from the Anglican parish church of Holy Trinity, Brompton, a fashionable London church adjacent to Harrod's Department store in stylish Knightsbridge. Here large numbers of people, professionally given to the fuller effect of money and markets, have been religiously converted, often in terms of a charismatic experience related to teaching focused on the Holy Spirit and in the context of small groups of people getting to know each other over a period of months. Many speak of discovering Christianity for themselves, and the language of authenticity replaces the post-modern context of 'image'. Theoretically speaking, plausibility is transcended, and the superplausibility of salvation attained. Almost exemplifying this, their former image-conscious social world is transcended by the 'Alpha' logo. The Alpha Course is, in fact, a copyright trademark, widely and expertly marketed. Research in England indicates that the great majority of people undergoing some form of religious change or conversion through the Alpha courses already had some church experience. Perhaps as few as 7 per cent had no church experience, while the majority (86 per cent) were clerical-administrative or professional in occupation (Hunt 2001:75, 79). This reinforces the theoretical idea of a shift from plausibility to super-plausibility within a relatively familiar world of meaning.

Another form of change associated with charismatic religion involves what I will call an escalation of plausibility; it is exemplified in the phenomenon of the Toronto Blessing (Percy 1996:151ff.). Once Charismatic religion is embraced as a divine action, devotees cannot simply let it fade away. The Charismatic movement of the late 1960s gave many a new form of experience grounded in a doctrine of the Holy Spirit as a dynamic force in the contemporary world. In Canada's Toronto Airport Church in the 1990s there emerged a dramatic form of charismatic religion in which people's behaviour displayed exaggerated sounds and movements. This came to be known as the Toronto Blessing, and, in terms of this chapter, it can be viewed as both validating and transcending earlier charismatic episodes that were not so dramatic. In this sense it serves as an ongoing legitimation of the charismatic style of religiosity in a process of escalation of Charismatic plausibility.

Celtic Christianity

Another contemporary growth point of religion emerged in the 1990s under the broad name of Celtic Christianity. Unlike Charismatic Christianity, its cultural background lies not in young urban professionals engaged in marketing, but in older people interested in the natural world and its sacramental capacity, a spiritual-ecological domain. Against the broad background of the ideology of *Gaia*, with its grammar of discourse on the nature of life, its survival and its flourishing, the 1990s witnessed Celtic spirituality coming to the fore. Here pilgrimage to sacred sites, a sense of historical association with a bygone era of indigenous saints, and distinctive forms of prayer and worship afford the means of transcending plausibility. Though more a form of spiritual retreat than of spiritual warfare, this outlook enables those already Christian to develop and expand their interest in the religious life. Both Charismatic and Celtic Christianities are forms of adaptation for survival. They both ground themselves in pre-existing forms, from which they gain a traditional type of legitimation, to which is brought a contemporary emotional dimension. The particular combination of past and present represents the transcendent element.

Holiness, Possession and Mysticism

Other religious phenomena open to interpretation in terms of super-plausibility and rebounding vitality include holiness movements, in which believers seek higher levels of commitment and morality. Quite different are groups in which spirit possession allows individuals a sense of transcendence through being possessed by an external power, exemplified in numerous anthropological studies of possession states (cf. Lewis 1986). Given their transitory nature, possession states are not, strictly, examples of conversion, but seem more to resemble moments of intensification of ideology. Mysticism is, in many senses, similar, in that it relates prime experiences to transitory moments – but moments that define the reality of the rest of life as lived less intensely.

New Age Groups

More popular than possession or mysticism, yet participating in elements of each, is a cluster of religious activities loosely described as New Age spirituality. Here the body assumes primacy of place as the individual sets about a search for an 'experience-rich' life. This is a personal pursuit with a private assessment of potentially validating leaders, groups or ideas and of a life-style option of engagement with a particular form of activity. There is a type of transcendence over the institutional world of religion, hierarchical authority, and mediated forms of grace. The network replaces the communal fellowship and the congregation. The body, rather than communal commitment or ideological obedience, comes to the fore. At the same time it also resonates with the wider framework of ecology

Ideologies of Superplausibility

Amongst other religious phenomena open to similar interpretation are the Eastern notions of *moksha* and *nibbana*, involving, as they do, a conquest of the old and a gaining of a new state of religious power. These notions also demonstrate the adaptability of the human animal through ever-increasingly complex conceptual, emotional and ethical environments. As forms of conversion they involve moral problem-solving, discovery, and adaptation, not only to the external and social environments, but also to the inner world, where the drive for meaning is not left without its destination or moral significance.

Dynamism of the Second Order of Life

Charisma may also be interpreted through the rebounding conquest model. As an attribute of a distinctive type of individual charisma denotes the magnetically attractive personality of one whom others are glad to follow. While, in a more particular sociological sense, it is wise to discuss the idea of charisma in terms of 'charismatic relations', my emphasis here is upon the leader and, especially, on the transformation that takes place in the production of such leaders.

In applying Bloch's rebounding conquest thesis to charismatic leaders I distinguish between the pre- and post-conquest sense of self in terms of a first and second order of life. The basis for this speculation lies in the fact that many founders of religious groups have undergone traumatic periods of life, often in their youth or young adulthood, when they suffered bereavement or some severe illness that is often described as almost bringing them to death. This they survive and, in that survival, are transformed. Experientially they have conquered death: this type of leader has passed from the first to the second order of life. The way such people speak and bear themselves expresses the presence of a power in their life, one that is attractive to a sufficient number of people to furnish a following. This dynamism of the second order of life, grounded in having survived trauma, is reflected in their prophetic message, and attracts many who lack a first-hand experience of triumph or who seek some form of initiation into it. Inherent in the message is an element of heroism and of the mythical hero motif.

David Aberbach has offered a psychological interpretation of charismatic leadership rooted in traumatic grief (1989, 1996.). For him charisma involves the bereaved individual's longing for support from followers, who serve as a kind of substitute for the lost parent underlying the leader's grief. Whether psychological processes contribute to charismatic leadership is, ultimately, for competent scholars to decide; but, from a simple descriptive perspective, death has played a significant part in the biography of major religious leaders, as I have demonstrated, for example, in the case of Joseph Smith, the prophetic founder of Mormonism (Davies 2000a:102–4). Other religious, political, economic and opportunistic factors are, doubtless, also important; but Aberbach's suggestion should not be ruled out of court, for religious leaders are almost always people of the second order of life, howsoever achieved. This applies not only to the founders of established movements, but also to leaders at local levels, especially in groups where status is accorded on the basis of manifest ability and life experience.

Individuals, trauma and distress behind them, announce to any who will listen a message of transcendence. They stand as living proof that the ills of life can be overcome. They embody the process of rebounding conquest, for they have touched the power enabling them to flee the first order of life and, through the liminality of trauma, to emerge with the power and knowledge enabling them to conquer first-order life wherever they encounter it. This leadership involves a conquest of the led, who gladly follow into the realm of salvation.

Symbolism and Sacrament

Symbolism underlies much of human life, as the immense literature on its history, theory and application shows. In four unequal parts, this chapter modestly introduces several key concepts of common interest to theologians and anthropologists, stressing the relationship between symbolism and embodiment. First we draw on Victor Turner and Dan Sperber's symbolic studies to expand the theme of human embodiment and to offer two brief analyses of major Christian sacraments. Then, secondly, we sketch Karl Rahner's Catholic and Paul Tillich's Protestant theological interest in symbolism, before exploring, in the third part, a series of topics closely linked to issues of symbolism and that directly inter-relate theological and anthropological concerns over the nature of human religiosity, not least in relation to time. Finally, and very briefly, we deal with a more technical issue on symbolism as an innate aspect of human competence.

Symbols and Brains

One of the clearest distinctions between two broad types of anthro-pologists of symbolism concerns psychology, for, while most operate solely with social explanations of human activity, a few see great advantage in drawing upon psychological theories. Behind this lies a theoretical debate originating in Durkheim and leading to a sharp divide between social scientific and psychological thought, a divide that is artificial and unnecessary (Moscovici 1993). The developing field of cognitive anthropology is one area that takes psychology seriously, as we have already seen in Chapter 2, while, in this chapter, both Turner and Sperber reflect some psychological influence. Sperber, in particular, draws from research on the brain and its mental operations affecting perception, embodiment and human action.

Turner and Sperber were amongst the more influential of later twentieth-century anthropologists to have advanced the study of symbolism and its ritual world of operation. Turner focuses on the cultural use of particular symbols, while Sperber is also interested in the way the human mind organizes its symbolic knowledge. While their terminology differs, there is much in each that complements the other, and, together, they provide a firm basis for gaining an initial competence in approaching the interpretation of symbols.

Turner's Polarity of a Symbol

Turner suggests viewing a symbol as possessing two poles, the ideological pole and the sensory pole. While reminiscent of the north and south poles of a magnet, they are not exclusive and repellent of each other, but interfuse and interpenetrate along a spectrum. Each may bear more than one significance, being multivocal or polysemic. The ideological pole refers to the ideology, doctrine and belief of a group, or it hosts the concepts of a movement and embraces the cognitive aspects of its thought. The sensory pole, by contrast, deals with the experiences and sensations of life. It concerns the bodily-felt aspects of life, and touches the major senses of the body.

We can extend Turner's scheme to say that the interfusing of idea and sense yields different moods, where 'mood' refers to a sense of embodiment. Here our stress lies on this interlinking, and does not follow those who criticize Turner for employing dichotomous categories to establish distinctions and then arguing that ritual exists to unite what is otherwise divided (Aune 1996:158–9). Two examples will help explain this scheme and take the argument into the world of the Christian sacraments, for it is in 'sacraments' that the theological concern with symbolism comes to its most explicit focus. First we consider baptism, and then the Eucharist.

Baptismal Symbols

Different Christian traditions practise baptism in different forms, sometimes of infants and sometimes only of adults. By following a rite of the Church of England, often noted for its middle way of spirituality, many features of other traditions may be illuminated.

The baptismal rite of the book of *Common Worship* of the year 2000 is particularly interesting as a liturgical text within the Church of England, because it marks a shift towards an explicitness of the rite, reflecting a growing self-consciousness about what people think they are doing. It may also be a mark of the increased secularization of society, in that symbolic activity has to be explained because of its unfamiliarity. In the 1662 *Book of Common Prayer* the brief introduction simply advises that baptism take place on a public occasion when others present may be reminded of their own profession of faith and that they may witness the reception of a new member of Christ's Church. That was in a society where the Catechism had to be learned by people before the rite of the Confirmation, and contained explicit teaching on sacraments that they consisted of two parts, 'the outward visible sign and the inward spiritual grace'. The water is given relatively little interpretation: it is simply that in which someone is baptized with the Trinitarian formula; but the inward and spiritual grace is defined as 'a death unto sin, and a new birth unto righteousness: for being by nature born in sin, and the children of wrath, we are hereby made the children of grace'.

In the 1980 *Alternative Service Book* there are no explicit statements prior to the service, and the Catechism has disappeared as a rite and as a cultural practice. By 2000 *Common Worship* contains a long 'pastoral introduction' explaining that baptism begins a lifelong journey with God, that it is a joyful moment for family and friends and that the congregation welcomes the new Christian, with each remembering their own baptism. It speaks of the rite as presenting 'many vivid pictures' reflecting this journey of faith: the sign of the cross is a badge of faith for the journey and a reminder of Christ's death, while there is also a 'drowning' in the baptismal waters, 'where we die to sin and are raised to new life'. This motif of drowning is rather stark in a liturgical text, and is, perhaps, a mark of an increasingly dramatic Church, at least in literary terms, even though, for example, there is no reference to the traditional idea that the waters of baptism wash away sin. In this liturgy there are additional sets of 'prayers over the waters' that add or emphasize theological ideas depending upon the season of the ecclesiastical year in which the baptism occurs. One of them also takes the Trinitarian form of a threefold prayer on the Father, Son and Holy Spirit and their relation to redemptive 'water'.

In the rite itself many more motifs are brought to bear in the special 'prayer over the water'. This is a classic example of what Turner describes as the process of 'condensation', in which many meanings come to be associated with a single phenomenon. Here a wide variety of biblical references to water focus on the water in the font around which priests, family and congregation are gathered. Accordingly, the multivocal water is spoken of as a gift that sustains, refreshes and cleanses. It reflects that water existing at the beginning of creation, when the Holy Spirit, echoing the Book of Genesis, moved over it. This is an interesting item, devoid of any explicit signification, but available for exegesis as the beginning of divine activity in the formation of order out of chaos. It also has the virtue of a reference to the 'beginning' of things. The language rapidly moves to another Old Testament feature, that of the waters of the Red Sea (not named) through which God led the captive Israelites to 'freedom in the Promised Land'. Then comes the baptism of Jesus by John the Baptist, linked with the recognition by the Holy Spirit to designate him as the Christ. Thanks are then given that, in this water of baptism, we are 'buried with Christ in his death' and also come to share in his resurrection. The priest then asks God to 'sanctify this water that, by the power of your Holy Spirit' the person may not only 'be cleansed from sin and born again' but also be renewed in God's image.

These many meanings constitute the ideological pole of the symbol of water used in this form of baptism. It is almost a compendium of the key doctrines of biblical theology: creation, deliverance from captivity, Jesus as the Christ, forgiveness of sin, conquest of death and the power of the Holy Spirit. But what of the sensory pole? This is a far more complex feature to describe, precisely because it concerns the actual experience of water, something that individuals do not discuss in normal social life. This includes the experience of drinking when thirsty, the sense of thirst itself and the anticipation of its being slaked on arrival at a source of water. There is even the sense that, when really thirsty, many seem to have a preference, and probably a physical need, for water rather than for some water-based beverage. Again, there is the experience of water in washing – the washing at the beginning of day as a basic cultural item that becomes second nature to people as part of their entry into the day. There are also other times of washing, bathing, or the taking a shower for the removal of sweat or other body fluids that practically never receive public or even much private comment, as also with the washing of babies at birth and of corpses at death. In British cultural history, and this is reflected in the cultural life of increasing numbers of societies, more people wash themselves more of the time than has probably ever been the case. People are now cleaner than they have ever been, which may, perhaps, make water a more potent symbol than it has been before. Not only so, but water itself, as a potable substance, is now cleaner and more healthy than in earlier times, most especially in urban society.

Other symbolic features, not all explicit, include a threefold Trinitarian emphasis upon the Father, Son and Holy Spirit, in a confession of faith of the congregation at large. In a new, democratic, liturgical act the priest may invite the parents and godparents to mark the child with the sign of the cross, something that, traditionally, was restricted to the priest. A large candle may be used to symbolize the light of Christ, and smaller candles may be lit from it to give to the baptismal candidates or to their sponsors. And there is the symbol of the congregation itself. This is the least explicitly referred to in terms of a symbol. Indeed, one might even speak of it as the hidden symbol of the rite; yet its significance is everywhere present, and comes into its own in the final greeting of the new member: 'We are all one in Christ Jesus. We belong to him through faith, heirs of the promise of the Spirit of peace.'

In baptism, then, theological ideas and practical experiences of life come together in the ideological and sensory poles of water. In terms of embodiment, the ritual act becomes a mode of thought, theology becomes action, liturgy is belief. And if this is the case in baptism, what of the Eucharist?

Eucharistic Symbols

The obvious eucharistic symbols are bread and wine, with water also often used to mix the wine and to wash the priest's hands before the prayer of consecration. Here we touch only briefly on the symbolic polarity of the eucharistic bread and wine, having already considered aspects of the theology of these elements in Chapter 4.

In terms of the ideological pole the bread and wine are spoken of as gifts 'that may be to us' Christ's body and blood. Their use at the Last Supper of Jesus with his disciples becomes the basis for their future 'remembrance of' him. Jesus's words 'this is my body which is given for you' are cited as the charter for the rite. With the wine the Master's words are, 'this is my blood of the new covenant which is shed for you and for many for the forgiveness of sins'. The doctrinal ideas that are condensed in the elements focus on the identity of Jesus as the one who forgives sins, and on the act of remembering him. They also include the idea of the Last Supper as a Passover meal, and herald a shift from the old covenant and Old Testament to a new covenant and the New Testament. All takes place in a context of a meal 'in the same night that he was betrayed'. This element of betrayal is, itself, one theological motif of the Eucharist that is seldom made explicit, except perhaps in liturgies associated with Maundy Thursday, the day before Good Friday, which is celebrated as the occasion of the institution of the Christian Eucharist. One example is the medieval Judas Cup ceremony, revived in the liturgy of Durham Cathedral in 1998 (Davies 2000b:61–76). It is interesting to see, in some of the variant forms of the eucharistic Prayer offered in *Common Worship*, a real divergence from the ecclesiastical tradition of the night of betrayal with clauses such as 'on the night before he died he had [came to] supper with his friends' (Prayers E & [G]), 'on the night he gave himself up for us all' (Prayer F), (*CW* 2000:198–203). What is of interest is that these verbal shifts express quite considerable theological changes of emphasis and indicate just how liturgical change can alter the deposit of faith condensed into ritual symbols.

As for the sensory pole of the rite, we enter, once more, the realm of personal experience, this time not of washing but of eating and drinking and of the sociability of so doing. The physical act of eating and drinking is so basic to human life that its diverse significance must elude any simple description. Still, the very fact of ingestion involves an awareness of the necessity of eating and drinking as repetitive, daily, events. Even in a culture where wine has not, traditionally, been a staple drink, that has still usually been the case for bread. There is a sense of well-being associated with eating, just as there is a degree of dis-ease linked to hunger. When the elements of commensality and perhaps even hospitality are added to the act, then eating becomes all the more pleasurable an experience. In the Eucharist these ideological doctrines and sensory awarenesses combine in the simple act of eating.

This is what Turner pursues through the notion of a symbol as a phenomenon that brings ideas and sensations into intimate association. It is no simple 'association of ideas', but a kind of association of thought and feeling that demonstrates the very notion of embodiment. This existential dimension of symbols relates closely to Turner's interpretation of ritual as the formal contexts within which symbols are utilized: indeed, it makes better sense to speak of symbols, or at least to think of symbols, as 'ritual symbols' or 'ritual-symbols', if only to stamp them firmly with the sense of context. And context is of prime concern for Turner, who shows that it is only through the wider ritual context that we can see the full part played by any symbol. In some contexts a symbol may be a dominant symbol and control most of the significance of the event, while in others it may play a much reduced role. This is the case for water in the two rites outlined above. In baptism water is the dominant symbol: it bears a multiplicity of meanings and controls the meaning available through the other symbols used. It plays an absolutely subsidiary role, by contrast, in the majority of the sacramental traditions where drops of water are added to the wine before the prayer of consecration. Interpretations vary on this addition: some see the combination of wine and water as representing the divine and human natures present in Christ. Some even use hot water, and interpret it as symbolizing the Holy Spirit in relation to Christ. The point is that the water plays a minor role, and is dominated by the symbol of the wine. By contrast, in the Mormon tradition of the Church of Jesus Christ of Latter-day Saints it is water and not wine that is used at the Sacrament Service. In that context it is more of a dominant symbol, and carries its own load of historical, theological and ethical significance that cannot be pursued here.

Sperber, Rethinking Symbolism

Where Turner deals with the relationship between ideas and emotions through the idea of the polarity of a symbol, Sperber approaches the same broad distinction by describing two forms of knowledge, one of which he calls 'encyclopaedic' and the other 'symbolic' knowledge. In this Sperber advocated a theory of symbolism of some significance for theology (1975). Following psychological theories of brain laterality, with their emphasis upon the linguistic and rational capacities of the left cerebral hemisphere and the imaginative creativity of the 'silent' right cerebral hemisphere, he concludes that 'symbolic data, no matter what their origin integrate themselves into a single system within a given individual' (1975:88). Distinguishing between symbolic and encyclo-paedic forms of knowledge, he argues that symbols are not learned in the way propositionally based knowledge is learned. At school information is taught as facts that cohere in discrete subject groups, as with biology, history or a language. Symbolic knowledge, he believes is different from this, and is perpetually integrated into one single system within an individual. So, for example, it is not possible to learn one set of symbols in one religious tradition and then pass on to learn another set in another tradition without there being some degree of relationship between the two. Each new element inevitably combines with what is already in the memory. This can be brought to sharper focus in the notion of a mood-memory, one way of referring to the combined affective and emotional aspects of symbolic knowledge.

Mood-memories

The religious experience of individuals can be viewed as a cumulative set of such mood-memories, which, together, help constitute someone's religious identity. When individuals move from one religious group to another they may change their doctrinal ideas with little difficulty, but certain aspects of the emotional base of their former ritual life change less easily, reflecting the cumulative development of mood-memories throughout life. Sometimes there is an active desire to change the mood-memories of a past life, especially if it holds a haunting or painful biography; but, in practice, it seems easier for people to shift their conceptual frame rather than their emotional deposit of faith.

Sperber's approach also conduces to a sense of intellectual humility, in that he believes that symbols cannot simply be matched with a propositional meaning: symbols are not signs, and cannot be paired with interpretations (1975:85). This marks the end of the period of dominance of the linguistic model. We can no longer assume that there is a 'language' waiting to be decoded lying behind all sorts of phenomena. There may, for example, be many postures and acts that an individual may adopt in totally private prayer or other behaviour that could not be 'explained' as 'meaning' this, that or the other. The purpose of the posture might simply be to facilitate the mood of prayer, and reflect an aspect of embodiment that does not seek to communicate with other people. There are moments that are ends in and of themselves, not least in worship.

Sperber exemplifies this through the topic of smell, arguing that smell is quite unlike, for example, the phenomenon of colour. Culture after culture possesses names for colours, but they do not possess names for smells. Smells are described as being 'like' something that does carry a name. Smell relates to an experience, marks the concreteness of life, and can be regarded as the very symbol of embodiment. By analogy we might say, for example, that the 'idea' is the symbol of philosophy. The philosopher is a thinker, and ideas are objects manipulated in the practice of philosophy. On that basis Descartes' famous *cogito ergo sum*, 'I think, therefore I am', even wants to ground our sense of being in the act of thought. If, however, we suggested the aphorism 'I smell, therefore I am' the image of humanity's prime endeavour would shift quite dramatically. In its unintended sense of giving off a smell it would serve as a reminder of the organic basis of human life, itself a worthy caution to overly abstract philosophy; but, more directly it would affirm the deeply personal grounding of memory that constitutes the human being. Sperber is, I think, quite correct in affirming the intensity of relationship between abstract concept and emotional sensation, and in reckoning the smell to be a prime focus of that interactive intensity. In a smell my emotion and my ideas cohere to yield a joy or sorrow, as the history of that smell may dictate. And it is just such smells that cannot be 'interpreted', language-like, for others to understand. As such, the concept of the smell serves a fundamental purpose as a symbol of and for an entire category of human life experiences that are profoundly important, but that cannot be directly 'interpreted' for others.

We might, for example, pose the question: 'How does grief resemble a smell?' At first glance this seems an absurd question; but, on consideration, it soon reveals itself as a question reflecting the way anthropology handles symbols and the symbolic equivalence of symbols. Here grief resemble smell, in that while an individual's grief is quite personal and cannot be 'understood' by anyone else, yet the fact of grief can be publicly shared and very well understood by others who have, themselves, been bereaved. This is on the basis that most people can say that they know what is meant by the power of a smell to evoke a memory without knowing anything of the actual content of that smell-memory for someone else. This type of mood-memory would apply to numerous aspects of life that are significant for religious groups.

Age, Symbolic Knowing, and Faith

The acquisition of symbolic awareness in mood-memories begins very early in life and, relating as it does to the sensed awareness of being, is better approached in terms of the development of *habitus* and *gestus*, technical terms already introduced in Chapter 2, than in the conventional language of socialization. On Sperber's basis babies and children acquire a symbolic memory of the sounds, movements and mood of an event, not least of the music and voices that play such a significant part in many religious groups from their earliest days. I sketched the significance of Sperber's view of the acquisition of symbolic knowledge some time ago for the particular case of admitting children to the Eucharist at a young age (Davies 1985b); subsequent study has only reinforced that point. The psychologically and sociologically dubious assumption that real religion begins with teenagers or young adults is easily conveyed to people of all ages when only those categories are admitted to eucharistic participation. There is little theological justification for thwarting symbolic learning in the young, and the practice of limiting youthful participation may be one reason why many Anglican congregations loose many teenagers shortly after Confirmation, precisely because they have not had a sufficiently long time to develop a eucharistic mood-memory into which to place the radical changes associated with adolescence. That at least is one hypothesis that is worthy of exploration and comparison with Roman Catholic congregations, where the young are admitted to the Mass much earlier.

In sectarian bodies where exclusivism rules this is intelligible, especially where membership presupposes intellectual assent to particular doctrines. But where the message of divine love and acceptance is paramount, the medium of participation might be regarded as a positive advantage rather than a disincentive. In terms of the psychology of symbolic knowledge, it would make sense to allow children to be free to grow their own symbolic meaning in and through eating and drinking sacred things and through the performance of other acts that induce a *habitus* and *gestus* of spirituality.

Symbolic awareness also facilitates the rational knowledge of religious believers, as exegesis flows through allusion, analogy, and parable, with verbal messages intertwined with liturgical acts of the liturgy. Ritual symbols act upon each other in different ways during the course of embodied life, reinforcing the advantage of the young as well as the sick in benefiting from the Eucharist, in that their mood-memory is cumulative within itself and yields a sense of unity at any one part of life. As Abner Cohen suggested, it is the ritual base, with its data feeding the human symbolic processes, that contributes much towards producing the totality of the self (1977:108). And that self changes over time, as rational and emotional sets of awareness merge within the embodiment of individuals and encounter novel circumstances. Protestant forms of Christianity have tended to address personal development in terms of years of discretion, somewhere near puberty, when youngsters are received into full membership of their community after assenting to the formal claims of their faith. In the more sacramental traditions youngsters are likely to be admitted to the Eucharist earlier than their Protestant counterparts, partly because of an understanding of the religious self as an entity that is growing and that needs to grow in relation to the liturgical patterns of the group. In both traditions periods of religious insight serve to combine the ideological and the sensory aspects of life, so that embodiment can easily be described as 'spirituality'. Here 'spirituality' refers to moods of embodiment, because 'mood' expresses an important combination of reason and emotion, of cognition and affect. A mood is not a pure or naked experience, but is interpreted as it is encountered and as it is recalled and transformed as mood-memories, often related to religious symbols.

Theological Symbolics

Symbols and symbolism have always been important within Christianity, because theologians of every age have known that in speaking of God they must use language that is other than God. In ritual practice, too, theologians, with all believers, have been immersed in symbolic activity related to the divine. So theological necessity and ritual experience highlight the nature of symbolic forms as the means of rendering the infinite in finite terms. While this symbolic necessity is often expressly asserted by theologians, it is sometimes hidden by those who assert the literal truth of their doctrine and practice as divinely given. The Catholic theologian Karl Rahner exemplifies the former view, and has argued in the strongest possible way that 'the whole of theology is incomprehensible if it is not essentially a theology of symbols', adding that this fact is seldom taken seriously within Christian circles (1972: 235, 45). At the centre of Rahner's rationale is the fundamental theological belief that the body is 'a symbol of man' and that human beings come to exist and to develop as themselves through or as bodies. Bodies are the basis of our expression, and it is by means of expressing ourselves that we come to be ourselves. It would be easy to criticize Rahner's view of the symbolic nature of persons; but his position is perfectly logical within the Thomist philosophical perspective that the body is the symbol and medium of expression of the soul. But Rahner's theological work remains important for its clear sense of the centrality of symbolism in any doctrine of humanity.

Similarly, the classical Protestant existentialist theology of Paul Tillich firmly acknowledges symbolic argument, clearly defining symbol as something that participates in that which it represents, while a sign 'bears no necessary relation to that to which it points' (1953:265). Tillich's definition of symbol and sign, and of their differentiation, is extremely useful, and is equally as applicable to anthropological as to theological analysis, a fact that reflects his own existential grounding. Interestingly, he is the one theologian extensively cited by Roy Rappaport in his magisterial anthropological study of ritual (1999). Tillich's work is important for the theology of symbolism because of the way he uses his existential theology to show how the finite realm may properly be the basis for revealing the infinite. There is, he argues, an analogy of being, an *analogia entis* in the technical language of philosophical theology, between finite things and the infinite. There is, in other words, a degree of affinity between them, allowing the one a degree of access to and reflection of the other. Here Tillich develops his idea that 'religious symbols are double edged', in that they are 'directed towards the infinite which they symbolise and towards the finite through which they symbolise it' (1953:267). His examples illustrate the power inherent in distinctively theological forms of argument, as in taking the examples of 'father' and 'king' to show that these terms are not simply derived from human figures and applied to notions of God but that, once used of God, they bring to human fatherhood or kingship a degree of significance they did not possess before.

Similarly with the idea of the 'word'. If, he argues, 'God's self manifestation is called "the word", this not only symbolises God's relation to man but also emphasises the holiness of all words as an expression of the spirit' (1953:267). This example demonstrates the major difference between anthropological and theological methods, showing systematic theology's basis in confessional theology. For Tillich that base lies in the affirmation that God is the ground of our being and is being itself

(1953:261). As mentioned in Chapter 1, he draws the technical distinction between being and existence to make the point that to say that 'God exists' is to reduce the deity to the level of the existence of mortals, which is to say much less than to say that God is being itself. An important feature of Tillich's theology is the assertion that 'God is being itself is a non-symbolic statement' (1953:264). This he regards as the basic utterance that quite simply says what it means and does not point beyond itself. He then argues that, in logical terms, after that has been said 'nothing else can be said about God as God which is not symbolic' (1953:265). These points highlight symbolism as a major concern both of anthropology and theology, remembering that anthropologists – as anthropologists – are usually involved in ritual as participant observers, while theologians have often been practising churchpeople engaged in their own regular ritual activity.

Symbolic Worlds

From these detailed considerations we pass to a variety of potential applications of the symbolic power of religious life, including the prime symbolic bodies of Christianity, the issue of post-modernity and mixed life-values, the symbolism of evil, the resources of art and music in religious life and, finally the issue of time and what we might call the ritual generation of time in Christianity.

Symbolic Bodies

Time, itself, becomes significant for Christianity through symbolic bodies, whether of Christ, the Apostles, Saints or exemplary leaders. Their embodiment of prime values presents one means of dealing with that special kind of time-reckoning called 'salvation history'. Both time and persons become media of and for revelation, itself a medium of salvation. The Latin and Greek derivations of Turner's 'multivocal' and 'polysemic' symbols express, respectively, the many voices and the many signs or meanings of a symbol. Each term may be pressed to indicate two rather different symbolic capacities with multivocality stressing the expression of a symbol, the way it – outwardly – addresses the world through its many-voiced communication. The polysemic dimension hints at the internal capacity of a symbol to integrate numerous meanings. The fact that several meanings may attach to a symbol allows for innovation to emerge as these ideas interlink in lateral and collateral thinking. The outward and inward aspects of symbols become increasingly important in changing social circumstances, when not all share the same value system. The variety of meanings inherent in symbols affords a pool of potential orientations available for different contexts (Davies 2000a: 247ff.). As circumstances change, groups with deeper pools of potential orientation from which to draw are more likely to succeed than groups with shallow pools of potential orientations.

Postmodernity and Muffled Dissonance

One feature of religion in contemporary cultures is that many believers live alongside others with different value orientations without any apparent sign of dissonance. It is characteristic of post-modern contexts that people co-exist while holding competing or mutually irrelevant values. The secularization argument has, broadly, insisted that religiosity is largely located within the leisure world and not the public life of society. In this sense there is a muffled dissonance between what many people believe and the belief they are prepared to express in public. While that muffling vanishes during conservative or fundamentalist opposition, often because of demographic shifts and the consequences of immigration, its normal effect is quite extensive.

Symbolism of Evil

Quite another aspect of embodiment involves evil and active responses to it rather than philosophizing over it, reminiscent of Evans-Pritchard's observation on the African Azande people, who knew what to do in response to evil rather than how to theorize over it. The Church of England, for example, established exorcists in each of its dioceses in the 1970s in response to a growing popular concern with spirits and malevolent supernaturalism in general, an atmosphere fostered by a spate of films such as *The Exorcist*. Within numerous Christian Churches in America and Europe the Charismatic movement emphasizes the experiential form of dealing with evil through various kinds of exorcisms and blessings. Although it is impossible to balance the difference between 'ideas' and 'actions', one is tempted to say that such religious groups have a more effective way of dealing with evil than do theologians and their formal arguments on the nature of evil. Indeed, it is characteristic of Western philosophical theology to speak of 'the problem of evil'. Ideas are, by their nature, more complex than bodily actions.

Art, Music and Life

Other worlds of action that frame embodiment are art and music, domains that tend to conquer rather than problematize evil. No sooner does the philosopher Gadamer begin his magisterial *Truth and Method* than he turns to art as an example of the fact that, no matter how insightful art critics may be, they know that they, 'can neither replace nor surpass the experience of art'. By emphasizing the point that 'through a work of art a truth is experienced that we cannot attain in any other way', he affirms the philosophical function of art as it 'asserts itself against all attempts to rationalize it away', and thereby admonishes the 'scientific consciousness to acknowledge its own limits' (1996:xxiii). For Gadamer art is particularly important precisely because 'the aesthetic attitude is more than it knows of itself', being 'part of the event of being that occurs in presentation, and belongs essentially to play' (1996:116.).

This capacity of art to stand above the critical theological and philosophical eye is reflected in anthropology by Pierre Bourdieu. When discussing the nature of the relationship anthropologists may have with the people they study he draws on Husserl's point that in the 'case of art history' which had never really 'broken with the tradition of the amateur', free rein is given to 'celebratory contemplation and [it] finds in the sacred character of its object every pretext for a hagiographic hermeneutic superbly indifferent to the question of the social conditions in which works are produced and circulate' (1977:1). Similarly, Lévi-Strauss begins his magisterial account of mythology in South America with an abstract discussion of music and, briefly, of art. His first volume, *The Raw and the Cooked* (1970), is organized in sections denoted by musical terms, from theme and variations through to a rustic symphony in three movements. One of the points Lévi-Strauss is making is that 'emotive function and musical language are coextensive' (1970:30). His mythology explores the human creative capacity of mind to engage the divide between good and evil in order to overcome them in a series of problem-solving steps.

This emphasis upon art and music, and to a degree on myth, contrasts verbal language as a code-based communication with a communication in which the participant senses an appreciation lying beyond any literal understanding of a text. The issue can be well expressed in the difference between the active and passive moods of grasping and being grasped. When engaged in the critical reading of a text one speaks of grasping its meaning: the reader is the subject and the text is the object of the total reading event. But there is a form of reading in which the reader comes to be grasped by the text, and that passivity of the self before pictures and music is even more apparent for music and art. Liturgy is the prime form of embodied activity in which text, art and music cohere as it 'speaks' or reveals values to the devotee.

Time

Part of the power that sustains Christian identity is derived from the sense of time generated by ritual. Here I emphasize ritual over the place of 'history' or 'tradition' in fostering Christian attitudes to time. Indeed, the very notion of tradition can be approached in two quite distinctive ways, either as the reception of tradition from the past or the contemporary generation of a sense of the significance of the past. The one takes what it receives, the other generates a sense of reception; one ascribes its own identity to the past, the other credits the past with significance. In the broadest of all possible terms the one reflects the Catholic and the other the Protestant view of time. These grand distinctions invite serious criticism; but they highlight the relationship between forms of Christian identity and notions of time fostered by ritual events. Four examples of types of time will illustrate this: they relate to (i) liturgical time; (ii) Millenarian time; (iii) Imperial time of the Kingdom of God; and (iv) Mystical time of Existential Faith.

These ideal types of Christian time illustrate how time comes to be told in different ways. Children learn to 'tell the time', thereby acknowledging the power of time as told through clocks to influence working, family and leisure life. In this sense time appears to be a very simple entity. But moral, aesthetic and existential values soon become attached to time, invading it in periods that are said to pass quickly or to drag slowly on. This 'speed' of time is dependent upon our experience, circumstances and expectations, and is not simply dependent upon the measured hours and minutes of chronological time. The very phrase 'quality time' has emerged as a secular designation of valued periods.

Dividing Time

In the study of religion it is often the case that time is divided very sharply into two kinds, 'linear time' and 'cyclical time'. Linear time is often associated with the Judaeo-Christian approaches to time interpreted as a single ongoing stream of events, often seen as marked by divine acts in marked dispensations as discussed in the preceding chapter. From the acts of creation, through periods when prophets brought divine messages to mankind, to the appearance of Jesus of Nazareth, viewed as the incarnate son of God, and on to the future judgement of mankind and the end of the world, time moves on. This broad tradition can be extended to embrace the more prophetic and ethical religions, involving a future judgement from Zoroastrianism to Islam and its prophetic outcome in Baha'ism. Cyclical time, by contrast, is often loosely associated with religions of Indian origin or with traditional societies, marking duration through recurring cycles of nature or of human generations. This stark division of time seldom does justice to the devotional and personal lives of devotees, for, more realistically, time embraces both sorts of division. While most live by the clock in such a way that time can never be repeated, they also experience life through repetitive events such as Christmas, birthdays, thanksgivings for babies, marriages and deaths. In terms of Christian theology the distinction between *chronos* as clock-time and *kairos* as moments of divine significance reflects the qualitative valuation of duration. With that in mind we can turn to four different characterizations of time that may be found within Christian traditions.

Liturgical Time

One largely ignored aspect of Christian ritual is that it helps generate a sense of time. This notion of the ritual generation of time may, at first, appear odd. To common sense time seems to have a life and reality of its own, being seemingly objective and lying outside us. In one sense this is true, since society presents each generation with a sense of time. But the more time is pondered the more abstract and fashioned by its cultural sources it appears. Christian Churches have been responsible for giving the passing days, weeks, and years distinctive significance, and through their ritual events has emerged a keen sense of time, especially of '*kairos*-time', periods of divine significance for humanity. Ritual actually generates and maintains these perspectives, with a creative capacity to form and inform human experience. Time shifts from being some abstract entity to being a personalized phenomenon aligned with one's autobiography.

Time comes to be subjective, part of shared group experience, and this is increasingly true for 'secular' time as well as for the religious valuation of time. The celebration of the chronological shift from 31 December 1999 to 1 January 2000, for example, involved some of the largest celebrations ever witnessed across the world, thanks to the television. Millions turned chronology into festivity and autobiography. Something similar is involved in the phrase-question 'Where were you when?', as used of the death of celebrities, whose theoretical significance lies in the emotional responses of individuals. The question is not essentially about location, but about emotional significance. It is one of those indirect aspects of language that speaks of one reality through another, in this case of reflective awareness through a place. Something similar lies in the hymn 'Were you there when they crucified my Lord?' This Spiritual is no question expecting the answer yes or no, but a demand upon one's emotional response to the sense of the events listed in that song.

'Ordinary-Time'

One observation of the quality of time related to ritual appears in the Church of England's *Common Worship* book (*CW* 2000). Like its predecessors, the *Book of Common Prayer* (1662) and the *Alternative Service Book* (1980), it contains special prayers for the seasons of the liturgical year; but, unlike its predecessors, it introduces the expression 'Ordinary Time' into certain page headings. To see the notion of 'ordinary time' set into pages of prayers of liturgical time is surprising, and might make for extensive theological debate, since in symbolic and ritual terms this could be identified as a category mistake. Obviously, these liturgical reformers have developed their analysis of time beyond that of their forebears.

'Ordinary time' begins at the end of the season of Epiphany, after Christmas and after The Presentation of Christ in the Temple. It covers the Sundays before Lent and ends at Ash Wednesday, itself described as a Principal Holy Day. Lent passes into Easter and on to Ascension Day and the Day of Pentecost, immediately after which 'Ordinary Time' recommences. The page foot-headings continue in such a way that they even, for example, set Trinity Sunday into 'Ordinary Time', even though it is also described as a Principal Feast. In the *Book of Common Prayer* the many Sundays that followed Trinity Sunday were numbered as the first, second Sunday after Trinity, etc., while in the *Alternative Service Book* a different theological perspective on time described them as Sundays after Pentecost, giving them numbers such as Pentecost 1, Pentecost 2, etc. On the page, such a Sunday was described as, for example, PENTECOST 2 (Trinity 1). It is striking to witness this shift from the seventeenth into the twenty-first century and to see the very notion of ordinariness entering into the liturgical description of time. A few lines of explanation in the text explain only that during, 'Ordinary Time there is no seasonal emphasis' (*CW* 2000:532). A further addition to this service book, set in its Preface, raises the theoretical question of the kind of framework into which the liturgical reformers set the notion of worship and of life itself as expressed in the motif of the 'journey'. The account runs thus: 'Worship is for the whole people of God, who are fellow pilgrims on a journey of faith, and those who attend services are all at different stages of that journey. Indeed, worship itself is a pilgrimage – a journey into the heart and love of God' (*CW* 2000: x).

This emphasized motif of the 'journey' involves an increased person-alizing of 'time', while the reference to different stages of this journey of faith both reflects a certain individualism and mirrors the popularity of stage-theories in several areas of life in the closing decades of the twentieth century, as, for example, in James Fowler's (1981) stages of faith develop-ment and in the stages of grief popularized through Elisabeth Kübler-Ross's work (1973). An appetite for stage theories expresses a cultural preference for individualism over the acceptance of the self as a uniform member of society, family or Church, and could be interpreted in terms of a post-modern framing of duration. There is, philosophically speaking, an ultimate dichotomy between the traditional view of Christianity as a 'plan for the fullness of time' (Eph.1:10) and post-modernity's distaste for any sense of totality, whether in ideology or time.

Millenarian Time

The history of Christianity is marked by periods of religiosity in which believers have held that the world order would soon end through divine intervention. The earliest Christian Church was probably such a com-munity, expectant of the Messianic return, judgement of the world and the construction of a new world order of the Kingdom of God. The Montanists of the second century, the Anabaptists of the Reformation era and numerous groups at the time of the Industrial Revolution all awaited a divine transformation of the world often associated with the Second Advent of Christ. This was the case for Mormonism in the nineteenth century and for the Jehovah's Witnesses in the twentieth.

One resurgence of this view occurred in the closing decades of the twentieth century amongst some Charismatic Christians belonging to a variety of mainstream denominations. The intensity of their religious experience, described in Chapter 5, involved the sense of an imminent divine intervention. As people spoke in tongues, rolled about in laughter and joy or received messages from God there was no question that God was real and active and that such activity presaged yet further outpourings of the Holy Spirit, inaugurating the Second Coming of Christ. The intense ritual forms of Charismatic worship expressed a compression of time, the days of the Acts of the Apostles were here again, the past was present and the future was not far ahead. Against that kind of spirituality the ongoingness of a liturgical calendar pales into insignificance.

Imperial Time of the Kingdom of God

Most Christian Churches adhere, formally, to eschatological doctrines, the doctrines of the 'last things' involving the return of Christ, the divine judgement and the life of heaven. Some emphasize the renewal of the earth, while others posit more 'otherworldly' dimensions of eternal life. For all practical purposes, however, this eschatology is not imminent, and most believers hardly ever give it much thought. More germane is the idea of the spread of the kingdom of God on earth, a practical vision fostered by the Holy Roman Empire, established by Charlemagne in 800 and lasting for a thousand years until, to all intents and purposes, Napoleon brought it to a close in 1806. The Reformation had, of course, intruded and created numerous independent princely states that, in time, led to the rise of missionary societies. These, while belonging to influential political authorities, produced a new form of concern to spread the Christian message throughout the world. Not only were these the very first 'examples of modern mass organisations, run by a professional staff, using and developing modern techniques of advertising and fund-raising', but they also marked the emergence of a new and distinctive form of Christianity as a 'world-wide community of believers, apart from the daily social world of existing political, social and ecclesiastical structures of authority' (van Rooden 1996:65–88). This outlook is one in which time becomes 'slower' and less intense than in millenarian groups. More attention is given to organization and long-term planning, with care given to a slower transformation of pre-existing cultures into those with a Christian ethos and ethic. And the practice of liturgical time enhances this perspective. Still, inherent within many missionary endeavours is the notion of conversion, and, in the more evangelical forms of Protestantism, this conversion is expected to involve an emotional shift associated with a new-birth and with a sense of life as possessing a 'before' and 'after'. That very personal experience of change, often ritualized in baptism or in testimony meetings, reinforces the idea that change in the world itself is possible, because change within the individual has manifestly occurred. A sense of regeneration of life mirrors a belief in a change in the quality of the time framing the world.

Mystical and Existential Faith

Another kind of transvaluation of time occurs in forms of mystical experience that confer a sense of unity of the self with all that is and of the timelessness of that experience. Aspects of existentialist religious faith also reflect this perspective, as the individual's conscious awareness of self does not engage with historical eras. Nicolas Berdyaev, writing from his own distinctive position within Russian Orthodoxy, affirmed the present as a time of spiritual awareness combining a desire to disintegrate the distinctions between past, present and future so as to live in an 'eternal and integral present' while, at the same time, holding a notion of the future Coming of Christ as the 'irruption within the relations of terrestrial phenomena of the celestial noumenon' (1936:198).

One of the clearest examples of ritual in relation to a privatized sense of faith and of time emerged in the mid-1970s British practice of bereaved people placing the cremated remains of their dead in sites of private significance, quite outside the liturgical rites of the Churches. This can be interpreted as a transition from the traditional eschatological fulfilment of Christian identity to a retrospective fulfilment of the identity of the dead through a place of intimate significance shared with the living (Davies 1997:31,188).

Another ritual dimension of funerals also raises the issue of time, and involves the desire of increasing numbers of people in Britain to be buried through what are sometimes called 'green funerals' or 'woodland burials'. The body is interred in a field with a tree buried over the grave, or else in small clearings in more established woodlands. Such rituals directly aligned with 'nature' shift the theological emphasis from salvation-history to the salvation of self in personal fulfilment and the salvation of nature, as in 'saving' natural species or the ozone layer. The ritual context of nature is somewhere where 'eternity' as a secular transcendence can be encountered; where the verbosity of post-modernity is rendered redundant and ritual achieves its pragmatic goal.

A similar symbolic association with nature occurs in New Age groups. Largely outside established Churches, these seek a sense of identity in relation to the natural world, and through rituals of an individual or small-group sort in which the body and its senses play a dominant role. The use of aromatherapy, of massage and of body manipulation, as well as of crystals or the reading of the power auras surrounding bodies, all express a focused interest on the self and its state of embodiment. Time ceases to be of concern, apart perhaps from the mythical conception of the Age of Aquarius in which we now live, as interest focuses on embodied consciousness.

Human Competence

We come finally to a more controversially technical aspect of symbolism that adds another dimension to the contemporary debate and paves the way for the final chapter. It concerns the acquisition of the symbolic knowledge utilized in ritual.

A few references have already been made to cognitive anthropology, or to what is sometimes called 'ethnoscience'. This concerns psychological aspects of human development and thought processes, and is likely to be increasingly fruitful for anthropology and theology. Some of this work already suggests that, for example, there is a great similarity between children in different cultures not only in the way they rapidly acquire language but also in the way they acquire a sense of the difference between living and non-living things. They are also able to classify animate and non-animate elements of the environment early in life in ways that suggest this to be a basic human competence grounded in innate dispositions, and not something that has to be 'forced' into them by extensive education. There are things that need such extensive education and training, and it is possible to distinguish between phenomena that belong to the 'core' and to the 'periphery' of human knowing (Atran 1993:48–96). The application of this approach to religion remains a potentially fruitful area for study. The crucial question is whether what we broadly call 'religious ideas' are instinctive and given, so that children accept that there is an unseen domain without having been taught about it. While this would not afford an argument for the existence of God, it would raise a discussion about the nature of what is easily reckoned to 'be there'. If that is the case we would need to consider the relationship between that given aptitude of perception and its subsequent cultivation, just as language is an aptitude, though children can still have their linguistic skills educated to a marked extent. Is this the case with religion? Another issue concerns the human capacity to think about thinking, to create meta-representations. Scott Atran, for example, talks of symbolism as drawing people 'ever deeper into unfathomable mysteries by pointedly outraging everyday experience', with the goal not of 'resolving phenomenal paradoxes' but of aiming 'at eternal truth' (1993:62). This echoes the last chapter's reflection on some kinds of conversion as a challenge to ordinariness and as an exploration of alternative views of the world. If there is a distinction to be made over core and peripheral phenomena in religion, and I suspect there may well be, the core element will be grounded in the acceptance of an 'otherness', much as we have explored in Chapter 2, and the periphery will involve the formal education that constitutes myth and theology. If we take seriously the interest that some cognitive anthropologists have in the distinction between personal or animate and inanimate phenomena in the process of human response to the world it may well be that 'core' religiosity shares in this perception of a 'personal' world. One wonders, even, whether this might not offer a clear connection with the earliest of interests in the anthropology of religion, namely, in Tylor's exploration of animism or Lévy-Bruhl's reflections on 'participation'. Another issue, that divide found by some people to exist between faith and theology, could then be described, if not actually explained, in terms of the distinction between the core and untaught perceptions of faith and the peripheral structures of theology. Such a distinction would also echo rather loudly Bloch's distinction between logico-sentiential and clustered forms of analysis of human experience explained in Chapter 2. It would also relate in a rather fundamental though indirect way to that distinction between 'alienable' and 'inalienable gifts' raised in Chapter 1, to which we now turn in greater detail in the closing chapter.

–8–

Gift and Charismata

To our conversation between anthropology and theology this final chapter brings the voices of Maurice Godelier and George Lindbeck, the former concluding our earlier considerations of gifts, merit and grace, and the latter providing a constructive theological framework grounded in an appreciation of the cultural base of knowledge.

The Inalienable Gift

Godelier's fundamentally anthropological account of gift-giving and human identity makes a valuable contribution to theological considerations of relationship with the divine. Though it is ultimately inextricable from our discussion of reciprocity in Chapter 3, Godelier's major contribution has been retained until now to emphasize the key distinction between things that are 'alienable' and explicitly 'given' through reciprocal acts and 'inalienable' things that can never be 'given' in exchange. These inalienable phenomena dominate Godelier's interpretation of Mauss, making it invaluable for theological use. By developing Mauss's notion of the 'fourth obligation', the obligation to give to the gods, rather than the first three obligations, to give, to receive, and to give in return, that pertain to human realms, Godelier shows how inalienable things serve as an 'anchorage in time', relating people to their past and to their origin, as they 'concentrate the greatest imaginary power and, as a consequence, the greatest symbolic value' (1999:32–3). Accordingly, while contractual exchange and non-contractual transmission make up the undercurrent of social life, it is the inalienable elements that help 'constitute an essential part' of the identity of specific groups (1999:120). They are as inalienable as the group's identity is inalienable, and to sell them would be tantamount to selling one's birthright in the most literal of senses.

One criticism that could be made of Godelier and Mauss is that they create too sharp a distinction between reciprocity amongst humans and between humans and the gods (Boyer 1994:32). Partly for this reason, my own discussion in Chapter 3 assumed that both Mauss's threefold and his fourth obligations may apply to religious realms. By so doing it was possible to show aspects of the inappropriateness of gift-discourse to analyses of grace. Now we can develop a model allowing for a more complex understanding of 'gift-language' within Christian soteriology, one that also brings added depth to the ritual of eucharistic liturgy. The heart of the matter is that Christ needs to be interpreted in terms of Godelier's inalienable gift, that can be 'given without really being "alienated" by the giver' (1999:37). Part of the giver is retained in the 'gift', and the giver retains some rights over it. Here Godelier's inalienable gift bears strong resemblance to St Paul's 'inexpressible gift' (II Cor. 9:15). Godelier does, albeit only in passing, refer to Christ's gift of his life for the forgiveness of sin as 'the supreme example of the absolutely free gift freely given', and sees it as one reason why gifts between friends remains important in Western society (1999:145). But here I suspect that Godelier does not fully appreciate the theological complexity of Christ 'as gift' in terms of the overall relationship between God as 'Father' and believers at large. To see Christ as God's gift in which the divine retains an interest, yet which alters the state of the recipient, is, precisely, to see him in terms of the inalienable gift, one that enhances the notion of grace as a quality of relationship and not as some kind of commodity that has been passed from one to another, even if spontaneously, or that needs repayment through 'faith' or 'good works'. But, in fact, Godelier's overall theory allows us to press this interpretation further than he does himself, and further than our earlier analysis in Chapter 3, which was restricted to Mauss's threefoldness of reciprocity without progressing to his 'fourth obligation', that of giving to the divine.

Before taking that final step it is worth recalling Georg Simmel's brief theoretical suggestions that presaged Mauss's division of gifts and Berger's insight into self-abnegation and masochism, discussed in Chapter 2, and the process of higher-order 'framing' of Chapter 6. Simmel's condensed style integrated these issues without spelling them out in any real sense. He speaks of a passing into the 'transcendental dimension' of certain elements basic to ordinary social relationships, especially the desire for 'surrender or acceptance', and it is this core that he reckons underlies the phenomenon of sacrifice (1997:158). Rhetorically, he asks whether this relationship between gods and their devotees is a 'metaphysical extension of the economic exchange of value and equivalent value? Rejecting that possibility, he suggests that it might 'derive from the spiritual significance that all giving has and which goes beyond the actual value of the gift'. This brings him to speak of an 'inner bond' that 'cannot be cancelled by returning something of the same outward value', and identifies 'the sociological relationship of giving and receiving' as being moulded by a general sense of religiousness into a transcendent phenomenon' (1997:159). Here Simmel explores what would become the broad duality of gifts in Mauss, elaborated in Godelier. First come things pertaining to economic exchange of known value, things that Mauss would have within his threefold obligation, and then phenomena involving the 'inner bond' that cannot be cancelled and in which is 'inherent . . . a sense of favour and goodwill', a clear expression of Mauss's fourth obligation (ibid.). It is sufficient to indicate this trend of thought in Simmel to show how economic models appeal to sociological minds, as they did to Weber, and yet hint at crucial constraints when they pass into relation with the divine.

Unlike Simmel, for whom the immediacy of encounter with deity furnished the very source of human creativity, Godelier defines the sacred as 'a certain kind of relationship with the origin' of a particular people (1999:169). He also prefers this approach to the sacred than to Durkheim's rather sharp distinction between the sacred and the profane as expressing the divide between the religious and the political. In this I think he is correct. Godelier then suggests that in societies where 'the bulk of social relationships take the form of personal relationships' a view of the world emerges in which 'things are also persons' generating a kind of 'enchanted' world (1999:105). Indeed, he coins the word 'thing-persons', or sometimes 'person-things', to cope with this phenomenon (1999:106, 69). This powerful analysis could benefit from the cognitive anthropologists' argument that human development in childhood involves an intuitive sense of the difference between animate things and artefacts. Pascal Boyer, for example, outlined three aspects of religious symbolism and its acquisition that are germane to this argument, its implicitness in being acquired rather than formally taught, the intrinsic vagueness and inconsistency of religious language, and the 'under-determined' nature of religious symbolism, which leaves much to the individual's 'intuitive heuristics' in arriving at a grasp of what is going on in the 'domain' of religious symbolism (Boyer 1993a: 34ff.; 1993b, 139–40).

This means that individuals know intuitively that a supernatural realm 'exists', and when people talk about it in a 'bits and pieces' fashion they are able to assemble those elements in a way that makes sense to them. The particularly informative speculation within this contribution of cognitive anthropology is the idea that the 'domain' of religiosity has to do with the perception of a 'personal' world. Without being taught that God is personal, people 'know' it. Problems emerge when explicit education includes knowledge that appears to be counter-intuitive, perhaps in notions such as that of the Holy Trinity or of the Buddhist notion of a non-enduring self. There is also a serious issue of method involved here, since it has generally been the philosophers of religion who have defined 'the idea of the holy', and cognitive psychology might indicate the inappropriateness of their form of logical consideration. This perspective also runs counter to a great deal of social learning theory, espoused in anthropology, which assumes that people learn all they know, and know it in culturally particular ways. Here, some might see theological pos-sibilities of another argument for the existence of God after the fashion of John Bowker's 'cues of meaning' (1973:45) or Peter Berger's 'signals of transcendence' (1971:75). My reason for including this discussion of the intuitive grasp of 'pseudo-natural kinds' is to indicate a possible theoretical way of interpreting Godelier's category of 'things as persons', for, if there is some truth in this intuitiveness of viewing the world, it would emphasize the importance of different kinds of 'gifts', and might add to the significant distinction between 'inalienable' and 'alienable' gifts.

Certainly, Christianity is typified by periods of intense personal relationships. From its birth in the disciple-group of Jesus and the subsequent expanded community described in the *Acts of the Apostles*, to many forms of religious communities, including the intense life of Charismatic and other Christian communities of the present, we witness a strong community organization and ethos. Sometimes this extends to a negative personification the world in terms of evil spirits; but, more positively, it embraces the world not as inert but as living, as in the ancient Jewish text and subsequent Christian hymn, the *Benedicite*. This offers an example in which all aspects of the universe, from sun and moon through to seasonal aspects of winter and snow, are called upon to bless the Lord and praise Him for ever. Within such a cosmic view gifts become increasingly dynamic, and forms of gift-giving easily become sacrificial. The Christian theology of creation ascribes a status to all things that have been created, bringing them into a distinctive mutual relationship with each other. This does not make it absurd for the *Benedicite* to exhort 'fire and hail' to praise the Lord. But neither does it become absurd for believers to consider themselves involved in forms of sacrifice and self-sacrifice, as things or circumstances are transformed into sacrificial gifts.

Inalienable Charismata?

There is, however, a paradox in all this: for Godelier implies that in societies where many relationships are impersonal, guided by market economies where money serves as the impersonal medium of transaction, the world ceases to be so enchanted. While this continues Max Weber's notion of the disenchantment of the world in an industrialized context, its very accuracy demands to be carried into post-industrial contexts. When the majority of people pass from being industrial operatives to service providers, we may expect their symbolic language of exchange and relationships to change. This is already a well-established process in most Western societies, and led me, some time ago, to argue that contemporary Charismatic movements exemplified the relational intimacy of service society rather than the formal mentality of industrial societies (Davies 1984c). This leads to the question, for example, of whether charismatic gifts belong to the alienable or inalienable form? As it happens, the New Testament furnishes an example that throws light on the subject.

In the *Acts of the Apostles* Simon, a former magician of Samaria, is converted and is amazed at the miracles performed by Philip. Shortly afterwards, the Apostles Peter and John arrive at Samaria and, through them, the believers there receive the Holy Spirit as a further development of their identity as already baptized people. When Simon sees that 'the Spirit was given through the laying on of hands' he offers the Apostles money so that he too could may pass on the Spirit when he lays hands on people. To this Peter replies, 'Your silver perish with you, because you thought you could obtain the gift of God with money' (Acts 8:20). The poor man is called upon to repent, and seems to have done so, adding to the English language in the process the very term 'simony'. The dramatic impact of this story shows that the Holy Spirit is not a commodity to be purchased. This episode marks a minor yet significant theme running through the *Acts* that seeks to establish the difference between money exchanges between human beings and the relationships inherent within the scheme of divine gift-giving, human reception and human response – whether to God in thanksgiving or in generosity towards fellow believers through the provision of alms. The theme emerges early in *Acts*, in Chapter 2, with the account of the day of Pentecost and the conferring of the archetypal divine gift of the Holy Spirit manifested in the 'gift' of speaking in tongues. The gifted believers are said to have sold their possessions, distributed to all as each had need, shared food in each other's homes and praised God (Acts 2:45–47). At the beginning of Chapter 3 Peter and John, the key Apostles at this point of the narrative, go up to the temple to pray, encounter a cripple who asks them for alms. Peter calls the man to pay attention to them and then addresses him, 'Silver and gold I have none, but what I have I give you; in the name of Jesus Christ of Nazareth, walk'. The man stands, walks, then leaps into the temple giving praise to God (Acts 3:1–10). Two chapters later there appears the story of the deceit of Ananias and Sapphira. Although we alluded to this earlier in terms of ritual purity and the Spirit its significance here falls squarely on the theme of money and gift. The couple are amongst those who sell their property to give to the needy but they only part with a portion of the proceeds under pretence that it is the full amount. Peter addresses Ananias in respect of his deceit, as one who had lied 'to the Holy Spirit' (Acts 5:3).

The 'gift' of the Holy Spirit in these cases is an example of Godelier's 'inalienable gift'. It comes from the donor, but is never separated from the donor. God is its source and remains its ultimate referent. The recipient is caught up into the intention of the donor, and must act with a similar intent. The gift is the very vehicle of and for divine power and, in theological terms, of grace. Accordingly, it must be held sincerely by the recipient, who, in turn, can share it by 'passing' it on to others; but it can never be sold for money, just as money can have no part in determining the characteristic feature of the community of grace. This, perhaps, is why Paul, the major protagonist of the latter part of the *Acts of the Apostles*, makes it clear that he had never coveted anyone's money, but had worked with his own hands to sustain his ministry, always, as he put it, 'remembering the words of the Lord Jesus, how he said that 'it is more blessed to give than to receive' (Acts 20:35). Even in the closing verses of the *Acts* it is recorded that Paul lived in Rome for two whole years 'at his own expense' preaching the kingdom of God (Acts 28:30). These monetary references are often ignored in biblical scholarship, but are powerful symbolic markers of the relational community founded on grace.

Eucharistic Inalienability

It is within the Eucharist that the absolute inalienability of the divine gift becomes apparent. Both its theology and its liturgy emphasize the contemporary 'power of the Spirit' in letting the bread and wine 'become for us' the body and blood of Christ. These material elements, transformed and received as a divine gift, become part of the recipient, with the consecrated bread or host being a quintessential example of Godelier's 'person-thing', an entity that is both familiar and unfamiliar and echoes our argument in Chapter 2 on the elective affinity between one's own sense of embodiment and the embodiment of the divine gift in Christ. The very 'mystery' of the sacred mysteries – as the Eucharist has been traditionally described – lies in the fact that believers know the very ideas at the heart of their grasp of the meaning of life to be enshrined within the phenomena of the rite. These mystery-meanings are not spelled out propositionally, but are encountered symbolically, and it is in that way that the Christian community 'reproduces its identity, ensures its continuity', and 'maintains a constant connection *with its origins'* through 'its gestures and ceremonies' (Godelier 1999:169, original stress).

Complementing the theme of the ritual generation of time introduced in Chapter 7, the eucharistic liturgy becomes the prime context within which the inalienable gift is given and received. The fact that we may speak of certain types of ritual as occurring 'out of time' makes perfect sense in this context, because we might argue that 'inalienable' gifts, themselves, belong 'out of time'. Ordinary processes of reciprocity take place in time, because it 'takes time' for acts of giving, receiving and giving again to take place. The Eucharist is 'timeless' in the sense that it is a true symbol of its originating events and participates in the Last Supper and sacrifice of Christ. And this is also the case as far as the negative dimension of the Eucharist is concerned, in terms of the question of sin. Having, in Chapter 2, briefly mentioned sin as a negative moral commodity that parallels merit, I can now suggest that there is a sense in which sin can also be analysed in terms of alienable and inalienable factors. The alienable aspects of sin are those accumulated through individual behaviour in the normal process of life. These sins take time to emerge. But, at the heart of most Christian theology, there is another way of speaking about sin, enshrined in the technical term Original Sin. Original Sin is interpreted as a tendency to evil that is the common lot of humanity due to the original sin of Adam and Eve in the biblical myth of creation. Whether expressed in a biblical literalism of inheriting sin from our 'fallen' parents or interpreted existentially as the flawed domain of the human condition, sin remains problematic. And it is this 'givenness' of sin that constitutes its inalienable variety. Original Sin is 'inalienable' sin and, as such, is also timeless. This is why it makes perfect sense for Christians to 'confess' their propensity to sin itself, let alone to confess their actual sins committed 'in time'.

In terms of symbolic analysis it is this 'inalienable' aspect of sin that comes to be related to the 'inalienable' domain of grace. For grace is not the result of accumulated merit. Unlike our emphasis upon the accumulated merit that makes up the treasury of merit of the Catholic Church explored in Chapter 3, we now need to assert that grace is not to be equated with that endless depth of accumulated goodness. This was expressed in Chapter 3 when using the simple model of reciprocity to argue that the processes of making merit and the reception of grace belonged to different categories. We intimated then that the notion of grace in God was of the same category of phenomenon as faith in humanity: grace and faith are mirror images. These distinctions now become even more apparent, for merit and 'works' can be seen to belong to the category of alienable gifts, while grace lies with the inalienable. It is the possession of the inalienable gift that confers Christian identity, that grounds it in the historical and mythical accounts of the life, death and resurrection of Jesus, and sets the believer in a position to pass it on, but in doing so to pass on that from which one can never be parted. Here tradition and commerce part company. Here, too, it would also be possible to extend Robert Hertz's slightly similar distinction between sin as an offence against God and crime as an offence against society (cf. Parkin 1996:131).

Our immediate purpose, however, takes a different direction, to suggest that a telling theoretical alignment may be made between Godelier's notion of inalienability and Bloch's rebounding conquest. Each deals with a sense of power that adds something to human ordinariness; each is related to transcendence. In Christian theology this is the meaning of grace. What is interesting about the history of Christian spirituality is the way in which that 'grace' can be used to frame charismatic gifts on the one hand and eucharistic gifts on the other; and, with time, circumstance and fashion, it becomes possible for the balance of emphasis to shift from one to the other. Yet underlying each is the sense that divinely sourced benefit comes to human beings and is not generated by them.

Human Divinity

For Bloch the sense of transcendence comes through contact with supernatural powers, which he is content simply to describe. Godelier, however, presses the dynamics of the supernatural further to explore that certain something that 'comes to' human beings. This, he acknowledges, is thought by people at large to be divine, but is identified by the social scientist as derivative from society itself. This, of course, is the classic expression of that process of human projection that lies hidden from its very authors, a fact of life that, in the modern era, reaches from the philosophical Feuerbach through the psychological Freud and the sociologists of knowledge to Godelier's description of the gods as the 'duplicate selves' of human beings, divine selves that 'individuals are not conscious of projecting and reifyng . . . [as] . . . part of their own social being' (1999:198, 169). For him, however, this conclusion is not the daunting demystification of Needham's (1972) anthropological exploration of belief and experience, but a celebration of the 'imaginary', of what 'human beings *add* in their minds to their real capacities' (1999:134). Here,

Godelier speaks of 'a considerable social force' present in myths and surrounding those 'person-things', those symbols that reflect human values and purpose and echo the idea of the super-plus of meaning, or that capacity of embodiment for transcendence pursued throughout earlier chapters. Rather like Freud, Godelier's all-embracing theory of alienable and inalienable gifts reaches back to the origin of religions, arguing that religion was the very source of the idea of asymmetrical hierarchies demanding 'both reciprocal obligations and a relationship of obedience situated beyond any possible reciprocity' (1999:194). To highlight this speculation is not to commit oneself to it; indeed, Godelier's interpretation can stand without it.

Underlying all ritual relations with the deity is a 'mental and bodily feeling', an 'attitude . . . of the believer' committed to the belief that there are '"true" gods'. Here we are in the same logical and sociological 'metaphysics' as Durkheim, with his certainty that the one absolute truth is 'society' and our human experience of society, albeit couched in terms of a deity. In terms of the existential consequence of social science we are in an intriguing situation, for while the general projectionist attitude might wish to abandon 'supernatural' religion to live authentically in the knowledge of the human source of religion, Godelier says 'we already "know" we cannot "believe" this, and we must not believe it' (1999:200). This paradoxical tension of consciousness – embracing the contradictory views of projection and revelation – leads into his final chapter, itself highly reminiscent of the closing chapter of James Frazer's *Golden Bough*; in fact, he dwells much on Frazer as he moves to a discussion of contemporary societies and the dominance of the money market within them. Godelier also echoes Mauss's original dismay at the decline of the personal and the rise of the market economy; yet he espouses a degree of cautious optimism in concluding that 'individuals as persons, as corporeal and spiritual singularities, cannot be put on the market as economic agents', despite the fact that even wombs are for hire in surrogate motherhood (1999:205). The ultimate dialectic in Godelier's scheme is between inalienable and alienable processes. For human life to be a successful medium of personhood there needs to be an inalienable base for alienable activities. There must, for example, be trust underlying market exchange. From his own cultural context he cites the political basis of France as a state that is the 'gift that free men and women bestow upon themselves', one in which 'the political sphere has taken the place of religion', yet it is one that can, itself, soon be 'secularised' (1999:207).

Ultimately Godelier's concluding thoughts root around within explicitly theological territory, pondering the nature of human social life and wondering what scope remains for the inalienable. The prime issue is that of reality and appearance. The loss of innocence on his own part, resulting from the knowledge that religion is a human invention, leads to the question of whether all human life now has to be grounded in contracts, in alienable transactions? He wants the answer to be 'no', but can see no obvious way out except that there is an inevitability about the fact that we have to 'produce society in order to live' (1999:210). This is the existential point at which sociological issues become both philosophical and religious, where the conversation between theology and anthropology becomes intimate and the partners decide issues to be either philosophical and ethical on the one hand or theological on the other, depending upon their personal predilections. But it is not stretching the word to say that this may be the point at which the most radical sense can be given to the word 'faith'. In terms of at least one strain of Christian theology, faith belongs to a group of ideas all bearing a strong family resemblance to each other, and including trust, hope and love, all typified by the property of being inalienable and not alienable. Neither trust, hope nor love can be bought; yet they combine in varying ways to provide the basis for many a market situation in which purchase is of the essence. What is more, these features belong to embodied lives grounded in commitment or, in Godelier's terms, to 'corporeal and spiritual singularities'. From a Christian theological perspective such embodiment is a venture in the kind of faith that is not grounded in certainties. This 'faith', when it is Christian, involves the symbol of Jesus as the Christ, the inalienable focus of identity for the individual and for the community within which belief becomes 'faith'. These issues of communal meaning-generation and identity-formation bring us directly to one of the few recent theologians to have taken the cultural nature of Christianity, seriously, George Lindbeck .

Knowing Action

Lindbeck's *The Nature of Doctrine* (1984) offers a sketched theory of both religion in general and Christianity in particular. Drawing upon several perspectives related to ideas on embodiment discussed earlier in this book, he affords a good example of dialogue between theology and the social sciences. He invokes Weber, Durkheim and Berger, and often refers to Geertz and the broad anthropological tradition of symbolic interpretation of social action to construct what he calls a cultural–linguistic theory of religion. This he differentiates from the pre-liberal propositionalist or propositionalist–cognitive scheme on the one hand and the experiential–expressionist on the other. The pre-liberal propositionalist resembles science or philosophy in making explicit truth claims about objective realities, and includes the type of theologian who uses biblical texts as clear statements of the truth (1984: 24, 36). The experiential–expressionist, by contrast, sees religion as the outward manifestation of a prior inner experience, with Schleiermacher and Rudolph Otto as prime sources in the philosophy of religion and Mircea Eliade for the history of religions. Theologically, he sees Rahner and Lonergan, to a degree at least, as upholding the same position (1984:32). He also argues, to some extent justifiably, that this expressionist view has been influential in cultural anthropology, in which forms of social organization, symbol and ritual are seen as an expression of an underlying cultural entity. In fact my own discussion in Chapter 2 of the way in which *gestus* is a manifestation of *habitus* could be described – and criticized – in these terms. He sees this position as well placed to interpret individual quests for meaning in contemporary life and as fitting well the need of academic markets in the study of religion, not to mention the more specifically religious domain of interfaith dialogue.

But all this experiential–expressivism will not do for Lindbeck, for whom religion is not some outworking of an inner experience. His cultural-linguistic perspective prefers to see religion as a kind of language, one that provides the opportunity for certain kinds of experience and not for others. In what can be taken as his definition of religion 'a religion can be viewed as a kind of cultural and/or linguistic framework or medium that shapes the entirety of life and thought' (1984:33). Religion is 'similar to an idiom that makes possible the description of realities, the formulation of beliefs and the experiencing of inner attitudes, feelings and sentiments. Like a culture or language, it is a communal phenomenon that shapes the subjectivities of individuals rather than being primarily an expression of those subjectivities' (idem). All this involves rituals and institutional forms, and performance is of the essence, indeed 'credibility comes from good performance' (1984:131). Here Lindbeck echoes the discussion of embodiment that runs through this book, as when he speaks of the 'interiorized skill, the skill of the saint' as the operating basis of Christianity (1984:36). So it is that 'just as an individual becomes human by learning a language, so he or she begins to be a new creature through hearing and interiorizing the language that speaks of Christ' (1984:62). He sees theological advantage as accruing from the comparison of religion and language, in that languages and their cultural base are relative in time and space and do not make unique truth claims: they also tend to focus on this-worldly ventures rather than defining themselves as transcendental (1984:23).

Another specific theological benefit for Lindbeck is that he can render redundant the Roman Catholic idea of anonymous Christianity, held by some since Vatican II. 'The notion of an anonymous Christianity present in the depths of other religions is . . . a nonsense, and a theory of the salvation of non-Christians built upon it seems thoroughly unreal' (1984:62). Still, he holds that there may be advantages in some languages, as in some religions, that furnish opportunities for experience and understanding that would otherwise not be available. To a qualified extent I agree with Lindbeck's view of religions as cultural linguistic processes within which individuals come to a sense of themselves and their world, though his scheme shows the marks of too keen a desire to avoid the cultural–expressive approach, which is not, I think, entirely separable. Lindbeck has his theological reasons for establishing a categorical divide between his and the expressivist position; but they are redundant as far as our reflections are concerned. In practical terms the complex inter-relation of cognitive development of thought with affective factors in the development of individual and group identity through embodiment cannot be too sharply isolated and ascribed to prior or learned sources.

Lindbeck's view of religion, useful as far as it goes, leaves untouched the dynamics of transcendence. In the terms of this book, there is nothing of conquest about it. It is all too apparent that in seeking to distance himself from both traditional dogmatic theology and liberal experiential–expressivism he remains too firmly wed to the cognitive mode of philosophical theology to break through into the real power of embodied performance. To justify the comparison between a religion and a language he would need either to identify a phenomenon within language that served to deny language and to replace it with a higher-order utterance or to describe how some aspect of language turned upon itself to yield a transcending insight. One might, perhaps, relate the idea of revelation to that of poetry or to that literature that 'comes to' an author, that 'dawns' upon the creative mind and transforms a view of the world. The creative power of language, the 'imaginary' power of Godelier, uses language to transcend itself. It is no accident that the prophetic word, the mystical word of the mantra or the confounding word-formula of the *koan* should be vehicles of personal and social change.

Loosely, we might simply invoke the notion of 'poetry' as exemplifying the rebounding conquest of language. Fancifully, perhaps, we might describe the poet as taking non-poetic language, languishing within it and, under the compelling constraints of the 'supernatural' poetic imagination, finally producing the line that kills and makes alive. Here 'poetry' expresses ideas that engage the mind and heart of the embodied self and evokes a sense of commitment to acting and to living. It sees the 'truth' of a stanza in its power to express how it feels to live, to relate to others, and to be free. And it will not do for the conservative critic to attempt to marginalize this vision of faith as mere idealism, romanticism or wishful thinking. For poets knows they speak the truth of life, albeit in a few words – words that others hear in such a way as to make them weep because someone else has also seen the same vision, felt the same agony or joy.

It is this power of poetic piety that really fires the fundamentalists who, beside their beloved doctrines of Papal or Biblical Infallibility, find the evocative truth of God emerging in Christ, whether in the uplifted host or the preached 'word'. Defence of conservative doctrines is often defence of the invisible house wherein poetry is known, loved and embraced. Their secret lies in the fact that the 'word' is heard in a ritual context, the ear existing not alone, embodied amidst complementary organs that conspire together in the joy of hearing.

Why anyone should believe will ever remain a variable of the individual; how they believe will, as Lindbeck rightly argues, ever involve culturally available symbols; but that a person may believe is an attribute of the human condition. The leap of faith remains a leap, because it involves that transcending of embodiment that we have spent much of this book exploring. In that act the human being becomes more of itself, and the wonder of this is not diminished by a knowledge that it is the case. A poem's mystery is not lost because we know it is written in words. This is precisely the point at which the word 'mystery' is not to be invoked as a timely theological escape from a narrow squeeze, but as a statement of the property of human beings. The religious life can be seen to be, can be felt and thought to be, a mysterious dwelling. Each religious tradition engages with this and announces it in its own way. Karl Barth, from quite a different theological style than Lindbeck, did just this in his epoch-making *Epistle to the Romans*, published at the close of the First World War. I invoke it here because it is a prime example of a style of Christian theological writing that uses language to transcend language. In the Protestant tradition of which it is a prime example it announces that God addresses humanity through the word of the scriptures, which, themselves, attest to the 'word' that is Jesus, the Christ and the Son of God. It is prophetic prose. It preaches as it reads. This commentary on *Romans*, itself perhaps the most influential of all scriptures upon the prophetic tradition of Christianity, is one of the best examples of the transcendence effected by faith, and can be read as documenting the process of rebounding vitality as the divine word takes its toll of human inadequacy and transforms it. In the person of Jesus the old man is conquered and the new man emerges. 'He is the invisible new man in God. He is the end of the old man as such, for he has put behind Him death and the whole relativity of historical and time-enveloped things . . . The new life cannot be extinguished and revoked' (1968:205).

Such literature can convert the reader. It exemplifies the literary genre of rebounding conquest. As for belief and its effects, some are given to it and some are not, just as not all love poetry or music. Just how or whether inspired literature may free potential believers from 'the traditions of men' to a life of uncertain 'faith' inspired by the poetic word and its performance remains an open question. Certainly it is a matter at the heart of religions at large, and not least of Christianity, as one final example will demonstrate.

Rebounding Conquest and Imago Christi

Throughout this book, we have used the rebounding conquest theme to interpret embodiment, and now, in conclusion, we offer an example of its use for glossing but one biblical text of St Paul (II Cor. 5:14–21). Here Paul argues that the love of Christ controls believers, who are convinced that, because Christ has died for all, all may be said both to have 'died' and now to live, not for themselves but for Christ. This prompts him to speak of his own transformed vision, in which he can no longer regard anyone from a human point of view. Having undergone his own change of mind on the identity of Jesus – whom once he regarded 'from a human' point of view – he now finds it inevitable that his view of the identity of ordinary men and women must also change. Indeed, he speaks of a new creation brought about by God through an act of reconciliation in Christ – an act that now passes over into the ministry of Christian leaders as 'ambassadors for Christ'. It is as such an ambassador that he appeals to others to be reconciled and to enter that new order of reality. The essentially self-centred or self-originating image of self gives way to an image expressed in the self-sacrificed Son of God. This involves a changed motivation and basis for action. The human sense of embodiment is deified as a result of the belief that the divine Word had been humanized. Men and women come to mean more and to have a higher value because of the belief that God has valued mankind through the Incarnation. There is, here, a form of exchange of attributes emerging as the result of God's reconciliation. The worthwhileness of individuals is seen as grounded in the worth of Jesus of Nazareth as the Christ of God. This leads to the strong ethical call to live for others, because 'the love of Christ controls us'.

This densely packed text clearly reflects the process of rebounding conquest. His old world-view is transformed through a symbolic death that participates in the actual death of Christ. Through that death, as a medium of contact with the supernatural power of God, Paul's new world-view emerged. His eyes are the eyes of one who has been conquered – though the theological language used is the language of reconciliation – and who now sets out to conquer that old, worldly and human view of things that once held his own gaze. Having come to see Jesus as the Christ, the human as the divinely appointed one, he can no longer see ordinary humans 'from a human point of view'. In seeking their conversion into this new creation he exemplifies the conquered conquering.

Concluding Pause

This picture of transcendence is entirely inspiring. It reflects the high optimism of faith, and embraces an ethic of relationships and communal support validated by nothing less than the divine source of all. It is a picture of intense communality not far removed from Robertson Smith's joyous sacrificial community of Chapter 2. Against this it would be easy to offset any number of post-modern images of fragmented individualism, talking of a shift from the religious to the secular as the shift from community to individualism. In her deeply humane essay on 'Rites of Passage' Barbara Myerhoff addressed the question of loneliness and isolation as the 'other side of freedom' and advocated a commitment to taking 'matters into our own hands' in 'furnishing meaning' and being 'attentive to the needs of the soul' (1982:132). These are ongoing ventures whose importance only grows by the year. They can never be concluded and, indicative of that, there can be no 'conclusion' to this little book.

I have sought a series of topics of conversation between anthropology and theology and, although the direction of flow has been more from the anthropological side, this has only been because it is sometimes good to take the words out of people's mouths to make our own argument. Many ideas have simply been raised or only partially explored, and no apology is made for that. In the present state of knowledge the venture of furnishing meaning and of being attentive to our very existence, with simplicity but without naiveté, demands that anthropologists and theologians acknowledge that they have much to ponder as the conversation continues.

Bibliography

Aberbach, David (1989), *Surviving Trauma: Loss, Literature and Psycho-analysis*, New Haven, CT and London: Yale University Press.

Aberbach, David (1996), *Charisma in Politics, Religion and the Media, Private Trauma, Public Ideals*, London: Macmillan.

Akinnaso, F. Niyi (1995), 'Bourdieu and the Diviner, Knowledge and Symbolic Power in Yoruba Divination', in *The Pursuit of Certainty*, ed. Wendy James, London: Routledge.

Aquili, E. G. d' and C. D. Laughlin Jr. and J. McManus (1979), *The Spectrum of Ritual*, NY: Columbia University Press.

Archer, Leonie J. (1990), 'Bound by Blood: Circumcision and Menstrual Taboo in Post-exilic Judaism', in Janet Martin Soskice ed., *After Eve: Women, Theology and the Christian Tradition*, London: Marshall-Collins.

Aristotle (1963), *Ethics*, ed. and trans. John Warrington, London: Dent, Everyman's Library.

Asad, Talal (1988), 'Towards a Genealogy of the Concept of Ritual', in Wendy James and Douglas Johnson eds, *Vernacular Christianity*, Oxford: JASO.

Asad, Talal (1993), *Genealogies of Religion: Discipline and Reasons of Power in Christianity and Islam*, Baltimore, MD and London: The John Hopkins University Press.

ASB (Alternative Service Book) (1980), London: SPCK and Cambridge: Cambridge University Press.

Atkins, Robert A. (1991), *Egalitarian Community, Ethnography and Exegesis*, Tuscaloosa, AL and London: The University of Alabama Press.

Atran, Scott (1993), 'Whither "Ethnoscience"?' *Cognitive Aspects of Religious Symbolism*, ed. Pascal Boyer, Cambridge: Cambridge University Press

Augustine (1945), *The City of God*, London: J. M. Dent.

Aune, Michael B. (1996), 'The Subject of Ritual', in *Religious and Social Ritual*, eds. Michael B. Aune and Valerie DeMarinis, Albany, NY: State University of NY Press.

Bibliography

Austin, J. L. (1961), *Philosophical Papers,* Oxford: Clarendon Press.

Babb, L. A. (1983), 'The Physiology of Redemption', in *History of Religions*, Vol. 22, No. 4, pp. 93–313.

Baily, John (1977), 'Movement Patterns in Playing the Herati Dutar', *The Anthropology of the Body*, ed. John Blacking, London: Academic Press.

Barker, E. (1944), 'Introduction', *St. Augustine, The City of God*, ed. R. V. G. Tasker, London: J. M. Dent.

Barrett, C. K. (1955), *The Gospel According to St. John*, London: SPCK.

Barth, K. (1956), *Church Dogmatics Vol. IV, The Doctrine of Reconciliation*, ed. G. W. Bromiley and T. F. Torrence, Edinburgh, T. & T. Clark.

Barth, Karl (1968), *The Epistle to the Romans*, London: Oxford University Press.

Barth, Karl (1981), *Ethics*, Edinburgh: T. and T. Clark.

Batson, C. D. and W. L. Ventis (1982), *The Religious Experience*, Oxford: Oxford University Press.

BCC (British Council of Churches) (1986), *Views from the Pews*, London: British Council of Churches.

Bauman, Zygmunt (1995), *Life in Fragments, Essays in Postmodern Morality*, Oxford: Blackwell.

Beattie, John (1980), 'On Understanding Sacrifice', in *Sacrifice*, ed. M. C. F. Bourdillon and Meyer Fortes, London: Academic Press.

Bechtel, Lyn M. (1991), 'Shame as a Sanction of Social Control in Biblical Israel: Judicial, Political and Social Shaming', *Journal for the Study of the Old Testament* No. 49: 47–76.

Bediako, Gillian M. (1997*), Primal Religion and the Bible: William Robertson Smith and His Heritage*, Sheffield: Sheffield Academic Press.

Begbie, Jeremy (2000), *Theology, Music and Time*, Cambridge: Cambridge University Press.

Bell, Catherine (1997), *Ritual Perspectives and Dimensions*, Oxford: Oxford University Press.

Bellah, R. N. (1970), *Beyond Belief*, NY: Harper and Row.

Benesh, Rudolph and Joan Benesh (1977), 'The Benesh Movement Notation' in *The Anthropology of the Body*, ed. John Blacking, London: Academic Press.

Berdyaev, Nicolas (1936), *The Meaning of History,* London: Geoffrey Bles.

Berger, Peter (1969), *The Social Reality of Religion*, Harmondsworth: Penguin Books.

Berger, Peter and Thomas Luckmann (1966), *The Social Construction of Reality*, Harmondsworth: Penguin Books.

Bernstein, Basil (1971), *Class, Codes and Control*, London: Routledge and Kegan Paul.

Bhardwaj, S. H. (1973), *Hindu Places of Pilgrimage in India*, Berkeley, CA: University of California Press.

Binns, C. A. P. (1979–80), 'The Changing Face of Power' *Man, Journal of the Royal Anthropological Institute*, Vol. 14: 585–606; Vol. 15: 170–87.

Blacking, John (1974), *How Musical is Man?* Seattle; WA and London: University of Washington Press.

Blacking, John (ed.) (1977), *The Anthropology of the Body*, London: Academic Press.

Blakeslee, Thomas R. (1980), *The Right Brain: A New Understanding of the Unconscious Mind and its Creative Powers*, London: Macmillan.

Bloch, Maurice (1992a), *Prey into Hunter*, Cambridge: Cambridge University Press.

Bloch, Maurice (1992b), 'What Goes Without Saying: The Conceptualization of Zafimaniry Society', in *Conceptualizing Society*, ed. Adam Kuper, London: Routledge.

Bloch, Maurice and Jonathan Parry (eds) (1982), *Death and the Regeneration of Life*, Cambridge: Cambridge University Press.

Bourdieu, Pierre (1977), *Outline of a Theory of Practice*, Cambridge: Cambridge University Press.

Bourdillon, M. C. F. and Meyer Fortes (1980), *Sacrifice*, London: Academic Press.

Bowie, Fiona (2000), *The Anthropology of Religion*, Oxford: Blackwell.

Bowker, John (1973), *The Sense of God*, Oxford: Oxford University Press.

Bowker, John (1981), *Believing in the Church: Report of the Doctrine Commission of the Church of England,* London: SPCK.

Boyer, Pascal (1993a), 'Cognitive Aspects of Religious Symbolism', in *Cognitive Aspects of Religious Symbolism*, ed. Pascal Boyer, Cambridge: Cambridge University Press.

Boyer, Pascal (1993b), 'Pseudo-natural Kinds', in *Cognitive Aspects of Religious Symbolism*, ed. Pascal Boyer, Cambridge: Cambridge University Press

Boyer, Pascal (1994), *The Naturalness of Religious Ideas, A Cognitive Theory of Religion*, Berkeley, CA: University of California Press.

Brunner, Emil (1937), *The Divine Imperative, A Study in Christian Ethics*, London: Lutterworth.

Brunner, Emil (1939), *Man in Revolt*, London: Lutterworth Press.

Buckley, Thomas and Alma Gottlieb (1988), *Blood Magic, The Anthropology of Menstruation*, Berkeley, CA: The University of California Press.

Bultmann, Rudolph (1971), *The Gospel of John*, Oxford: Basil Blackwell.

Burridge, Kennelm (1969), *New Heaven, New Earth*, Oxford: Blackwell.

Bynum, Caroline Walker (1992), *Fragmentation and Redemption: Essays on Gender and the Human Body in Medieval Religion*, NY: Zone Books.

Campbell, A. (1981), *Rediscovering Pastoral Care*, London: Darton. Longman and Todd.

Carey, S. (1978), 'A Case Study: Face Recognition', in *Explorations in the Biology of Language*, ed. Edward Walker, Sussex: Harvester Press.

Carrithers, M., S. Collins, S. and S. Lukes (1985), *The Category of the Person: Anthropology, Philosophy, History*, Cambridge: Cambridge University Press.

Casey, Maurice (1991), *From Jewish Prophet to Gentile God*, Cambridge: James Clarke.

Catechism of the Catholic Church (1994), London: Geoffrey Chapman.

Chalcraft, David J. (ed.) (1997), *Social-Scientific Old Testament Criticism: A Sheffield Reader*, Sheffield: Sheffield Academic Press.

Chapple, E. D. and C. S. Coon. (1942) *Principles of Anthropology*, NY: Henry Holt and Company.

Chardin, Pierre Teilhard de (1959), *The Phenomenon of Man*, London: William Collins and Co.

Chardin, Pierre Teilhard de (1965), *Hymn of the Universe*, London: William Collins and Co.

Cheal, David (1988), *The Gift Economy*, London: Routledge.

Christian, William A. Jr. (1982), 'Provoked Religious Weeping in Early Modern Spain', in *Religious Organization and Religious Experience*, ed. J. Davis, London, NY: Academic Press.

Cohen, Abner (1977), 'Symbolic Action and the Structure of the Self', in *Symbols and Sentiments*, ed. Ioan Lewis, London: Academic Press.

Cranmer, Thomas (1907), *The True and Catholic Doctrine and Use of the Lord's Supper*, London: C. J. Thynne.

Csikszentmihalyi, Mihaly (1991[1974]), *Flow: The Psychology of Optimal Experience*, New York: Harper Perennial.

CW (Common Worship) (2000), *Common Worship, Services and Prayers for the Church of England*, London: Church House Publishing.

Danforth, L. M. (1982), *The Death Rituals of Rural Greece*, Princeton, NJ: Princeton University Press.

Das, Veena (1977), *Structure and Cognition*, Oxford: Oxford University Press.

Das, Veena (1983), 'Language of Sacrifice', *Journal of the Royal Anthropological Institute*, Vol. 18. No. 3.

Davies, D. J. (1976), 'Social Groups, Liturgy, and Glossolalia', *Churchman*, Vol. 90, No. 3.

Davies, D. J. (1977), 'Sacrifice in Leviticus', *Zeitschrift fur die Alttestamentliche Wissenschaft*, 1977. Reprinted as 'Interpretation of Sacrifice in Leviticus' (1985), in *Anthropological Approaches to Old Testament*, ed. Bernhard Lang, London, SPCK and Fortress Press.

Davies, D. J. (1978), 'The Notion of Salvation in the Comparative Study of Religion', *Religion*, Vol. 8.

Davies, D. J. (1981), 'Theologies in Code', *Research Bulletin, Birmingham University Institute for Worship*, ed. J. G. Davies.

Davies, D. J. (1982), 'Sacrifice in Theology and Anthropology', in *Scottish Journal of Theology*, Vol. 35.

Davies, D. J. (1983a), 'Rites of Passage in Training Non-Stipendiary Ministers', in *Training for Diversity of Ministry*, ed. P. Vaughan, Nottingham: University of Nottingham.

Davies, D. J. (1983b), 'Pastoral Theology and "Folk-Religion" as a Clerical Category of Self-Absolution', in *Research Bulletin, Institute of Worship and Religious Architecture*, Birmingham: University of Birmingham.

Davies, D. J. (1984a), *Meaning and Salvation in Religious Studies,* Leiden: E. J. Brill.

Davies, D. J. (1984b), 'Pastoral Theology and Folk-Religion', *Research Bulletin, Birmingham University Institute for Worship*, ed. J. G. Davies.

Davies, D. J. (1984c), 'The Charismatic Ethic and the Spirit of Post-Industrialism', in *Strange Gifts*, ed. D. Martin and P. Mullen, London: SPCK.

Davies, D. J (1985a), 'Natural and Christian Priesthood in Folk Religiosity', *Anvil*, Spring, 1985.

Davies, D. J. (1985b), 'Symbolic Thought and Religious Knowledge', *British Journal of Religious Education,* Vol. 7. No. 2.

Davies, D. J. (1986), *Studies in Pastoral Theology and Social Anthropology*, Birmingham: University of Birmingham, Institute for Study of Worship and Religious Architecture.

Davies, D. J. (1995), 'Rebounding Vitality: Resurrection and Spirit in Luke–Acts', in *The Bible in Human Society*, ed. M. D. Carroll, D. J. A. Clines, and R. Davies, Sheffield: Sheffield Academic Press.

Davies, D. J. (1997), *Death, Ritual and Belief*, London: Cassell.

Davies, D. J. (2000a), *The Mormon Culture of Salvation*, Aldershot: Ashgate.

Davies, D. J. (2000b), *Private Passions: Betraying Discipleship on the Journey to Jerusalem*, Norwich: Canterbury Press.

Davies, D. J. (2000c), 'Health, Morality and Sacrifice: The Sociology of Disasters', in *The Blackwell Companion to the Sociology of Religion*, ed. R. K. Fenn, Oxford: Blackwell.

Davies, Douglas and Mathew Guest (2000), *Modern Christianity*, Reading: South Street, Press.

Davies, Douglas and Alastair Shaw (1995), *Reusing Old Graves, A Report of Popular British Attitudes*, Crayford, Kent: Shaw and Sons.

Davies, D. J., C. Pack, S. Seymour, C. Short, C. Watkins, and M. Winter (1990), *Rural Church Project Volume IV, The Views of Rural Parishioners*, Centre for Rural Studies, Royal Agricultural College, Cirencester and The Department of Theology, University of Nottingham.

Davis, John (1992), *Exchange*, Buckingham: Open University Press.

Deng, Francis M. (1988), 'Dinka Response to Christianity: The Pursuit of Well-being in a Developing Society', in Wendy James and Douglas H. Johnson (eds), *Vernacular Christianity*, Oxford: JASO.

Derrida, Jacques (1997), 'The Time of the King', in *The Logic of the Gift*, ed. Alan D. Schrift, New York, London: Routledge.

Derrida, Jacques (1998), 'Faith and Knowledge: The Two Sources of "Religion" at the Limits of Reason Alone', in Jacques Derrida and Gianni Vattimo (eds), *Religion*, Cambridge: Polity Press.

Dicken, Trueman (1963), *The Crucible of Love*, London: Darton, Longman and Todd.

Dijk, van, Rijk and Peter Pels (1996), 'Contesting Authorities and the Politics of Perception: Deconstructing the Study of Religion in Africa, in *Postcolonial Identities in Africa*, eds. Richard Werbner and Terence Ranger, London: Zed Books.

Dimock, N. (1895), *The "Ego Berengarius" in Relation to the Development of the Doctrine of the Eucharist*, London: Elliot Stock.

Doctrine Commission of the Church of England (1981), *Believing in the Church, The Corporate Nature of Faith*, London: SPCK.

Douglas Mary (1966), *Purity and Danger*, London: Routledge and Kegan Paul.

Douglas, Mary (1970), *Natural Symbols*, London: Pelican Books.

Douglas, Mary (1982), *In the Active Voice*, London: Routledge and Kegan Paul.

Droogers, André (1993), 'Power and Meaning in Three Brazilian Popular Religions', in *The Popular Use of Popular Religion in Latin America*, eds. Susanna Rostas and André Droogers, The Hague: Centre for Latin American Research and Documentation and Free University Amsterdam.

Duffield, I .K. (ed.) (1997), *Urban Christ*, Sheffield: Urban Theology Unit.

Dulles, Avery (1980), 'Symbolic Structures of Revelation', *Theological Studies*, Vol. 41, No. 1: 51–73.

Dumont, Louis (1986), *Essays on Individualism*, Chicago and London: University of Chicago Press.

Durkheim, Emile (1915), *The Elementary Forms of the Religious Life*, trans. J. W. Swain, London: Allen and Unwin Ltd.

Edwards, Jonathan (1966), *Basic Writings*, ed. O. A. Winslow, NY: New American Library.

Eilberg-Schwartz, Howard (1997), 'The Problem of the Body for the People of the Book', in *Reading Bibles, Writing Bodies*, eds. Timothy K. Beal and David M. Gunn, London and NY: Routledge.

Elford, John (1999), *The Pastoral Nature of Theology, An Upholding Presence*, London: Cassell.

Eliade, Mircea (1968), *Myths, Dreams and Mysteries*, NY: Fontana.

Eliade, Mircea (1970), *Myths, Dreams and Mysteries*, London: Collins.

Eliott, John (1995), *Social-Scientific Criticism of the New Testament*, London: SPCK.

Eliott, T. S. (1939), *The Idea of a Christian Society*, London: Faber and Faber.

Epstein, A. L. (1978), *Ethos and Identity*, London: Tavistock.

Evans-Pritchard, E. E. (1937), *Witchcraft, Oracles and Magic Among the Azande*, Oxford: Clarendon Press.

Evans-Pritchard, E. E. (1956), *Nuer Religion*, Oxford: Clarendon Press.

Evans-Pritchard, E. E. (1965), *Theories of Primitive Religion*, Oxford: Clarendon Press.

Faith in the City, London: Church House Publishing.

Farmer, H. H. (1936), *The World and God*, London: Nesbit.

Farmer, H. H. (1954), *Revelation and Religion*, London: Nesbit.

Feuerbach, Ludwig (1957 [1841]), *The Essence of Christianity*, London: Harper and Row.

Firth, Raymond (1964), *Essays on Social Organization and Values*, London: Athlone.

Firth, Raymond (1996), *Religion, a Humanist Interpretation*, London and NY: Routledge.

Flanagan, Kieran (1991), *Sociology and Liturgy: Re-presentations of the Holy*, Basingstoke: Macmillan.

Fontaine, J. S. La (1998), *Speak of the Devil: Tales of Satanic Abuse in Contemporary England*, Cambridge: Cambridge University Press.

Foster, M. L. and S. H. Brandes (1980), *Symbol as Sense*, London: Academic Press.

Fowler, James (1981), *Stages of Faith*, San Francisco: Harper and Row.

Friedrich, Paul (1997), 'The Prophet Isaiah in Pushkin's "Prophet",' in *Poetry and Prophecy: The Anthropology of Inspiration*, ed. John Leavitt. Ann Arbor, MI: University of Michigan Press.

Frijda, Nico H. (1993), *The Emotions*, Cambridge: Cambridge University Press.

Fukuyama, Francis (1992), *The End of History and the Last Man*, London: Penguin Books.

Fulton, John (2000a), 'Young Adults, Contemporary Society and Catholicism', in J. Fulton, M. Abela, I. Borowik, T. Doling, P. L. Marler and L. Tomasi (eds), *Young Catholics at the New Millennium*, Dublin: University College Dublin Press.

Fulton, John (2000b), 'Young Adults in Catholic England', in J. Fulton, M. Abela, I. Borowik, T. Doling, P. L. Marler and L. Tomasi (eds), *Young Catholics at the New Millennium*, Dublin: University College Dublin Press.

Fürer-Haimendorf, Christoph von (1969), *Morals and Merit*, London: Weidenfeld and Nicolson.

Gadamer, Hans-Georg (1996), *Truth and Method*, London: Sheed & Ward.

Gardner, Helen (1972), *The Faber Book of Religious Verse*, London: Faber and Faber Ltd.

Geertz, Clifford (1973), 'Religion as a Cultural System', in Michael Banton (ed.), *Anthropological Approaches to the Study of Religion*, London: Tavistock.

Gennep, Arnold van (1960), *The Rites of Passage*, trans, M. K. Vizedom and G. Caffee, London: Routledge Kegan Paul.

Girard, R. (1977), *Violence and the Sacred*, London: Johns Hopkins University Press.

Godelier, Maurice (1999), *The Enigma of the Gift*, Oxford: Blackwell.

Goldman, R. (1964), *Religious Thinking from Childhood to Adolescence*, London: Routledge and Kegan Paul.

Goody, Jack (1977), 'Against Ritual', in *Secular Ritual*, ed. Sally Moore and Barbara Myerhoff, Amsterdam: Van Gorcum.

Gooren, Henri (1998), *Rich among the Poor: Church, Firm and Household among Small-scale Entrepreneurs in Guatamala City*, Utrecht: Thela Latin America Series.

Gribben, Emmanuel (2000), 'Making Music for the Lord', in Jeff Astley, Timothy Hone and Mark Savage (eds), *Creative Chords, Studies in Music, Theology and Christian Formation*, Leominster: Gracewing.

Griffiths, J. (1914), *Certain Sermons or Homilies*, London: SPCK.

Grimes, Ronald L. (1990), *Ritual Criticism: Case Studies in Its Practice, Essays on Its Theory*, Columbia, SC: University of South Carolina Press.

Hagan, George P. (1988), 'Divinity and Experience: The Trance and Christianity in Southern Ghana', in Wendy James and Douglas H. Johnson (eds), *Vernacular Christianity*, Oxford: JASO.

Hauerwas, Stanley and W. H. Willimon (1989), *Resident Aliens: Life in the Christian Colony*, Nashville, TN: Abingdon.

Hay, David (1982), *Exploring Inner Space*, London: Penguin.

Hay, David (1990), *Religious Experience Today*, London: Mowbray.

Hayley, Audrey (1980), 'A Commensal Relationship with God: The Nature of the Offering in Assamese Vaishnavism', *Sacrifice*, ed. M. C. F. Bourdillon and Meyer Fortes, London: Academic Press.

Heelas, Paul (1996), *The New Age Movement*, Oxford: Blackwell.

Heffner, Robert O. (1993), *Conversion to Christianity*, Berkeley, CA: University of California Press.

Heiler, F. (1932), *Prayer*, Oxford: Oxford University Press.

Hertz, Robert (1994[1922]), *Sin and Expiation in Primitive Societies*, trans. Robert Parkin, Oxford: British Centre for Durkheimian Studies, Occasional Papers No. 2.

Hick, John (1966), *Evil and the God of Love*, London: Macmillan.

Hick, John (ed.) (1977), *The Myth of God Incarnate*, London: SCM.

Hocart, A. M. (1935), 'The Purpose of Ritual', in *The Life-Giving Myth and Other Essays*, ed. Lord Raglan, London: Tavistock Publications with Methuen and Co. (2nd edition 1952, with Introduction by Rodney Needham).

Hodgson, L. (1928), *And was made Man*, London: Longman.

Hodgson, L. (1968), *For Faith and Freedom*, London: SCM.

Hooker, Richard (1865), *The Works of Richard Hooker*, Oxford: Clarendon Press.

Hubert, Henri and Marcel Mauss (1964), *Sacrifice, its Nature and Function*, trans. W. D. Halls, London: Cohen and West.

Hughes, Glyn Tegai (1983), *Williams Pantycelyn*, Cardiff: University of Wales Press.

Hunt, Stephen (2001), *Anyone for Alpha? Evangelism in a Post-Christian Society*, London: Darton, Longman and Todd.

Ingold, Tim (1986), *The Appropriation of Nature*, Manchester: Manchester University Press.

Irigaray, Luce (1997), 'Women of the Market', in *The Logic of the Gift*, ed. Alan D. Schrift, New York, London: Routledge.

James, Wendy (1988), 'Music and the Spread of the Gospel', in *Vernacular Christianity*, ed. Wendy James and Douglas H. Johnson, Oxford: JASO.

James, Wendy (1998), '"One of us: Marcel Mauss and 'English' Anthropology"', in *Marcel Mauss A Centenary Tribute*, ed. Wendy James and Nick Allen, New York and Oxford: Berghahn Books.

Bibliography

James, William (1902), *The Varieties of Religious Experience*, London: Longman.

Jankowiak, William (ed.) (1995), *Romantic Passion*, NY: Columbia University Press.

Jenkins, Timothy (1999), *Religion in English Everyday Life*, Oxford: Berghahn Books.

Jobling, David (1984), 'Lévi-Strauss and the Structural Analysis of the Hebrew Bible', in *Anthropology and the Study of Religion*, ed. Robert L. Moore and Frank E. Reynolds, Chicago: Centre for the Scientific Study of Religion.

Johnstone, William (ed.) (1995), *William Robertson Smith: Essays in Reassessment*, Sheffield: Sheffield Academic Press.

Jones, Rufus M. (1909), *Studies in Mystical Religion*, London: Macmillan and Co.

Kee, Howard C. (1980), *Christian Origins in Sociological Perspective*, London: SCM Press.

Keesing, R. M. (1993), *Cultural Anthropology*, New York: Harcourt College Publications.

Kellner, Roger Y. (1993), 'Christian Gods and Mapuche Witches: The Retention of Indigenous Concepts of Evil among Mapuche Pentecostals', in *The Popular Use of Popular Religion in Latin America*, ed. Susanna Rostas and André Droogers, Amsterdam: CEDLA Publication.

Kent, Jack (1999), *The Psychological Origins of the Resurrection*, London: Open Gate Press.

Kerr, Hugh T. (ed.) (1943), *A Compend of Luther's Theology*, London: SCM Press

Kübler-Ross, Elisabeth (1973), *On Death and Dying*, London: Tavistock-Routledge.

Kunik, Gerhard (1977), 'Pattern of Body Movement in the Music of Boys' Initiation in South-East Angola', in *The Anthropology of the Body*, ed. John Blacking, London: Academic Press.

Lambek, Michael (1995), 'Choking on the Quran', in *The Pursuit of Certainty*, ed. Wendy James, London: Routledge.

Lang, Bernhard (1985), *Anthropological Approaches to the Old Testament*, London: SPCK.

Lange, Roderyk (1977), 'Some Notes on the Anthropology of Dance', in *The Anthropology of the Body*, ed. John Blacking, London: Academic Press.

Langer, Susanne K. (1951[1942]), *Philosophy in a New Key*, London: Oxford University Press.

Lawrence, D. H. and M. L. Skinner (1963) *The Boy in the Bush*, Harmonds-worth: Penguin.

Lawson, E. T. and R. N. McCauley (1990) *Rethinking Religion*, Cambridge: Cambridge University Press.

Leach, E. R. (ed.) (1968), *Dialectic in Practical Religion*, Cambridge: Cambridge University Press

Leach, Edmund (1976), *Culture and Communication*, Cambridge: Cambridge University Press.

Leach, Edmund (1985), 'The Logic of Sacrifice', in *Anthropological Approaches to the Old Testament*, ed. Bernhard Lang, London: SPCK.

Leavitt, John (1997), 'The Language of the Gods: Craft and Inspiration in Central Himalayan Ritual Discourse', in *Poetry and Prophecy, The Anthropology of Inspiration*, ed. John Leavitt, Ann Arbor, MI: The University of Michigan Press.

Leeuw, Gerardus van der (1967[1933]), *Religion in Essence and Manifestation*, Gloucester, MA: Peter Smith. (First published in 1933 as *Phänomenologie der religion.*)

LeFevre, Perry D. (1956), *The Prayers of Kierkegaard*, Chicago: University of Chicago Press.

Levin, D. M. (1985), *The Body's Recollection of Being: Phenomenological Psychology and the Destruction of Nihilism*, London: Routledge and Kegan Paul.

Lévi-Strauss, Claude (1962), *Totemism*, London: Merlin Press.

Lévi-Strauss, Claude (1969[1949]), *The Elementary Structures of Kinship*, trans. J. H. Bell and J. R. Von Sturmer, ed. Rodney Needham, London: Eyre and Spottiswoode, Boston: Beacon Press.

Lévi-Strauss, Claude (1970), *The Raw and the Cooked*, London: Jonathan Cape.

Lewis, Gilbert (1970), *Day of Shining Red*, Cambridge: Cambridge University Press.

Lewis, Ioan (ed.) (1977), *Symbols and Sentiments*, London: Academic Press.

Lewis, Ioan (1986), *Religion in Context,* Cambridge: Cambridge University Press.

Lex, B. (1979), 'The Neurobiology of Ritual Trance', in E.G. d'Aquili, C. D. Laughlin Jr. and J. McManus (eds), *The Spectrum of Ritual*, NY: Columbia University Press.

Lienhardt, Godfrey (1982), 'The Dinka and Catholicism', in *Religious Organization and Religious Experience*, ed. J. Davies, London and New York: Academic Press.

Lindbeck, George (1948), *The Nature of Doctrine: Religion and Theology in a Postliberal Age*, London: SPCK.

Lindholm, Charles (1995), 'Love as an Experience of Transcendence', in *Romantic Passion*, ed. William Jankowiak, New York: Columbia University Press.

Luckman, Thomas (1967), *The Invisible Religion,* Harmondsworth: Penguin.

Lukács, Georg (1971), *History and Class Consciousness: Studies in Marxist Dialectics,* London: Merlin Press.

Luther, Martin (1957), *The Bondage of the Will*, trans. and ed. J. I. Packer and O. R. Johnston, London: James Clarke and Co. Ltd.

Maquarrie, John (1977), *Principles of Christian Theology*, London: SCM Press.

Mageo, Jeanette Marie and Alan Howard (1996), *Spirits in Culture, History and Mind*, New York and London: Routledge.

Malbon, Elizabeth Struthers (1984), 'The Text and Time: Lévi-Strauss and New Testament Studies', in Robert L. Moore and Frank E. Reynolds (eds) *Anthropology and the Study of Religion*, Chicago: Centre for the Scientific Study of Religion.

Malina, Bruce J. (2001), *The New Testament World, Insights from Cultural Anthropology*, Louisville, KY: Westminster John Knox Press.

Malinowski, Bronislaw (1974[1948]), *Magic, Science and Religion and Other Essays*, London: Souvenir Press.

Martin, David (1990), *Tongues of Fire: The Explosion of Pentecostalism in Latin America*, Oxford: Blackwell.

Martineau, Robert (1981), *The Office and Work of a Priest*, London: Mowbrays.

Martinson, Mattias (2000), *Perseverance without Doctrine: Adorno, Self-Critique, and the End of Academic Theology*, Frankfurt, Oxford: Peter Lang.

Mauss, Marcel (1954[1925]), *The Gift: Forms and Functions of Exchange in Archaic Societies*, trans. I. Cunnison, London: Cohen and West.

Mauss, Marcel (1979[1936]), 'Body Techniques', in *Sociology and Psychology*, trans. Ben Brewster, London: Routledge and Kegan Paul.

Mauss, Marcel (1979), *Sociology and Psychology*, London: Routledge and Kegan Paul.

McKinnon, Donald (1969), *The Stripping of the Altars*, London: Collins, Fontana Library.

McNeill, J. T. (1977), *A History of the Cure of Souls*, New York: Harper and Row.

Merriam, Alan P. (1964), *The Anthropology of Music*, Evanston, IL: Northwestern University Press.

Milbank, John. (1990), *Theology and Social Theory*, Oxford: Blackwell.

Mol, Hans (1976), *Identity and the Sacred*, Oxford: Blackwell.

Mol, Hans (1978), *Identity and Religion*, London: Sage.

Moltmann, J. (1974), *The Crucified God*, London: SCM Press.

Moltmann, J. (1981), *The Trinity and the Kingdom of God*, London: SCM Press.

Moore, Robert L. and Frank E. Reynolds (eds) (1984), *Anthropology and the Study of Religion*, Chicago: Centre for the Scientific Study of Religion.

Moscovici, Serge (1993), *The Invention of Society*, Cambridge, MA: Polity Press.

Muddiman, John (1996), 'Celibacy', in P. B. Clarke, and A. Linzey, (eds), *A Dictionary of Ethics, Theology and Society*, London and New York, Routledge.

Myerhoff, Barbara (1982), 'Rites of Passage: Process and Paradox', in *Celebration, Studies in Festivity and Ritual*, ed. Victor Turner, Washington, DC: Smithsonian Institution Press.

Navone, John (1977), *Towards a Theology of Story*, Surrey: St Paul Publications.

Needham, Rodney (ed. and trans.) (1967), *The Semi-Scholars,* by Arnold van Gennep, London: Routledge and Kegan Paul.

Needham, Rodney (1972), *Belief, Language and Experience*, Oxford: Blackwell.

Needham, Rodney (1974), *Remarks and Inventions, Skeptical Essays about Kinship*, London: Tavistock.

Needham, Rodney (1980), *Reconnaissances*, Toronto: University of Toronto Press.

Needham, Rodney (1985), *Exemplars*, California: University of California Press.

New Blackfriars (1992), Vol. 78, No. 913.

Niebuhr, H. Richard (1929), *The Social Sources of Denominationalism*, NY: Harper and Row.

Niebuhr, Reinhold (1943), *The Nature and Destiny of Man, Vol. 2, Human Destiny*, London: Nisbet.

Nouwen, H. J. M. (1969), *Intimacy*, San Francisco: Haper and Row.

Nouwen, H. J. M. (1972), *The Wounded Healer*, New York: Doubleday.

Obeyesekere, G. (1968), 'Theodicy, Sin and Salvation in a Sociology of Buddhism', in *Dialectic in Practical Religion*, ed. E. R. Leach, Cambridge: Cambridge University Press.

Oden, T. C. (1984), *Cure of Souls in the Classic Tradition*, Philadelphia, PA: Fortress Press.

Ohnuki-Tierney, Emiko (1981), *Illness and Healing among the Sakhalin Ainu*, Cambridge: Cambridge University Press.

Bibliography

Ortner, Sherry (1978), *The Sherpas through their Rituals*, Cambridge: Cambridge University Press.

Otto, Rudolph (1924), *The Idea of the Holy*, Oxford: Oxford University Press.

Overholt, Thomas W. (1996) *Cultural Anthropology and the Old Testament*, Minneapolis, MN: Fortress Press.

Parkin, Robert (1996), *The Dark Side of Humanity: The World of Robert Hertz and its Legacy*, Australia, United Kingdom: Harwood Academic Publishers.

Pannenberg, Wolfhart (1985), *Anthropology in Theological Perspective*, Edinburgh: T. and T. Clark.

Parry, J. P. (1994), *Death in Banaras*, Cambridge: Cambridge University Press.

Patterson, Daniel W. (1982), 'Word, Song and Motion: Instruments of Celebration among Protestant Radicals in Early Nineteenth-Century America', in *Celebration*, ed. Victor Turner, Washington DC: Smithsonian Institution Press.

Pattison, S. (1988), *A Critique of Pastoral Care*, London: SCM Press.

Percy, Martin (1996), *Words, Wonders and Power*, London: SPCK.

Poulain, A. (1921), *The Graces of Interior Prayer*, London: Kegan Paul, Trench, Trubner and Co.

Radford Ruether, Rosemary (1969), *Gregory of Nazianzus: Rhetor and Philosopher*, Oxford: Clarendon Press.

Rahner, Karl (1972), *Theological Investigations*, trans. Graham Harrison, London: Darton, Longman and Todd.

Rambo, Lewis R. (1993), *Understanding Religious Conversion*, New Haven, CT: Yale University Press.

Rappaport, Roy (1999), *Ritual and Religion in the Making of Humanity*, Cambridge: Cambridge University Press.

Repstadt, Pål (1999), 'Theology and Sociology-Discourses in Conflict or Reconciliation under Postmodernism?,' in *Religion and Social Transitions*, ed. Eila Helander, Helsinki: University of Helsinki, Practical Theology Department.

Ricoeur, Paul (1976), *Interpretation Theory: Discourse and the Surplus of Meaning*, Fort Worth, TX: Texas Christian University Press.

Rieff, Philip (1966), *The Triumph of the Therapeutic*, Harmondsworth: Penguin Books.

Rogerson, J. W. (1974), *Myth in Old Testament Interpretation*, Berlin: De Gruyter.

Rogerson, J. W. (1978), Anthropology and the Old Testament, Oxford: Basil Blackwell.

Rowland, Chris (1997), 'Journey Downwards', in *Urban Christ*, ed. I. K. Duffied, Sheffield: Urban Theology Unit.

Rooden, Peter van (1996), 'Nineteenth-Century Representations of Missionary Conversion and the Transformation of Western Christianity', in *Conversion to Modernities, The Globalization of Christianity*, ed. Peter van der Veer, London: Routledge.

Rouget, Gilbert (1977), 'Music and Possession Trance', in *The Anthropology of the Body*, ed. John Blacking, London: Academic Press.

Ryle, John (1988), 'Miracles of the People: Attitudes to Catholicism in an Afro-Brazilian Religious Centre, in *Vernacular Christianity*, ed. Wendy James and Douglas H. Johnson, Oxford: JASO.

Sack, Daniel (1999), 'Food and Eating in American Religious Culture', in *Perspectives on American Religious Culture*, ed. Peter Williams, Oxford: Blackwell.

Salamone, Frank A. and Walter Randolph Adams (1997), *Explorations in Anthropology and Theology*, NY, Oxford: University Press of America.

Schneider, Mark A. (1993), *Culture as Enchantment*, Chicago: Chicago University Press.

Schutz, Alfred and Thomas Luckmann (1973), *The Structures of the Life-World* (trans. R. M. Zaner and H. Tristram Engelhardt Jr.), London: Heinemann.

Sheppard, David (1983), *Bias to the Poor*, London: Hodder and Stoughton.

Simmel, Georg (1997), *Essays on Religion*, ed. and trans. Horst Jurgen Helle with Ludwig Nieder, New Haven, CT and London: Yale University Press.

Skultans, Vieda (1999), 'Narrative of the Body and History: Illness in Judgement on the Soviet Past', *Sociology of Health and Illness*, Vol. 21, No. 3: 310–28.

Sloboda, John (2000), 'Music and Worship: A Psychologist's Perspective', in *Creative Chords, Studies in Music, Theology and Christian Formation*, ed. Jeff Astley, Timothy Hone and Mark Savage, Leominster: Gracewing.

Slough, Rebecca J. (1996), 'Let Every Tongue, by Art Refined, Mingle its Soft Notes with Mine: An Exploration of Hymn-Singing Events and Dimensions of Knowing', in *Religious and Social Ritual*, ed. M. B. Aune and Valerie DeMarinis, Albany, NY: State University of New York Press.

Smith, William Robertson (1894[1889]), *The Religion of the Semites*, Edinburgh: A. & C. Black.

Southwold, Martin (1982), 'True Buddhism and Village Buddhism', in *Religious Organization and Religious Experience*, ed. J. Davis, London, NY: Academic Press.

Spencer, Paul (1985), *Society and the Dance*, Cambridge: Cambridge University Press.

Sperber, Dan (1975), *Rethinking Symbolism*, trans. Alice L. Morton. Cambridge: Cambridge University Press.

Sperber, Dan (1982), *On Anthropological Knowledge*, Cambridge: Cambridge University Press.

Spurgeon, C. H. (1887), *Lectures to my Students, Second Series*, London: Passmore and Alabaster.

Steere, Douglas (1961), 'Translator's Note', in Søren Kierkegaard, *Purity of Heart*, London: Fontana.

Steiner, George. (1989), *Real Presences: Is There Anything in What We Say?* London and Boston: Faber and Faber.

Stocking, George W. (1971), 'Animism in Theory and Practice, E. B. Tylor's Unpublished "Notes on Spiritualism"', *Man* 6, No. 1. (March 1971): 89–91.

Storr, Anthony (1992), *Music and the Mind*, London: Harper-Collins.

Strathern, Marilyn (1988), *The Gender of the Gift*, London: University of California Press.

Stringer, Martin (1999), *On the Perception of Worship*, Birmingham: Birmingham University Press.

Stroebe, W. and M. S. Stroebe (1987), *Bereavement and Health: The Psychological and Physical Consequences of Partner Loss*, Cambridge: Cambridge University Press.

Stroupe, George W. (1981), *The Promise of Narrative Theology*, London: SCM Press.

Stuckenberg, J. H. W. (1881), *Christian Sociology*, London: R. D. Dickinson.

Sutton, Brett (1988), 'Speech, Chant, and Song: Patterns of Language and Action in a Southern Church', in R. W. Tyson, J. L. Peacock and D. W. Patterson (eds), *Diversities of Gifts: Field Studies in Southern Religion*, Urbana IL and Chicago: University of Illinois Press.

Sykes, Stephen (1980), 'Sacrifice in the New Testament and Christian Theology', in *Sacrifice,* ed. M. C. F. Bourdillon and Meyer Fortes, London: Academic Press.

Tagore, Rabindranath (1924), *Thought Relics and Stray Birds*, NY: Macmillan Company.

Tambiah, S. J. (1968), 'The Ideology of Merit and the Social Correlates of Buddhism in a Thai Village', in *Dialectic in Practical Religion*, ed. E. R. Leach, Cambridge: Cambridge University Press.

Taves, Ann (1999), *Fits, Trances and Visions*, Princeton, NJ: Princeton University Press.

Temple, William (1934), *Nature, Man and God*, London: Macmillan.

Theissen, Gerd (1982) *The Social Setting of Pauline Christianity*, Edinburgh: T. & T. Clark.

Tillich, Paul (1959), *Theology of Culture*, New York: Oxford University Press.

Toren, Christina (1993), 'Sign into Symbol, Symbol as Sign: Cognitive Aspects of a Social Process', in Pascal Boyer, (ed.) *Cognitive Aspects of Religious Symbolism*, Cambridge: Cambridge University Press.

Toulis, Nicole R. (1997), *Believing Identity: Pentecostalism and the Mediation of Jamaican Ethnicity and Gender*, Oxford: Berg.

Troeltsch, Ernst (1931), *The Social Teachings of the Christian Churches*.

Turner, Edith *et al.* (1992), *Experiencing Ritual, A New Interpretation of African Healing*, Philadelphia: University of Pennsylvania Press.

Turner, Victor and Edith Turner (1978), *Image and Pilgrimage in Christian Culture*, Oxford: Basil Blackwell.

Turner, Victor (1969), *The Ritual Process*, London: Routledge and Kegan Paul.

Turner, Victor (1974), *Dramas, Fields and Metaphors,* Ithaca, NY: Cornell University Press.

Turner, Victor (1975), *Revelation and Divination in Ndembu Ritual*, Ithaca, NY: Cornell University Press.

Turner, Victor (1982), *From Ritual to Theatre,* New York City: Performing Arts Journal Publications.

Turner, Victor (1985), 'Liminality, Kabbalah, and the Media', *Religion,* Vol. 15, July.

Tylor, E. B. (1958[1871]), *Religion in Primitive Culture*, Part Two of "Primitive Culture", New York: Harper and Brothers, Torchbook.

Tyson, R. W., J. L. Peacock and D. W. Patterson (eds) (1988), *Diversities of Gifts: Field Studies in Southern Religion*, Urbana, IL and Chicago: University of Illinois Press.

Ven, Johannes van der (1998), *Practical Theology, An Empirical Approach*, The Hague: Peeters Press.

Vizedom, Monika B. and Gabrielle L. Caffee (translators) (1960), *The Rites of Passage*, by Arnold Van Gennep, London: Routledge & Kegan Paul.

Weber, Max (1965[1922]), *The Sociology of Religion*, London: Methuen.

Westra, A. D. W. (1993), 'Religion as a System of Flows: An Organisational Analysis of Brazilian Condomble', in *The Popular Use of Popular Religion in Latin America*, ed. Susanna Rostas and André Droogers, The Hague: Centre for Latin American Research and Documentation and Free University of Amsterdam.

Williams, Rowan (2000), *On Christian Theology*, Oxford: Blackwell.
Willis, Roy (1974), *Man and Beast*, London: Hart-Davis, MacGibbon.
Winquist, C. E. (1978), *Homecoming*, Ann Arbor, MI: Scholars Press.
Winquist, C. E. (1995), *Desiring Theology*, Chicago and London: University of Chicago Press.

Index

Subject and Name

Index

Epstein, A. L. 146
ethical vitality, 57, 66
Eucharist, 24, 49, 63, 82–90, 105, 126, 131, 139, 177–8, 196, 200
evangelism, 135
Evans-Pritchard, E. E. 33, 96, 185
evil, 84, 86, 155–6, 185, 198
excitement, 135, 136
exclusivism, 16
exorcism, 32, 94, 185

faith, 24, 70, 101–2, 104, 202, 204, 209
Falklands War, 121
fear, 81
Feuerbach, L. 2, 4, 202
fieldwork, 7
Firth, R. 33, 82
Flanagan, K. 86
flesh-spirit, 105, 138
flow, 132, 133, 136, 140
Fontaine, J. 34
food, 81, 83, 95, 98, 101, 107, 199
force, 140, 203
Fortes, M. 82
Fowler, J. 190
frame (ing), 154–6, 158, 162, 191, 196, 202
Frazer, J. 81, 203.
free-gift, 70
Freud, S. 2, 28, 82, 148, 202–3
Frijda, N. H. 20
Fukuyama, F. 132
Fulton, J. 61, 140
funerals, 55, 122
Fürer-Haimendorf, C. 58, 68

Gadamer, Hans-Georg, 186
Gaia, 169
Geertz, C. 6, 15, 50, 159, 204
gender, 2, 7, 19, 23, 26
Genesis, 175
Gennep, A. van, 123, 137
Gentiles, 99, 100–1
gesture, 41, 201
gestus, 40, 181, 205
Gethsemane, 89
gift-theory, 45, 54, 195–204
Girard, R. 82
globalization, 27

glossolalia, 38–40, 91, 94, 100, 107, 135–6, 141, 199
gnosticism, 30
God, 13, 26–7, 30–1, 60, 65, 103, 149, 155, 161, 182–3, 196
Godelier, M. 76–9, 195–8
Goldman, R. 37
Gooren, H. 165
grace, 10, 54, 77, 93, 99, 102, 129, 138, 166, 196, 200–2
great-little traditions, 24
Greek Orthodoxy, 43, 47, 79
Gribben, E. 85
grid-group, 35
grief, 157, 171, 180

habitus, 40, 181, 205
Hagan, G. 155
Hauerwas, S. 86
Hay, D. 37
Hayley, A. 83
healing, 47, 91, 92
health, 130
Heelas, P. 39, 136
Heffner, R. O. 160
Herbert, G. 75
Hertz, R. 45, 50, 57, 202
Hinduism, 43, 44, 47, 71, 83
Hocart, A. M. 163
Hodgson, L. 149
holiness, 97, 103, 169
Holy Roman Empire, 191
Holy Spirit, 32, 60, 70, 72, 81, 88, 92, 94, 99, 102–4, 106, 109, 126, 132, 138, 150, 156, 167–8, 175, 178, 190, 199
Homo duplex, 28, 47
Homo religiosus, 43
hope, 81, 162
Hubert, H. 45, 82
Hughes, G. T. 163
human nature, 102, 103
humility, 148, 152
Hunt, S. 168
hymns, 104, 139

ideal-type, 104
identity, 68, 71, 90, 99, 104, 107, 109, 145, 152, 163, 192

Biblical Texts